LONG WALK TO FREEDOM

'This life of a man who has been a political activist for fifty years, in one of the most difficult and complex conflicts of the twentieth century, is a major achievement'

Martin Meredith, *The Observer*

'The authentic voice of Mandela shines through this book . . . humane, dignified and magnificently unembittered'

R.W. Johnson, *The Times*

'The autobiography succeeds because the vicissitudes Mandela has gone through in the course of his life are so dramatic that the reader cannot help responding to them as if to a fairy tale or moral fable of some kind. No hero of legend ever went through such protracted trials in order to arrive at so improbable a victory'

Dan Jackson, *Sunday Telegraph*

'This is a splendid book . . . Justice, freedom, goodness and love have prevailed spectacularly in South Africa and one man has embodied that struggle and its vindication. This is his story and the story of that struggle and a people's victory. It is a fitting monument. It will help us never to forget, lest we in our turn repeat the ghastliness of apartheid'

Desmond Tutu, *The Tablet*

'A compelling book . . . both a brilliant description of a diabolical system and a testament to the power of the spirit to transcend it . . . One of the most remarkable lives of the twentieth century'

Washington Post

'A work of literature as well as an important document'

Angus Calder, *S_____ ___day*

'Most searing in its p_____ ___ ____ __d prison and the author'___ _____ _____ ___ng in its descriptions of M_ _____ _____ __ng his clandestine journey__ _____

_____ator

'An engrossing tapestry of recent South African history that grips the reader from the first pages . . . Riveting and sometimes painfully honest'

San Francisco Chronicle

'Mandela writes with rare and moving candour'

The Economist

'*Long Walk to Freedom* is, unexpectedly, a sociological treasure trove . . . a work of constant revelations'

Wole Soyinka, *Times Higher Education Supplement*

'A remarkable document'

Cape Times

'One of those masterpieces, perhaps the greatest of twentieth century autobiographical literature, which is a sharp, poignant, elegant and eloquent counter to the prevailing cynicism about the rottenness of politics'

G.D. Gorender, *Caribbean Times*

'An enthralling tale told simply, the story of one man's remarkable life and of a people which finally became free'

Sunday Tribune

'Mr Mandela's narrative is perhaps most striking for its self-revealing candour and sensitivity'

Geoffrey Howe, *Country Life*

'*Long Walk to Freedom* is a story that is at once appalling and inspirational: appalling in its depiction of the waste of human potential; inspirational in the triumph of the human spirit'

Canberra Times

'Irresistible describes *Long Walk to Freedom*, which must be one of the few political biographies that's also a page-turner'

Los Angeles Times

'Absorbing reading . . . . the work of a great politician who still retains the ability to reflect on himself as a mere mortal'

Beverley Naidoo, *The Times Educational Supplement*

LONG WALK TO FREEDOM

THE AUTOBIOGRAPHY OF
NELSON MANDELA

Volume One

1918–1962

ABACUS

An *Abacus* Book

First published in Great Britain in 1994
by Little, Brown and Company
First published in Great Britain by Abacus in 1995

This edition published by Abacus in 2002

Reader's note: for editorial reasons, three sections, 49 to 51, which in the
original 1994 edition belonged to Part Seven: Rivonia, have been
incorporated at the end of Part Six: The Black Pimpernel. No text,
however, has been omitted in this two-volume edition.

A CIP catalogue record for this book
is available from the British Library.

ISBN 0 349 11602 4

Typeset in New Baskerville by
Hewer Text Limited, Edinburgh
Printed and bound in Great Britain by
Clays Ltd, St Ives plc

Abacus
An imprint of
Time Warner Books UK
Brettenham House
Lancaster Place
London WC2E 7EN

www.TimeWarnerBooks.co.uk

CONTENTS

I dedicate this book to my six children, Madiba and Makaziwe (my first daughter), who are now deceased, and to Makgatho, Makaziwe, Zenani and Zindzi, whose support and love I treasure; to my twenty-nine grand-children and six great-grandchildren, who give me great pleasure; and to all my comrades, friends and fellow South Africans whom I serve and whose courage, determination and patriotism remain my source of inspiration.

ACKNOWLEDGEMENTS

As readers will discover, this book has a long history. I began writing it clandestinely in 1974 during my imprisonment on Robben Island. Without the tireless labour of my old comrades Walter Sisulu and Ahmed Kathrada for reviving my memories, it is doubtful the manuscript would have been completed. The copy of the manuscript which I kept with me was discovered by the authorities and confiscated. However, in addition to their unique calligraphic skills, my co-prisoners Mac Maharaj and Isu Chiba had ensured that the original manuscript safely reached its destination. I resumed work on it after my release from prison in 1990.

Since my release, my schedule has been crowded with numerous duties and responsibilities, which have left me little free time for writing. Fortunately, I have had the assistance of dedicated colleagues, friends and professionals who have helped me complete my work at last, and to whom I would like to express my appreciation. Thanks again to my comrade Ahmed Kathrada for the long hours spent revising, correcting and giving accuracy to the story.

I am deeply grateful to Richard Stengel who collaborated with me in the creation of this book, providing invaluable assistance in editing and revising the first parts and in the writing of the latter parts. I recall with fondness our early morning walks in the Transkei and the many hours of interviews at Shell House in

Johannesburg and my home in Houghton. A special tribute is owed to Mary Pfaff who assisted Richard in his work. I have also benefited from the advice and support of Fatima Meer, Peter Magubane, Nadine Gordimer and Ezekiel Mphahlele.

Many thanks to my ANC office staff who patiently dealt with the logistics of the making of this book, but in particular to Barbara Masekela for her efficient co-ordination. Likewise, Iqbal Meer has devoted many hours to watching over the business aspects of the book. I am grateful to my editor, William Phillips of Little, Brown, who has guided this project from early 1990 on, and edited the text. He was ably assisted by Jordan Pavlin and Steve Schneider. I would also like to thank Professor Gail Gerhart for her factual review of the manuscript.

LONG WALK
TO FREEDOM

Volume One

1918–1962

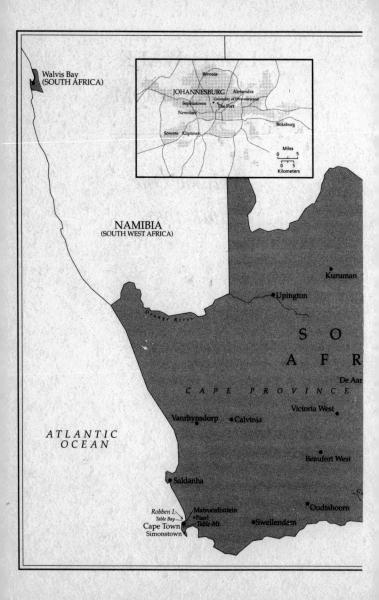

Walvis Bay
(SOUTH AFRICA)

Rivonia

JOHANNESBURG Alexandra

University of Witwatersrand

Sophiatown The Fort

Newclare

Soweto Kliptown

Boksburg

Miles
0   5

0   5
Kilometers

NAMIBIA
(SOUTH WEST AFRICA)

Kuruman

Upington

Orange River

S O

A F R

De Aar

CAPE PROVINCE

Victoria West

Vanrhynsdorp   Calvinia

ATLANTIC
OCEAN

Beaufort West

Saldanha

Robben I.   Matroosfontein
Table Bay   Paarl
Cape Town   *Table Mt.*
Simonstown

Oudtshoorn

Swellendam

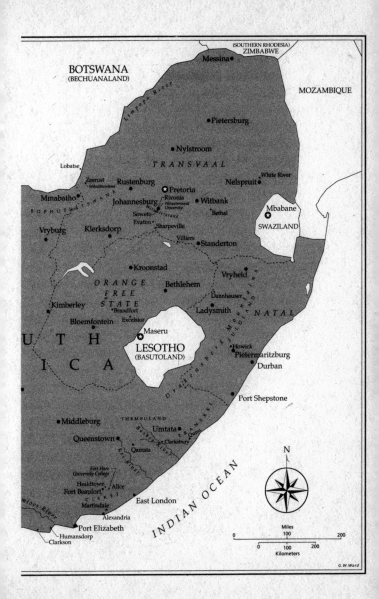

PART ONE

———

A Country Childhood

1

Apart from life, a strong constitution and an abiding connection to the Thembu royal house, the only thing my father bestowed upon me at birth was a name, Rolihlahla. In Xhosa, Rolihlahla literally means 'pulling the branch of a tree', but its colloquial meaning more accurately would be 'troublemaker'. I do not believe that names are destiny or that my father somehow divined my future, but in later years, friends and relatives would ascribe to my birth name the many storms I have both caused and weathered. My more familiar English or Christian name was not given to me until my first day of school. But I am getting ahead of myself.

I was born on 18 July 1918 at Mvezo, a tiny village on the banks of the Mbashe River in the district of Umtata, the capital of the Transkei. The year of my birth marked the end of the Great War; the outbreak of an influenza epidemic that killed millions throughout the world; and the visit of a delegation of the African National Congress to the Versailles peace conference to voice the grievances of the African people of South Africa. Mvezo, however, was a place apart, a tiny precinct removed from the world of great events, where life was lived much as it had been for hundreds of years.

The Transkei is 800 miles east of Cape Town, 550 miles south of Johannesburg, and lies between the Kei River and the Natal border, between the rugged

Drakensberg mountains to the north and the blue waters of the Indian Ocean to the east. It is a beautiful country of rolling hills, fertile valleys, and a thousand rivers and streams which keep the landscape green even in winter. The Transkei used to be one of the largest territorial divisions within South Africa, covering an area the size of Switzerland, with a population of about three and a half million Xhosas and a tiny minority of Basothos and whites. It is home to the Thembu people, who are part of the Xhosa nation, of which I am a member.

My father, Gadla Henry Mphakanyiswa, was a chief by both blood and custom. He was confirmed as chief of Mvezo by the king of the Thembu tribe but, under British rule, his selection had to be ratified by the government, which in Mvezo took the form of the local magistrate. As a government-appointed chief, he was eligible for a stipend as well as a portion of the fees the government levied on the community for vaccination of livestock and communal grazing land. Although the role of chief was a venerable and esteemed one, it had, even seventy-five years ago, become debased by the control of an unsympathetic white government.

The Thembu tribe reaches back for twenty generations to King Zwide. According to tradition, the Thembu people lived in the foothills of the Drakensberg mountains and migrated towards the coast in the sixteenth century, where they were incorporated into the Xhosa nation. The Xhosa are part of the Nguni people who have lived, hunted and fished in the rich and temperate southeastern region of South Africa, between the great interior plateau to the north and the

Indian Ocean to the south, since at least the eleventh century. The Nguni can be divided into a northern group – the Zulu and the Swazi people – and a southern group, which is made up of amaBaca, amaBomvana, amaGcaleka, amaMfengu, amaMpodomise, amaMpondo, abeSotho and abeThembu, and together they comprise the Xhosa nation.

The Xhosa are a proud and patrilineal people with an expressive and euphonious language and an abiding belief in the importance of laws, education and courtesy. Xhosa society was a balanced and harmonious social order in which every individual knew his or her place. Each Xhosa belongs to a clan that traces its descent back to a specific forefather. I am a member of the Madiba clan, named after a Thembu chief who ruled in the Transkei in the eighteenth century. I am often addressed as Madiba, my clan name, as a sign of respect.

Ngubengcuka, one of the greatest monarchs, who united the Thembu tribe, died in 1832. As was the custom, he had wives from the principal royal houses: the Great House, from which the heir is selected, the Right Hand House, and the Ixhiba, a minor house that is referred to by some as the Left Hand House. It was the task of the sons of the Ixhiba or Left Hand House to settle royal disputes. Mthikrakra, the eldest son of the Great House, succeeded Ngubengcuka and among his sons were Ngangelizwe and Matanzima. Sabata, who ruled the Thembu from 1954, was the grandson of Ngangelizwe a senior to Kalzer Daliwonga, better known as K.D. Matanzima, the former chief minister of the Transkei – my nephew, by law and custom – who was a descendant of Matanzima. The eldest son of the

Ixhiba house was Simakade, whose younger brother was Mandela, my grandfather.

Although over the decades there have been many stories that I was in the line of succession to the Thembu throne, the simple genealogy I have just outlined exposes those tales as a myth. Although I was a member of the royal household, I was not among the privileged few who were trained for rule. Instead, as a descendant of the Ixhiba house, I was groomed, like my father before me, to counsel the rulers of the tribe.

My father was a tall, dark-skinned man with a straight and stately posture, which I like to think I inherited. He had a tuft of white hair just above his forehead and, as a boy, I would take white ash and rub it into my hair in imitation of him. My father had a stern manner and did not spare the rod when disciplining his children. He could be exceedingly stubborn, another trait that may unfortunately have been passed down from father to son.

My father has sometimes been referred to as the prime minister of Thembuland during the reigns of Dalindyebo, the father of Sabata, who ruled in the early 1900s, and that of his son, Jongintaba, who succeeded him. That is a misnomer in that no such title existed, but the role he played was not so different from what the designation implies. As a respected and valued counsellor to both kings, he accompanied them on their travels and was usually to be found by their sides during important meetings with government officials. He was an acknowledged custodian of Xhosa history, and it was partly for that reason that he was valued as an adviser. My own interest in history had early roots and was encouraged by my father. Although my father could neither read nor write, he was reputed to be an excellent orator who captivated his audiences by entertaining them as well as teaching them.

In later years, I discovered that my father was not only an adviser to kings but a kingmaker. After the untimely death of Jongilizwe in the 1920s, his son Sabata, the infant of the Great Wife, was too young to ascend to the throne. A dispute arose as to which of Dalindyebo's three most senior sons from other mothers – Jongintaba, Dabulamanzi and Melithafa – should be selected to succeed him. My father was consulted and recommended Jongintaba on the ground that he was the best educated. Jongintaba, he argued, would not only be a fine custodian of the crown but an excellent mentor to the young prince. My father, and a few other influential chiefs, had the great respect for education that is often present in those who are uneducated. The recommendation was controversial, for Jongintaba's mother was from a lesser house, but my father's choice was ultimately accepted by both the Thembus and the British government. In time, Jongintaba would return the favour in a way that my father could not then imagine.

All told, my father had four wives, the third of whom, my mother, Nosekeni Fanny, the daughter of Nkedama from the amaMpemvu clan of the Xhosa, belonged to the Right Hand House. Each of these wives – the Great Wife, the Right Hand wife (my mother), the Left Hand wife and the wife of the Iqadi or support house – had her own kraal. A kraal was a homestead and usually included a simple fenced-in enclosure for animals, fields for growing crops, and one or more thatched huts. The kraals of my father's wives were separated by many miles and he commuted among them. In these travels, my father sired thirteen children in all, four boys and nine girls. I am the eldest child of the Right Hand House, and the youngest of my father's four sons. I have three sisters, Baliwe, who was the oldest girl, Notancu, and Makhutswana. Although the eldest of my father's sons was Mlahlwa, my father's heir as chief was Daligqili, the son of the Great House, who died in the early 1930s. All of his sons, with the exception of myself, are now deceased, and each was my senior not only in age but in status.

When I was not much more than a newborn child, my father was involved in a dispute that deprived him of his chieftainship at Mvezo and revealed a strain in his character I believe he passed on to his son. I maintain that nurture, rather than nature, is the primary moulder of personality, but my father possessed a proud rebelliousness, a stubborn sense of fairness, that I recognize in myself. As a chief – or headman, as it was often known among the whites – my father was compelled to account for his stewardship not only to the Thembu king but to the local magistrate. One day one of my father's subjects lodged a complaint against him involving an ox that had strayed from its owner. The magistrate accordingly sent a message ordering my father to appear before him. When my father received the summons, he sent back the following reply: '*Andizi, ndisaqula*' ('I will not come, I am still girding for battle'). One did not defy magistrates in those days. Such behaviour would be regarded as the height of insolence – and in this case it was.

My father's response bespoke his belief that the

magistrate had no legitimate power over him. When it came to tribal matters, he was guided not by the laws of the king of England, but by Thembu custom. This defiance was not a fit of pique, but a matter of principle. He was asserting his traditional prerogative as a chief and was challenging the authority of the magistrate.

When the magistrate received my father's response, he promptly charged him with insubordination. There was no inquiry or investigation; that was reserved for white civil servants. The magistrate simply deposed my father, thus ending the Mandela family chieftainship.

I was unaware of these events at the time, but I was not unaffected. My father, who was a wealthy nobleman by the standards of his time, lost both his fortune and his title. He was deprived of most of his herd and land, and the revenue that came with them. Because of our straitened circumstances, my mother moved to Qunu, a slightly larger village north of Mvezo, where she would have the support of friends and relations. We lived in a less grand style in Qunu, but it was in that village near Umtata that I spent some of the happiest years of my boyhood and whence I trace my earliest memories.

2

The village of Qunu was situated in a narrow, grassy valley crisscrossed by clear streams, and overlooked by green hills. It consisted of no more than a few hundred people who lived in huts, which were beehive-shaped structures of mud walls, with a wooden pole in the centre holding up a peaked grass roof. The floor was made of crushed ant-heap, the hard dome of excavated earth above an ant colony, and was kept smooth by smearing it regularly with fresh cow dung. The smoke from the hearth escaped through the roof, and the only opening was a low doorway one had to stoop to walk through. The huts were generally grouped in a residential area that was some distance away from the maize fields. There were no roads, only paths through the grass worn away by barefooted boys and women. The women and children of the village wore blankets dyed in ochre; only the few Christians in the village wore Western-style clothing. Cattle, sheep, goats and horses grazed together in common pastures. The land around Qunu was mostly treeless except for a cluster of poplars on a hill overlooking the village. The land itself was owned by the state. With very few exceptions, Africans at that time did not enjoy private title to land in South Africa but were tenants paying rent annually to the government. In the area, there were two small primary schools, a general store, and a dipping tank to rid the cattle of ticks and diseases.

Maize (what we called mealies and people in the West call corn), sorghum, beans and pumpkins formed the largest portion of our diet, not because of any inherent preference for these foods, but because the people could not afford anything richer. The wealthier families in our village supplemented their diets with tea, coffee and sugar, but for most people in Qunu these were exotic luxuries far beyond their means. The water used for farming, cooking and washing had to be fetched in buckets from streams and springs. This was women's work and, indeed, Qunu was a village of women and children: most of the men spent the greater part of the year working on remote farms or in the mines along the Reef, the great ridge of gold-bearing rock and shale that forms the southern boundary of Johannesburg. They returned perhaps twice a year, mainly to plough their fields. The hoeing, weeding and harvesting were left to the women and children. Few if any of the people in the village knew how to read or write, and the concept of education was still a foreign one to many.

My mother presided over three huts at Qunu which, as I remember, were always filled with the babies and children of my relations. In fact, I hardly recall any occasion as a child when I was alone. In African culture, the sons and daughters of one's aunts or uncles are considered brothers and sisters, not cousins. We do not make the same distinctions among relations practised by whites. We have no half-brothers or half-sisters. My mother's sister is my mother; my uncle's son is my brother; my brother's child is my son, my daughter.

Of my mother's three huts, one was used for cooking, one for sleeping and one for storage. In the hut in which we slept, there was no furniture in the Western sense. We slept on mats and sat on the ground. I did not discover pillows until I went to Mqhekezweni. My mother cooked food in a three-legged iron pot over an open fire in the centre of the hut or outside. Everything we ate we grew and made ourselves. My mother planted and harvested her own mealies. Mealies were harvested from the field when they were hard and dry. They were stored in sacks or pits dug in the ground. When preparing the mealies, the women used different methods. They could ground the kernels between two stones to make bread, or boil the mealies first, producing *umphothulo* (mealie flour eaten with sour milk) or *umngqusho* (samp, sometimes plain or mixed with beans). Unlike mealies, which were sometimes in short supply, milk from our cows and goats was always plentiful.

From an early age, I spent most of my free time in the veld playing and fighting with the other boys of the village. A boy who remained at home tied to his mother's apron strings was regarded as a sissy. At night, I shared my food and blanket with these same boys. I was no more than five when I became a herd-boy looking after sheep and calves in the fields. I discovered the almost mystical attachment that the Xhosa have for cattle, not only as a source of food and wealth, but as a blessing from God and a source of happiness. It was in the fields that I learned how to knock birds out of the sky with a slingshot, to gather wild honey and fruits and edible roots, to drink warm, sweet milk straight from the udder of a cow, to swim in the clear, cold streams, and to catch fish with twine and sharpened bits of wire. I learned to stick-fight – essential knowledge to any rural African boy – and became adept at its various techniques, parrying blows, feinting in one direction and striking in another, breaking away from an opponent with quick footwork. From these days I date my love of the veld, of open spaces, the simple beauties of nature, the clean line of the horizon.

As boys, we were mostly left to our own devices. We played with toys we made ourselves. We moulded animals and birds out of clay. We made ox-drawn sledges out of tree branches. Nature was our playground. The hills above Qunu were dotted with large smooth rocks which we transformed into our own roller-coaster. We sat on flat stones and slid down the face of the large rocks. We did this until our backsides were so sore we could hardly sit down. I learned to ride by sitting atop weaned calves – after being thrown to the ground several times, one got the hang of it.

I learned my lesson one day from an unruly donkey. We had been taking turns climbing up and down its back and when my chance came I jumped on and the donkey bolted into a nearby thornbush. It bent its head, trying to unseat me, which it did, but not before the thorns had pricked and scratched my face, embarrassing me in front of my friends. Like the people of the East, Africans have a highly developed sense of dignity, or what the Chinese call 'face'. I had lost face among my friends. Even though it was a donkey that unseated me, I learned that to humiliate another person is to make him suffer an unnecessarily cruel fate. Even as a boy, I defeated my opponents without dishonouring them.

Usually the boys played among themselves, but we

sometimes allowed our sisters to join us. Boys and girls would play games like *ndize* (hide and seek) and *icekwa* (tag). But the game I most enjoyed playing with the girls was what we called *khetha*, or choose-the-one-you-like. This was not so much an organized game, but a spur-of-the-moment sport that took place when we accosted a group of girls our own age and demanded that each select the boy she loved. Our rules dictated that the girl's choice be respected and once she had chosen her favourite, she was free to continue on her journey escorted by the lucky boy she loved. But the girls were nimble-witted – far cleverer than we doltish lads – and would often confer among themselves and choose one boy, usually the plainest fellow, and then tease him all the way home.

The most popular game for boys was *thinti*, and like most boys' games it was a youthful approximation of war. Two sticks, used as targets, would be driven firmly into the ground in an upright position about a hundred feet apart. The goal of the game was for each team to hurl sticks at the opposing target and knock it down. We each defended our own target and attempted to prevent the other side from retrieving the sticks that had been thrown over. As we grew older, we organized matches against boys from neighbouring villages and those who distinguished themselves in these fraternal battles were greatly admired, as generals who achieve great victories in war are justly celebrated.

After games such as these, I would return to my mother's kraal where she was preparing supper. Whereas my father once told stories of historic battles and heroic Xhosa warriors, my mother would enchant us with Xhosa legends and fables that had come down from numberless generations. These tales stimulated my childish imagination, and usually contained some moral lesson. I recall one my mother told us about a traveller who was approached by an old woman with terrible cataracts on her eyes. The woman asked the traveller for help, and the man averted his eyes. Then another man came along and was approached by the old woman. She asked him to clean her eyes, and even though he found the task unpleasant, he did as she asked. Then, miraculously, the scales fell from the old woman's eyes and she became young and beautiful. The man married her and became wealthy and prosperous. It is a simple tale, but its message is an enduring one: virtue and generosity will be rewarded in ways that one cannot know.

Like all Xhosa children, I acquired knowledge mainly through observation. We were meant to learn through imitation and emulation, not through questions. When I first visited the homes of whites, I was often dumbfounded by the number and nature of questions that children asked their parents – and their parents' unfailing willingness to answer them. In my household, questions were considered a nuisance; adults imparted such information as they considered necessary.

My life, and that of most Xhosas at the time, was shaped by custom, ritual and taboo. This was the alpha and omega of our existence, and went unquestioned. Men followed the path laid out for them by their fathers; women led the same lives as their mothers had before them. Without being told, I soon assimilated the elaborate rules that governed the relations between men and women. I discovered that a man may not enter a house where a woman has recently given birth, and that a newly married woman would not enter the kraal of her new home without elaborate ceremony. I also learned that to neglect one's ancestors would bring ill-fortune and failure in life. If you dishonoured your ancestors in some way, the only way to atone for that lapse was to consult a traditional healer or tribal elder, who communicated with the ancestors and conveyed profound apologies. All of these beliefs were perfectly natural to me.

I came across few whites as a boy at Qunu. The local magistrate, of course, was white, as was the nearest shopkeeper. Occasionally white travellers or policemen passed through our area. These whites appeared as grand as gods to me, and I was aware that they were to be treated with a mixture of fear and respect. But their role in my life was a distant one, and I thought little if at all about the white man in general or relations between my own people and these curious and remote figures.

The only rivalry between different clans or tribes in our small world at Qunu was that between the Xhosas and the amaMfengu, a small number of whom lived in our village. AmaMfengu arrived on the eastern Cape after fleeing from Shaka Zulu's armies in a period known as the iMfecane, the great wave of battles and migrations between 1820 and 1840 set in motion by the rise of Shaka and the Zulu state, during which the Zulu warrior sought to conquer and then unite all the tribes under military rule. The amaMfengu, who were not originally Xhosa-speakers, were refugees from the iMfecane and were forced to do jobs that no other African would do. They worked on white farms and in white businesses, something that was looked down upon by the more established Xhosa tribes. But the amaMfengu were an industrious people, and because of their contact with Europeans, they were often more educated and 'Western' than other Africans.

When I was a boy, the amaMfengu were the most advanced section of the community and furnished our clergymen, policemen, teachers, clerks and inter-preters. They were also among the first to become Christians, to build better houses and to use scientific methods of agriculture, and they were wealthier than their Xhosa compatriots. They confirmed the mission-aries' axiom, that to be Christian was to be civilized, and to be civilized was to be Christian. There still existed some hostility towards the amaMfengu, but in retrospect I would attribute this more to jealousy than tribal animosity. This local form of tribalism that I observed as a boy was relatively harmless. At that stage, I did not witness nor even suspect the violent tribal rivalries that would subsequently be promoted by the white rulers of South Africa.

My father did not subscribe to the local prejudice towards the amaMfengu and befriended two ama-Mfengu brothers, George and Ben Mbekela. The brothers were an exception in Qunu: they were edu-cated and Christian. George, the elder, was a retired teacher and Ben was a police sergeant. Despite the proselytizing of the Mbekela brothers, my father re-mained aloof from Christianity and instead reserved his own faith for the great spirit of the Xhosas, Qamata, the God of his fathers. My father was an unofficial priest and presided over ritual slaughtering of goats and calves and officiated at local traditional rites con-cerning planting, harvest, birth, marriage, initiation ceremonies and funerals. He did not need to be ordained, for the traditional religion of the Xhosas is characterized by a cosmic wholeness, so that there is little distinction between the sacred and the secular, between the natural and the supernatural.

While the faith of the Mbekela brothers did not rub off on my father, it did inspire my mother, who became a Christian. In fact, Fanny was literally her Christian name, for she had been given it in church. It was due to the influence of the Mbekela brothers that I myself was baptized into the Methodist, or Wesleyan Church as it was then known, and sent to school. The brothers would often see me playing or minding sheep and come over to talk to me. One day, George Mbekela paid a visit to my mother. 'Your son is a clever young fellow,' he said. 'He should go to school.' My mother remained silent. No one in my family had ever attended school and my mother was unprepared for Mbekela's suggestion. But she did relay it to my father who, despite – or perhaps because of – his own lack of education, immediately decided that his youngest son should go to school.

The schoolhouse consisted of a single room, with a Western-style roof, on the other side of the hill from Qunu. I was seven years old, and on the day before I was to begin, my father took me aside and told me that I must be dressed properly for school. Until that time, I, like all the other boys in Qunu, had worn only a blanket, which was wrapped round one shoulder and pinned at the waist. My father took a pair of his trousers and cut them at the knee. He told me to put them on, which I did, and they were roughly the correct length, although the waist was far too large.

My father then took a piece of string and drew the trousers in at the waist. I must have been a comical sight, but I have never owned a suit I was prouder to wear than my father's cut-off trousers.

On the first day of school my teacher, Miss Mdingane, gave each of us an English name and said that thenceforth that was the name we would answer to in school. This was the custom among Africans in those days and was undoubtedly due to the British bias of our education. The education I received was a British education, in which British ideas, British culture and British institutions were automatically assumed to be superior. There was no such thing as African culture.

Africans of my generation – and even today – generally have both a Western and an African name. Whites were either unable or unwilling to pronounce an African name, and considered it uncivilized to have one. That day, Miss Mdingane told me that my new name was Nelson. Why she bestowed this particular name upon me I have no idea. Perhaps it had something to do with the great British sea captain Lord Nelson, but that would be only a guess.

3

One night, when I was nine years old, I was aware of a commotion in the household. My father, who took turns visiting his wives and usually came to us for perhaps one week a month, had arrived. But it was not at his accustomed time, for he was not scheduled to be with us for another few days. I found him in my mother's hut, lying on his back on the floor, in the midst of what seemed like an endless fit of coughing. Even to my young eyes, it was clear that my father was not long for this world. He was ill with some type of lung disease, but it was not diagnosed, as my father had never visited a doctor. He remained in the hut for several days without moving or speaking, and then one night he took a turn for the worse. My mother and my father's youngest wife, Nodayimani, who had come to stay with us, were looking after him, and late that night he called for Nodayimani. 'Bring me my tobacco,' he told her. My mother and Nodayimani conferred, and decided that it was unwise that he have tobacco in his current state. But he persisted in calling for it, and eventually Nodayimani filled his pipe, lit it, and then handed it to him. My father smoked and became calm. He continued smoking for perhaps an hour, and then, his pipe still lit, he died.

I do not remember experiencing great grief so much as feeling cut adrift. Although my mother was the centre of my existence, I defined myself through my father. My father's passing changed my whole life in a way that I did not suspect at the time. After a brief period of mourning, my mother informed me that I would be leaving Qunu. I did not ask her why, or where I was going.

I packed the few things that I possessed and early one morning we set out on a journey westward to my new residence. I mourned less for my father than for the world I was leaving behind. Qunu was all that I knew, and I loved it in the unconditional way that a child loves his first home. Before we disappeared behind the hills, I turned and looked for what I imagined was the last time at my village. I could see the simple huts and the people going about their chores; the stream where I had splashed and played with the other boys; the maize fields and green pastures where the herds and flocks were lazily grazing. I imagined my friends out hunting for small birds, drinking the sweet milk from the cow's udder, cavorting in the pond at the end of the stream. Above all else, my eyes rested on the three simple huts where I had enjoyed my mother's love and protection. It was these three huts that I associated with all my happiness, with life itself, and I rued the fact that I had not kissed each of them before I left. I could not imagine that the future I was walking towards could compare in any way with the past that I was leaving behind.

We travelled by foot and in silence until the sun was sinking slowly towards the horizon. But the silence of the heart between mother and child is not a lonely one. My mother and I never talked very much, but we did not need to. I never doubted her love or questioned her support. It was an exhausting journey, along rocky dirt roads, up and down hills, past numerous villages, but we did not pause. Late in the afternoon, at the bottom of a shallow valley surrounded by trees, we came upon a village at the centre of which was a large and gracious home that so far exceeded anything that I had ever seen that all I could do was marvel at it. The buildings consisted of two *iingxande* (or rectangular houses) and seven stately rondavels (superior huts), all washed in white lime, dazzling even in the light of the setting sun. There was a large front garden and a maize field bordered by rounded peach trees. An even more spacious garden spread out behind it, which boasted apple trees, a vegetable garden, a strip of flowers and a patch of wattles. Nearby was a white stucco church.

In the shade of two gum trees that graced the doorway of the front of the main house sat a group of about twenty tribal elders. Encircling the property, contentedly grazing on the rich land, was a herd of at least fifty cattle and perhaps five hundred sheep. Everything was beautifully tended, and it was a vision of wealth and order beyond my imagination. This was the Great Place, Mqhekezweni, the provisional capital of Thembuland, the royal residence of Chief Jongintaba Dalindyebo, acting regent of the Thembu people.

As I contemplated all this grandeur an enormous motor car rumbled through the western gate and the men sitting in the shade immediately doffed their hats and then jumped to their feet shouting, '*Bayete a-a-a, Jongintaba!*' ('Hail, Jongintaba!'), the traditional salute of the Xhosas for their chief. Out of the motor car (I learned later that this majestic vehicle was a Ford V8) stepped a short, thickset man wearing a smart suit. I could see that he had the confidence and bearing of a man who was used to the exercise of authority. His name suited him, for Jongintaba literally means 'One who looks at the mountains', and he was a man with a sturdy presence upon whom all eyes gazed. He had a dark complexion and an intelligent face, and he casually shook hands with each of the men beneath the tree, men who as I later discovered comprised the highest Thembu Court of Justice. This was the regent who was to become my guardian and benefactor for the next decade.

In that moment of beholding Jongintaba and his court I felt like a sapling pulled root and branch from the earth and flung into the centre of a stream whose strong current I could not resist. I felt a sense of awe mixed with bewilderment. Until then I had had no thoughts of anything but my own pleasures, no higher ambition than to eat well and become a champion stick-fighter. I had no thought of money, or class, or fame, or power. Suddenly a new world opened before me. Children from poor homes often find themselves beguiled by a host of new temptations when suddenly confronted by great wealth. I was no exception. I felt many of my established beliefs and loyalties begin to ebb away. The slender foundation built by my parents began to shake. In that instant, I saw that life might hold more for me than being a champion stick-fighter.

I learned later that, in the wake of my father's death, Jongintaba had offered to become my guardian. He would treat me as he treated his other children, and I would have the same advantages as they. My mother had no choice; one did not turn down such an overture from the regent. She was satisfied that, although she would miss me, I would have a more advantageous upbringing in the regent's care than in her own. The regent had not forgotten that it was due to my father's intervention that he had become acting paramount chief.

My mother remained in Mqhekezweni for a day or two before returning to Qunu. Our parting was without fuss. She offered no sermons, no words of wisdom, no kisses. I suspect she did not want me to feel bereft at her departure and so was matter-of-fact. I knew that my father had wanted me to be educated and prepared for a wide world, and I could not do that in Qunu. Her tender look was all the affection and support I needed, and as she departed she turned to me and said, '*Uqinisufokotho, Kwedini!*' ('Brace yourself, my boy!'). Children are often the least sentimental of creatures, especially if they are absorbed in some new pleasure. Even as my dear mother and first friend was leaving, my head was swimming with the delights of my new home. How could I not be braced up? I was already wearing the handsome new outfit purchased for me by my guardian.

I was quickly caught up in the daily life of Mqhe-kezweni. A child adapts rapidly, or not at all – and I had taken to the Great Place as though I had been raised there. To me, it was a magical kingdom; everything was delightful; the chores that were tedious in Qunu be-came an adventure in Mqhekezweni. When I was not in school, I was a ploughboy, a waggon guide, a shepherd. I rode horses and shot birds with slingshots and found boys to joust with, and some nights I danced the evening away to the beautiful singing and clapping of Thembu maidens. Although I missed Qunu and my mother, I was completely absorbed in my new world.

I attended a one-room school next door to the palace and studied English, Xhosa, history and geography. We read *Chambers English Reader* and did our lessons on black slates. Our teachers, Mr Fadana and, later, Mr Giqwa, took a special interest in me. I did well in school not so much through cleverness as through doggedness. My own self-discipline was reinforced by my aunt Phathiwe, who lived in the Great Place and scrutinized my homework every night.

Mqhekezweni was a mission station of the Methodist Church and far more up-to-date and Westernized than Qunu. People dressed in modern clothes. The men wore suits and the women affected the severe Protestant style of the missionaries: thick long skirts and high-necked blouses, with a blanket draped over the shoulder and a scarf wound elegantly around the head.

If the world of Mqhekezweni revolved around the regent, my smaller world revolved around his two children. Justice, the elder, was his only son and heir to the Great Place, and Nomafu was the regent's daughter. I lived with them and was treated exactly as they were. We ate the same food, wore the same clothes, performed the same chores. We were later joined by Nxeko, the older brother to Sabata, the heir to the throne. The four of us formed a royal quartet. The regent and his wife No-England brought me up as if I were their own child. They worried about me, guided me and punished me, all in a spirit of loving fairness. Jongintaba was stern, but I never doubted his love. They called me by the pet name of Tatomkhulu, which means 'Grandpa', because they said when I was very serious, I looked like an old man.

Justice was four years older than me and became my first hero after my father. I looked up to him in every way. He was already at Clarkebury, a boarding school about sixty miles away. Tall, handsome and muscular, he was a fine sportsman, excelling in track and field events, cricket, rugby and soccer. Cheerful and outgoing, he was a natural performer who enchanted audiences with his singing and transfixed them with his ballroom dancing. He had a bevy of female admirers – but also a coterie of critics, who considered him a dandy and a playboy. Justice and I became the best of friends, though we were opposites in many ways: he was extroverted, I was introverted; he was lighthearted, I was serious. Things came easily to him; I had to drill myself. To me, he was everything a young man should be and everything I longed to be. Though treated alike, our destinies were different: Justice would inherit one of the most powerful chieftainships of the Thembu tribe, while I would inherit whatever the regent, in his generosity, decided to give me.

Every day I was in and out of the regent's house doing errands. Of those I did for the regent, the one I enjoyed most was pressing his suits, a job in which I took great pride. He owned half a dozen Western suits, and I spent many an hour carefully making the creases in his trousers. His palace, as it were, consisted of two large Western-style houses with tin roofs. In those days, very few Africans had Western houses and they were considered a mark of great wealth. Six rondavels stood in a semicircle around the main house. They had wooden floorboards, something I had never seen before. The regent and the queen slept in the right-hand rondavel, the queen's sister in the centre one, and the left-hand hut served as a pantry. Under the floor of the queen's sister's hut was a beehive, and we would sometimes take up a floorboard or two and feast on its honey. Shortly after I moved to Mqhekezweni, the regent and his wife moved to the *uxande* (middle house), which automatically became the Great House. There were three small rondavels near it; one for the regent's mother, one for visitors and one shared by Justice and myself.

The two principles that governed my life at Mqhekezweni were chieftaincy and the Church. These two doctrines existed in uneasy harmony, although I did not then see them as antagonistic. For me, Christianity was not so much a system of beliefs as it was the powerful creed of a single man: Reverend Matyolo. For me, his powerful presence embodied all that was alluring in Christianity. He was as popular and beloved as the regent, and the fact that he was the regent's superior in spiritual matters made a strong impression on me. But the Church was as concerned with this world as the next: I saw that virtually all of the achievements of Africans seemed to have come about through the missionary work of the Church. The mission schools trained the clerks, the interpreters and the policemen, who at the time represented the height of African aspirations.

Reverend Matyolo was a stout man in his mid-fifties, with a deep and potent voice that lent itself to both preaching and singing. When he preached at the simple church at the western end of Mqhekezweni, the hall was always brimming with people. The hall rang with the hosannas of the faithful, while the

women knelt at his feet to beg for salvation. The first
tale I heard about him when I arrived at the Great
Place was that he had chased away a dangerous ghost
with only a Bible and a lantern as weapons. I saw
neither implausibility nor contradiction in this story.
The Methodism preached by Reverend Matyolo was of
the fire-and-brimstone variety, seasoned with a bit of
African animism. The Lord was wise and omnipotent,
but He was also a vengeful God who let no bad deed go
unpunished.

At Qunu, the only time I had ever attended church
was on the day that I was baptized. Religion was a ritual
that I indulged in for my mother's sake and to which I
attached no meaning. But at Mqhekezweni, religion
was a part of the fabric of life and I attended church
each Sunday along with the regent and his wife. The
regent took his religion very seriously. In fact the only
time that I was ever given a hiding by him was when I
dodged a Sunday service to take part in a fight against
boys from another village, a transgression I never
committed again.

That was not the only rebuke I received on account
of my trespasses against the reverend. One afternoon, I
crept into Reverend Matyolo's garden and stole some
maize, which I roasted and ate on the spot. A young girl
saw me eating the corn in the garden and immediately
reported my presence to the priest. The news quickly
made the rounds and reached the regent's wife. That
evening, she waited until prayer time – which was a
daily ritual in the house – and confronted me with my
misdeed, reproaching me for taking the bread from a
poor servant of God and disgracing the family. She said
the devil would certainly take me to task for my sin. I

felt an unpleasant mixture of fear and shame – fear that I would get some cosmic comeuppance and shame that I had abused the trust of my adopted family.

Because of the universal respect the regent enjoyed – from both black and white – and the seemingly untempered power that he wielded, I saw chieftaincy as being the very centre around which life revolved. The power and influence of chieftaincy pervaded every aspect of our lives in Mqhekezweni and was the preeminent means through which one could achieve influence and status.

My later notions of leadership were profoundly influenced by observing the regent and his court. I watched and learned from the tribal meetings that were regularly held at the Great Place. These were not scheduled, but were called as needed, and were held to discuss national matters such as a drought, the culling of cattle, policies ordered by the magistrate, or new laws decreed by the government. All Thembus were free to come – and a great many did, on horseback or by foot.

On these occasions, the regent was surrounded by his *amaphakathi*, a group of councillors of high rank who functioned as the regent's parliament and judiciary. They were wise men who retained the knowledge of tribal history and custom in their heads and whose opinions carried great weight.

Letters advising these chiefs and headmen of a meeting were dispatched from the regent, and soon the Great Place became alive with important visitors and travellers from all over Thembuland. The guests would gather in the courtyard in front of the regent's house and he would open the meeting by thanking everyone for coming and explaining why he had summoned them. From that point on, he would not utter another word until the meeting was nearing its end.

Everyone who wanted to speak did so. It was democracy in its purest form. There may have been a hierarchy of importance among the speakers, but everyone was heard: chief and subject, warrior and medicine man, shopkeeper and farmer, landowner and labourer. People spoke without interruption and the meetings lasted for many hours. The foundation of self-government was that all men were free to voice their opinions and were equal in their value as citizens. (Women, I am afraid, were deemed second-class citizens.)

A great banquet was served during the day, and I often gave myself a bellyache by eating too much while listening to speaker after speaker. I noticed how some speakers rambled and never seemed to get to the point. I grasped how others came to the matter at hand directly, and who made a set of arguments succinctly and cogently. I observed how some speakers used emotion and dramatic language, and tried to move the audience with such techniques, while others were sober and even, and shunned emotion.

At first, I was astonished by the vehemence – and candour – with which people criticized the regent. He was not above criticism – in fact, he was often the principal target of it. But no matter how serious the charge, the regent simply listened, not defending himself, showing no emotion at all.

The meetings would continue until some kind of consensus was reached. They ended in unanimity or not at all. Unanimity, however, might be an agreement to disagree, to wait for a more propitious time to propose a solution. Democracy meant all men were to be heard, and a decision was taken together as a people. Majority rule was a foreign notion. A minority was not to be crushed by a majority.

Only at the end of the meeting, as the sun was setting, would the regent speak. His purpose was to sum up what had been said and form some consensus among the diverse opinions. But no conclusion was forced on people who disagreed. If no agreement could be reached, another meeting would be held. At the very end of the council, a praise-singer or poet would deliver a panegyric to the ancient kings, and a mixture of compliments to and satire on the present chiefs; the audience, led by the regent, would roar with laughter.

As a leader, I have always followed the principles I first saw demonstrated by the regent at the Great Place. I have always endeavoured to listen to what each and every person in a discussion had to say before venturing my own opinion. Oftentimes, my own opinion will simply represent a consensus of what I heard in the discussion. I always remember the regent's axiom: a leader, he said, is like a shepherd. He stays behind the flock, letting the most nimble go on ahead, whereupon the others follow, not realizing that all along they are being directed from behind.

It was at Mqhekezweni that I developed my interest in African history. Until then I had heard only of Xhosa heroes, but at the Great Place I learned of other African heroes like Sekhukhune, king of the Bapedi, the Basotho king, Moshoeshoe, and Dingane, king of the Zulus, and others such as Bambatha, Hintsa and Makana, Montshiwa and Kgama. I learned of these men from the chiefs and headmen who came to the Great Place to settle disputes and try cases. Though not lawyers, these men presented cases and then adjudicated them. Some days, they would finish early and sit around telling stories. I hovered silently and listened. They spoke in an idiom that I'd never heard before. Their speech was formal and lofty, their manner slow and unhurried, and the traditional clicks of our language were long and dramatic.

At first, they shooed me away and told me I was too young to listen. Later they would beckon me to fetch fire or water for them, or to tell the women they wanted tea, and in those early months I was too busy running errands to follow their conversation. But, eventually, they permitted me to stay, and I discovered the great African patriots who fought against Western domination. My imagination was fired by the glory of these African warriors.

The most ancient of the chiefs who regaled the gathered elders with ancient tales was Zwelibhangile Joyi, a son from the Great House of King Ngubengcuka. Chief Joyi was so old that his wrinkled skin hung on him like a loose-fitting coat. His stories unfolded slowly and were often punctuated by a great wheezing cough, which would force him to stop for minutes at a time. Chief Joyi was the great authority on the history of the Thembus in large part because he had lived through so much of it.

But as grizzled as Chief Joyi often seemed, the decades fell off him when he spoke of the *impis*, or warriors, in the army of King Ngangelizwe. In pantomime, Chief Joyi would fling his spear and creep along the veld as he narrated the victories and defeats. He spoke of Ngangelizwe's heroism, generosity and humility.

Not all of Chief Joyi's stories revolved around the Thembus. When he first spoke of non-Xhosa warriors, I wondered why. I was like a boy who worships a local soccer hero and is not interested in a national soccer star with whom he has no connection. Only later was I moved by the broad sweep of African history, and the deeds of all African heroes regardless of tribe.

Chief Joyi railed against the white man, whom he believed had deliberately sundered the Xhosa tribe, dividing brother from brother. The white man had told the Thembus that their true chief was the great white queen across the ocean and that they were her subjects. But the white queen brought nothing but misery and perfidy to the black people; if she was a chief, she was an evil chief. Chief Joyi's war stories and his indictment of the British made me feel angry and cheated, as though I had already been robbed of my own birthright.

Chief Joyi said that the African people lived in relative peace until the coming of the *abelungu*, the white people, who arrived from across the sea with fire-breathing weapons. Once, he said, the Thembu, the Pondo, the Xhosa, and the Zulu were all children of one father, and lived as brothers. The white man shattered the *abantu*, the fellowship, of the various tribes. The white man was hungry and greedy for land, and the black man shared the land with him as they shared the air and water; land was not for man to possess. But the white man took the land as you might seize another man's horse.

I did not yet know that the real history of our country was not to be found in standard British textbooks, which claimed South Africa began with the landing of Jan van Riebeeck at the Cape of Good Hope in 1652. It was from Chief Joyi that I began to discover that the history of the Bantu-speaking peoples began far to the north, in a country of lakes and green plains and valleys, and that slowly over the millennia we made our way down to the very tip of this great continent. However, I later discovered that Chief Joyi's account of African history, particularly after 1652, was not always so accurate.

In Mqhekezweni, I felt not unlike the proverbial country boy who comes to the big city. Mqhekezweni was far more sophisticated than Qunu, whose residents were regarded as backward by the people of Mqhekezweni. The regent was loath for me to visit Qunu, thinking I would regress and fall into bad company back in my old village. When I did visit, I sensed that my mother had been briefed by the regent, for she would question me closely as to whom I was playing with. On many occasions, however, the regent would arrange for my mother and sisters to be brought to the Great Place.

When I first arrived in Mqhekezweni, I was regarded by some of my peers as a yokel who was hopelessly unequipped to exist in the rarefied atmosphere of the Great Place. As young men will, I did my best to appear suave and sophisticated. In church one day, I had noticed a lovely young woman who was one of the daughters of the Reverend Matyolo. Her name was Winnie and I asked her out and she accepted. She was keen on me, but her eldest sister, nomaMpondo, regarded me as hopelessly backward. She told her

sister that I was a barbarian who was not good enough
for the daughter of Reverend Matyolo. To prove to her
younger sister how uncivilized I was, she invited me to
the rectory for lunch. I was still used to eating at home,
where we did not use a knife and fork. At the family
table, this mischievous older sister handed me a plate
that contained a single chicken wing. But the wing,
instead of being soft and tender, was a bit tough, so the
meat did not fall easily off the bone.

I watched the others using their knives and forks with
ease and slowly picked up mine. I observed the others
for a few moments, and then attempted to carve my
little wing. At first I just moved it around the plate,
hoping that the flesh would fall from the bone. Then I
tried in vain to pin the thing down and cut it, but it
eluded me, and in my frustration I was clanking my
knife on the plate. I tried this repeatedly and then
noticed that the older sister was smiling at me and
looking knowingly at the younger sister as if to say, 'I
told you so.' I struggled and struggled and became wet
with perspiration, but I did not want to admit defeat
and pick the infernal thing up with my hands. I did not
eat much chicken that day at luncheon.

Afterwards the older sister told the younger, 'You will
waste your whole life if you fall in love with such a
backward boy,' but I am happy to say the young lady did
not listen – she loved me, backward as I was. Eventually,
of course, we went different ways and drifted apart. She
attended a different school, and qualified as a teacher.
We corresponded for a few years and then I lost track
of her, but by that time I had considerably improved
my table etiquette.

4

When I was sixteen, the regent decided that it was time that I became a man. In Xhosa tradition, this is achieved through one means only: circumcision. In my tradition, an uncircumcised male cannot be heir to his father's wealth, cannot marry or officiate in tribal rituals. An uncircumcised Xhosa man is a contradiction in terms, for he is not considered a man at all, but a boy. For the Xhosa people, circumcision represents the formal incorporation of males into society. It is not just a surgical procedure, but a lengthy and elaborate ritual in preparation for manhood. As a Xhosa, I count my years as a man from the date of my circumcision.

The traditional ceremony of the circumcision school was arranged principally for Justice. The rest of us, twenty-six in all, were there mainly to keep him company. Early in the new year, we journeyed to two grass huts in a secluded valley on the banks of the Mbashe River, known as Tyhalarha, the traditional place of circumcision for Thembu kings. The huts were seclusion lodges, where we were to live isolated from society. It was a sacred time; I felt happy and fulfilled taking part in my people's customs and ready to make the transition from boyhood to manhood.

We had moved to Tyhalarha by the river a few days before the actual circumcision ceremony. These last few days of boyhood were spent with the other initiates, and I found the camaraderie enjoyable. The lodge was near the

home of Banabakhe Blayi, the wealthiest and most popular boy at the circumcision school. He was an engaging
fellow, a champion stick-fighter and a glamour boy, whose
many girlfriends kept us all supplied with delicacies.
Although he could neither read nor write, he was one
of the most intelligent among us. He regaled us with
stories of his trips to Johannesburg, a place that none of us
had ever been to. He so thrilled us with tales of the mines
that he almost persuaded me that to be a miner was more
alluring than to be a monarch. Miners had a mystique; to
be a miner meant to be strong and daring: the ideal of
manhood. Much later, I realized that it was the exaggerated tales of boys like Banabakhe that caused so many
young men to run away to work in the mines of Johannesburg, where they often lost their health and their lives. In
those days, working in the mines was almost as much of a
rite of passage as circumcision school, a myth that helped
the mine-owners more than it helped my people.

A custom of circumcision school is that one must
perform a daring exploit before the ceremony. In days
of old, this might have involved a cattle raid or even a
battle, but in our time the deeds were more mischievous than martial. Two nights before we moved to
Tyhalarha, we decided to steal a pig. In Mkhekezweni,
there was a tribesman with a typical old pig. To avoid
making a noise and alarming the farmer, we arranged
for the pig to do our work for us. We took handfuls of
sediment from homemade African beer, which has a
strong scent much favoured by pigs, and placed it
upwind of the animal. It was so aroused by the scent
that he came out of the kraal, following a trail we had
laid and gradually made his way to us, wheezing and
snorting, and eating the sediment. When he got near

us, we captured the poor pig, slaughtered it, and then built a fire and ate roast pork underneath the stars. No piece of pork has ever tasted as good before or since.

The night before the circumcision, there was a ceremony near our huts with singing and dancing. Women came from the nearby villages and we danced to their singing and clapping. As the music became faster and louder, our dance turned more frenzied and we forgot for a moment what lay ahead.

At dawn, when the stars were still in the sky, we began our preparations. We were escorted to the river to bathe in its cold waters, a ritual that signified our purification before the ceremony. The ceremony was at midday, and we were commanded to stand in a row in a clearing some distance from the river where a crowd of parents and relatives, including the regent, as well as a handful of chiefs and counsellors, had gathered. We were clad only in our blankets and as the ceremony began, with drums pounding, we were ordered to sit on a blanket on the ground with our legs spread out in front of us. I was tense and anxious, uncertain of how I would react when the critical moment came. Flinching or crying out was a sign of weakness and stigmatized one's manhood. I was determined not to disgrace myself, the group or my guardian. Circumcision is a trial of bravery and stoicism; no anaesthetic is used; a man must suffer in silence.

To the right, out of the corner of my eye, I could see a thin, elderly man emerge from a tent and kneel in front of the first boy. There was excitement in the crowd, and I shuddered slightly, knowing that the ritual was about to begin. The old man was a famous *ingcibi*, a circumcision expert, from Gcalekaland, who would use his assegai to change us from boys to men with a single blow.

Suddenly I heard the first boy cry out, '*Ndiyindoda!*' ('I am a man!'), which we had been trained to say at the moment of circumcision. Seconds later, I heard Justice's strangled voice pronounce the same phrase. There were now two boys before the *ingcibi* reached me, and my mind must have gone blank because, before I knew it, the old man was kneeling in front of me. I looked directly into his eyes. He was pale, and though the day was cold, his face was shining with perspiration. His hands moved so fast they seemed to be controlled by an otherworldly force. Without a word, he took my foreskin, pulled it forward, and then, in a single motion, brought down his assegai. I felt as if fire was shooting through my veins; the pain was so intense that I buried my chin in my chest. Many seconds seemed to pass before I remembered the cry, and then I recovered and called out, '*Ndiyindoda!*'

I looked down and saw a perfect cut, clean and round like a ring. But I felt ashamed because the other boys seemed much stronger and firmer than I had been; they had called out more promptly than I had. I was distressed that I had been disabled, however briefly, by the pain, and I did my best to hide my agony. A boy may cry; a man conceals his pain.

I had now taken the essential step in the life of every Xhosa man. Now I might marry, set up my own home and plough my own field. I could now be admitted to the councils of the community; my words would be taken seriously. At the ceremony, I was given my circumcision name, Dalibhunga, meaning 'Founder of the Bungha', the traditional ruling body of the Transkei. To Xhosa traditionalists, this name is more acceptable than either of my two previous given names,

Rolihlahla or Nelson, and I was proud to hear my new name pronounced: Dalibhunga.

Immediately after the blow had been delivered, an assistant who followed the circumcision master took the foreskin that was on the ground and tied it to a corner of our blankets. Our wounds were then dressed with a healing plant, the leaves of which were thorny on the outside but smooth on the inside, which absorbed the blood and other secretions.

At the conclusion of the ceremony, we returned to our huts, where a fire was burning with wet wood that cast off clouds of smoke, which was thought to promote healing. We were ordered to lie on our backs in the smoky huts, with one leg flat, and one leg bent. We were now *abakwetha*, initiates into the world of manhood. We were looked after by an *amakhankatha*, or guardian, who explained the rules we had to follow if we were to enter manhood properly. The first chore of the *amakhankatha* was to paint our naked and shaved bodies from head to foot in white ochre, turning us into ghosts. The white chalk symbolized our purity, and I still recall how stiff the dried clay felt on my body.

That first night, at midnight, an attendant, or *ikhankatha*, crept around the hut, gently waking each of us. We were then instructed to leave the hut and go tramping through the night to bury our foreskins. The traditional reason for this practice was so that our foreskins would be hidden before wizards could use them for evil purposes, but, symbolically, we were also burying our youth. I did not want to leave the warm hut and wander through the bush in the darkness, but I walked into the trees and, after a few minutes, untied my foreskin and buried it in the earth. I felt as though I had now discarded the last remnant of my childhood.

We lived in our two huts – thirteen in each – while our wounds healed. When outside the huts, we were covered in blankets, for we were not allowed to be seen by women. It was a period of quietude, a kind of spiritual preparation for the trials of manhood that lay ahead. On the day of our re-emergence, we went down to the river early in the morning to wash away the white ochre in the waters of the Mbashe. Once we were clean and dry, we were coated in red ochre. The tradition was that one should sleep with a woman, who later might become one's wife, and she rubs off the pigment with her body. In my case, however, the ochre was removed with a mixture of fat and lard.

At the end of our seclusion, the lodges and all their contents were burned, destroying our last links to childhood, and a great ceremony was held to welcome us as men to society. Our families, friends and local chiefs gathered for speeches, songs and gift-giving. I was given two heifers and four sheep, and felt far richer than I ever had before. I, who had never owned anything, suddenly possessed property. It was a heady feeling, even though my gifts were paltry next to those of Justice, who inherited an entire herd. I was not jealous of Justice's gifts. He was the son of a king; I was merely destined to be a counsellor to a king. I felt strong and proud that day. I remember walking differently on that day, straighter, taller, firmer. I was hopeful, and thinking that I might some day have wealth, property and status.

The main speaker of the day was Chief Meligqili, the son of Dalindyebo, and after listening to him, my gaily coloured dreams suddenly darkened. He began conventionally, remarking how fine it was that we were continuing a tradition that had been going on for as long as anyone could remember. Then he turned to us and his tone suddenly changed. 'There sit our sons,' he said, 'young, healthy and handsome, the flower of the Xhosa tribe, the pride of our nation. We have just circumcised them in a ritual that promises them manhood, but I am here to tell you that it is an empty, illusory promise, a promise that can never be fulfilled. For we Xhosas, and all black South Africans, are a conquered people. We are slaves in our own country. We are tenants on our own soil. We have no strength, no power, no control over our own destiny in the land of our birth. They will go to cities where they will live in shacks and drink cheap alcohol, all because we have no land to give them where they could prosper and multiply. They will cough their lungs out deep in the bowels of the white man's mines, destroying their health, never seeing the sun, so that the white man can live a life of unequalled prosperity. Among these young men are chiefs who will never rule because we have no power to govern ourselves; soldiers who will never fight for we have no weapons to fight with; scholars who will never teach because we have no place for them to study. The abilities, the intelligence, the promise of these young men will be squandered in their attempt to eke out a living doing the simplest, most mindless chores for the white man. These gifts today are naught, for we cannot give them the greatest gift of all, which is freedom and independence. I well know that Qamata [God] is all-seeing and never sleeps, but I have a suspicion that Qamata may in fact be dozing. If this is the case, the sooner I die the better, because then I can meet him and shake him awake and tell him that the children of Ngubengcuka, the flower of the Xhosa nation, are dying.'

The audience had become more and more quiet as Chief Meligqili spoke and, I think, more and more angry. No one wanted to hear the words that he spoke that day. I know that I myself did not want to hear them. I was cross rather than aroused by the chief's remarks, dismissing his words as the abusive comments of an ignorant man who was unable to appreciate the value of the education and benefits that the white man had brought to our country. At the time, I looked on the white man not as an oppressor but as a benefactor, and I thought the chief was enormously ungrateful. This upstart chief was ruining my day, spoiling the proud feeling with wrong-headed remarks.

But without exactly understanding why, his words soon began to work on me. He had sown a seed, and though I let that seed lie dormant for a long season, it eventually began to grow. Later I realized that the ignorant man that day was not the chief but myself.

After the ceremony, I walked back to the river and watched it meander on its way to where, many miles distant, it emptied into the Indian Ocean. I had never crossed that river, and I knew little or nothing of the world beyond it, a world that beckoned me that day. It was almost sunset and I hurried on to where our seclusion lodges had been. Though it was forbidden to look back while the lodges were burning, I could not resist. When I reached the area, all that remained were two pyramids of ashes by a large mimosa tree. In these ash heaps lay a lost and delightful world, the world of my childhood, the world of sweet and irresponsible days at Qunu and Mqhekezweni. Now I was a man, and I would never again play *thinti*, or steal maize, or drink milk from a cow's udder. I was already in mourning for my own youth. Looking back, I know that I was not a man that day and would not truly become one for many years.

5

Unlike most of the others with whom I had been at circumcision school, I was not destined to work in the gold mines on the Reef. The regent had often told me, 'It is not for you to spend your life mining the white man's gold, never knowing how to write your name.' My destiny was to become a counsellor to Sabata, and for that I had to be educated. I returned to Mqhekezweni after the ceremony, but not for very long, for I was about to cross the Mbashe River for the first time on my way to Clarkebury Boarding Institute in the district of Engcobo.

I was again leaving home, but I was eager to see how I would fare in the wider world. The regent himself drove me to Engcobo in his majestic Ford V8. Before leaving, he had organized a celebration for my having passed Standard V and being admitted to Clarkebury. A sheep was slaughtered and there was dancing and singing – it was the first celebration that I had ever had in my own honour, and I greatly enjoyed it. The regent gave me my first pair of boots, a sign of manhood, and that night I polished them anew, even though they were already shiny.

Founded in 1825, the Clarkebury Institute was located on the site of one of the oldest Wesleyan missions in the Transkei. At the time, Clarkebury was the highest institution of learning for Africans in Thembuland. The regent himself had attended Clarkebury, and

Justice had followed him there. It was both a secondary school and a teacher-training college, but it also offered courses in more practical disciplines such as carpentry, tailoring and tin-smithing.

During the trip, the regent advised me on my behaviour and my future. He urged me to behave in a way that brought only respect to Sabata and to himself, and I assured him that I would. He then briefed me on the Reverend C. Harris, the governor of the school. Reverend Harris, he explained, was unique: he was a white Thembu, a white man who in his heart loved and understood the Thembu people. The regent said when Sabata was older, he would entrust the future king to Reverend Harris, who would train him as both a Christian and a traditional ruler. He said that I must learn from Reverend Harris because I was destined to guide the leader that Reverend Harris was to mould.

At Mqhekezweni I had met many white traders and government officials, including magistrates and police officers. These were men of high standing, and the regent received them courteously, but not obsequiously; he treated them on equal terms as they did him. At times, I even saw him upbraid them, though this was extremely rare. I had very little experience in dealing directly with whites. The regent never told me how to behave, and I observed him and followed his example. In talking about Reverend Harris, however, the regent, for the first time, gave me a lecture on how I was to conduct myself. He said I must afford the reverend the same respect and obedience that I gave to him.

Clarkebury was far grander even than Mqhekezweni. The school itself consisted of a cluster of two dozen or so graceful, colonial-style buildings, which included individual homes as well as dormitories, the library and various instructional halls. It was the first place I'd lived that was Western, not African, and I felt I was entering a new world whose rules were not yet clear to me.

We were taken in to Reverend Harris's study, where the regent introduced me and I stood to shake his hand, the first time I had ever shaken hands with a white man. Reverend Harris was warm and friendly, and treated the regent with great deference. The regent explained that I was being groomed to be a counsellor to the king and that he hoped the reverend would take a special interest in me. The reverend nodded, adding that Clarkebury students were required to do manual labour after school hours, and he would arrange for me to work in his garden.

At the end of the interview, the regent bade me good-bye and handed me a pound note for pocket money, the largest amount of money I had ever possessed. I bade him farewell and promised that I would not disappoint him.

Clarkebury was a Thembu college, founded on land given by the great Thembu king Ngubengcuka; as a descendant of Ngubengcuka I presumed that I would be accorded the same deference at Clarkebury that I had come to expect in Mqhekezweni. But I was painfully mistaken, for I was treated no differently from everyone else. No one knew or even cared that I was a descendant of the illustrious Ngubengcuka. The housemaster received me without a blowing of trumpets and my fellow students did not bow and scrape before me.

At Clarkebury, plenty of the boys had distinguished lineages, and I was no longer unique. This was an important lesson, for I suspect I was a bit stuck-up in those days. I quickly realized that I had to make my way on the basis of my ability, not my heritage. Most of my classmates could outrun me on the playing field and outthink me in the classroom, and I had a good deal of catching up to do.

Classes commenced the following morning, and along with my fellow students I climbed the steps to the first floor where the classrooms were located. The room itself had a beautifully polished wooden floor. On this first day of classes I sported my new boots. I had never worn boots before of any kind, and that first day I walked like a newly shod horse. I made a terrible racket walking up the steps and almost slipped several times. As I clomped into the classroom, my boots crashing on that shiny wood floor, I noticed two female students in the first row were watching my lame performance with great amusement. The prettier of the two leaned over to her friend and said loud enough for all to hear: 'The country boy is not used to wearing shoes,' at which her friend laughed. I was blind with fury and embarrassment.

Her name was Mathona, and she was a bit of a smart Aleck. That day I vowed never to talk to her. But as my mortification wore off (and I became more adept at walking with boots) I also got to know her, and she was to become my greatest friend at Clarkebury. She was my first true female friend, a woman I met on equal terms with whom I could confide and share secrets. In many ways, she was the model for all my subsequent friendships with women, for with women I found I could let my hair down and confess to weaknesses and fears I would never reveal to another man.

I soon adapted to life at Clarkebury. I participated in sports and games as often as I could, but my performances were no more than mediocre. I played for the love of sport, not the glory, for I received none. We played lawn tennis with home-made wooden rackets and soccer with bare feet on a field of dust.

For the first time, I was taught by teachers who had themselves been properly educated. Several of them held university degrees, which was extremely rare. One day, I was studying with Mathona, and I confided to her my fear that I might not pass my exams in English and history at the end of the year. She told me not to worry because our teacher, Gertrude Ntlabathi, was the first African woman to obtain a BA. 'She is too clever to let us fail,' Mathona said. I had not yet learned to feign knowledge that I did not possess, and as I had only a vague idea what a BA was, I questioned Mathona. 'Oh, yes, of course,' she answered. 'A BA is a very long and difficult book.' I did not doubt her.

Another African teacher with a bachelor of arts degree was Ben Mahlasela. We admired him not only because of his academic achievement, but because he was not intimidated by Reverend Harris. Even the white faculty behaved in a servile manner to Reverend Harris, but Mr Mahlasela would walk into the reverend's office without fear, and sometimes would even fail to remove his hat! He met the reverend on equal terms, disagreeing with him where others simply assented. Though I respected Reverend Harris, I admired the fact that Mr Mahlasela would not be cowed by him. In those days, a black man with a BA was expected to scrape before a white man with a primary school education. No matter how high a black man advanced, he was still considered inferior to the lowest white man.

Reverend Harris ran Clarkebury with an iron hand and an abiding sense of fairness. Clarkebury functioned more like a military school than a teacher-training college. The slightest infractions were swiftly punished. In assemblies, Reverend Harris always wore a forbidding expression, and was not given to levity of any kind. When he walked into a room, members of the staff, including white principals of the training and secondary schools, together with the black principal of the industrial school, rose to their feet.

Among students, he was feared more than loved. But in the garden, I saw a different Reverend Harris. Working in his garden had a double benefit: it planted in me a lifelong love of gardening and growing vegetables, and it helped me get to know the reverend and his family – the first white family with whom I had ever been on intimate terms. In that way, I saw that Reverend Harris had a public face and a private manner that were quite different from one another.

Behind the reverend's mask of severity was a gentle, broad-minded individual who believed fervently in the importance of educating young Africans. Often, I found him lost in thought in his garden. I did not disturb him and rarely talked to him, but as an example of a man unselfishly devoted to a good cause, Reverend Harris was an important model for me.

His wife was as talkative as he was taciturn. She was a lovely woman and she would often come into the garden to chat with me. I cannot for the life of me remember what we talked about, but I can still taste the delicious warm scones that she brought out to me in the afternoons.

After my slow and undistinguished start, I managed to get the hang of things, and accelerated my programme, completing the junior certificate in two years instead of the usual three. I developed the reputation of having a fine memory, but in fact I was simply a diligent worker. When I left Clarkebury, I lost track of Mathona. She was a day scholar, and her parents did not have the means to send her for further education. She was an extraordinarily clever and gifted person, whose potential was limited because of her family's meagre resources. This was an all too typical South African story. It was not lack of ability that limited my people, but lack of opportunity.

My time at Clarkebury broadened my horizons, yet I would not say that I was an entirely open-minded, unprejudiced young man when I left. I had met students from all over the Transkei, as well as a few from Johannesburg and Basutoland, as Lesotho was then known, some of whom were sophisticated and cosmopolitan in ways that made me feel provincial. Though I emulated them, I never thought it possible for a boy from the countryside to rival them in their worldliness. Yet I did not envy them. Even as I left Clarkebury, I was still, at heart, a Thembu, and I was proud to think and act like one. My roots were my destiny, and I believed that I would become a counsellor to the Thembu king, as my guardian wanted. My horizons did not extend beyond Thembuland and I believed that to be a Thembu was the most enviable thing in the world.

6

In 1937, when I was nineteen, I joined Justice at Heald-town, the Wesleyan College in Fort Beaufort, about 175 miles southwest of Umtata. In the nineteenth century, Fort Beaufort was one of a number of British outposts during the so-called Frontier Wars, in which a steady encroachment of white settlers systematically dispossessed the various Xhosa tribes of their land. Over a century of conflict, many Xhosa warriors achieved fame for their bravery, men like Sandile, Makhanda and Moqoma, the last two of whom were imprisoned on Robben Island by the British authorities, where they died. By the time of my arrival at Healdtown there were few signs of the battles of the previous century, except the main one: Fort Beaufort was a white town where once only the Xhosa lived and farmed.

Located at the end of a winding road overlooking a verdant valley, Healdtown was far more beautiful and impressive than Clarkebury. It was, at the time, the largest African school south of the equator, with more than a thousand students, both male and female. Its graceful ivy-covered colonial buildings and tree-shaded courtyards gave it the feeling of a privileged academic oasis, which is precisely what it was. Like Clarkebury, Healdtown was a mission school of the Methodist Church, and provided a Christian and liberal arts education based on an English model.

The principal of Healdtown was Dr Arthur Wellington, a stout and stuffy Englishman who boasted of his connection to the Duke of Wellington. At the outset of assemblies, Dr Wellington would walk on stage and say, in his deep bass voice, 'I am the descendant of the great Duke of Wellington, aristocrat, statesman, and general, who crushed the Frenchman Napoleon at Waterloo and thereby saved civilization for Europe – and for you, the natives.' At this, we would all enthusiastically applaud, each of us profoundly grateful that a descendant of the great Duke of Wellington would take the trouble to educate natives such as ourselves. The educated Englishman was our model; what we aspired to be were 'black Englishmen', as we were sometimes derisively called. We were taught – and believed – that the best ideas were English ideas, the best government was English government and the best men were Englishmen.

Healdtown life was rigorous. First bell was at 6 a.m. We were in the dining hall by 6.40 for a breakfast of dry bread and hot sugar water, watched over by a sombre portrait of George VI, the king of England. Those who could afford butter on their bread bought it and stored it in the kitchen. I ate dry toast. At eight we assembled in the courtyard outside our dormitory for 'observation', standing to attention as the girls arrived from separate dormitories. We remained in class until 12.45, and then had a lunch of samp, sour milk and beans, seldom meat. We then studied until 5 p.m., followed by an hour's break for exercise and dinner, and then studied again from seven until nine. Lights went out at 9.30.

Healdtown attracted students from all over the country, as well as from the protectorates of Basutoland, Swaziland and Bechuanaland. Though it was a mostly

Xhosa institution, there were also students from different tribes. After school and at weekends, students from the same tribe kept together. Even the members of various Xhosa tribes would gravitate together, such as the amaMpondo with the amaMpondo, and so on. I adhered to this same pattern, but it was at Healdtown that I made my first Sotho-speaking friend, Zachariah Molete. I remember feeling quite bold at having a friend who was not a Xhosa.

Our zoology teacher, Frank Lebentlele, was also Sotho-speaking and was very popular among the students. Personable and approachable, Frank was not much older than us and mixed freely with students. He even played in the college's first soccer team, where he was a star performer. But what most amazed us about him was his marriage to a Xhosa girl from Umtata. Marriages between tribes were then extremely unusual. Until then, I had never known of anyone who had married outside his tribe. We had been taught that such unions were taboo. But seeing Frank and his wife began to undermine my parochialism and loosen the hold of the tribalism that still imprisoned me. I began to sense my identity as an African, not just a Thembu or even a Xhosa. But this was still a nascent feeling.

Our dormitory had forty beds in it, twenty on either side of a central passageway. The housemaster was the delightful Reverend S.S. Mokitimi, who later became the first African president of the Methodist Church of South Africa. Reverend Mokitimi, who was also Sotho-speaking, was much admired among students as a modern and enlightened fellow who understood our complaints.

Reverend Mokitimi impressed us for another reason:

he stood up to Dr Wellington. One evening, a quarrel broke out between two prefects on the main thoroughfare of the college. Prefects were responsible for preventing disputes, not provoking them. Reverend Mokitimi was called in to make peace. Dr Wellington, returning from town, suddenly appeared in the midst of this commotion, and his arrival shook us considerably. It was as if a god had descended to solve some humble problem.

Dr Wellington pulled himself to a great height and demanded to know what was going on. Reverend Mokitimi, the top of whose head did not even reach Dr Wellington's shoulders, said very respectfully, 'Dr Wellington, everything is under control and I will report to you tomorrow.' Undeterred, Dr Wellington said with some irritation, 'No, I want to know what the matter is right now.' Reverend Mokitimi stood his ground: 'Dr Wellington, I am the housemaster and I have told you that I will report to you tomorrow, and that is what I will do.' We were stunned. We had never seen anyone, much less a black man, stand up to Dr Wellington, and we waited for an explosion. But Dr Wellington simply said, 'Very well', and left. I realized then that Dr Wellington was less than a god and Reverend Mokitimi more than a lackey, and that a black man did not have to defer automatically to a white, however senior he was.

Reverend Mokitimi sought to introduce reforms to the college. We all supported his efforts to improve the diet and the treatment of students, including his suggestion that students be responsible for disciplining themselves. But one change worried us, especially students from the countryside. This was Reverend

Mokitimi's innovation of having male and female students dine together in hall at Sunday lunch. I was very much against this for the simple reason that I was still inept with a knife and fork, and I did not want to embarrass myself in front of these sharp-eyed girls. But Reverend Mokitimi went ahead and organized the meals, and every Sunday I left the hall hungry and depressed.

I did, however, enjoy myself on the playing fields. The quality of sports at Healdtown was far superior to that of Clarkebury. In my first year I was not skilled enough to make any of the teams. But during my second year my friend Locke Ndzamela, Healdtown's champion hurdler, encouraged me to take up a new sport: long-distance running. I was tall and lanky, which Locke said was the ideal build for a long-distance runner. With a few hints from him, I began training. I enjoyed the discipline and solitariness of long-distance running, which allowed me to escape from the hurly-burly of school life. At the same time, I also took up a sport that I seemed less suited for, and that was boxing. I trained in a desultory way, and only years later, when I had put on a few more pounds, did I begin to box in earnest.

During my second year at Healdtown, I was appointed a prefect by Reverend Mokitimi and Dr Wellington. Prefects had different responsibilities, and the newest prefects had the least desirable duties. In the beginning, I supervised a group of students who worked as window cleaners during our manual work time in the afternoon, and led them to different buildings each day.

I soon graduated to the next level of responsibility, which was night duty. I have never had a problem in staying up all night, but during one such night I was put in a moral quandary that has remained in my memory. We did not have toilets in the dormitory, but there was an outhouse about a hundred feet behind the residence. On rainy evenings, when students woke up in the middle of the night, they wouldn't want to trudge through the grass and mud to the outhouse. Instead, students would stand on the veranda and urinate into the bushes. This practice, however, was strictly against regulations and one job of the prefect was to take down the names of students who indulged in it.

One night, I was on duty when it was pouring with rain, and I caught quite a few students – perhaps fifteen or so – relieving themselves from the veranda. Towards dawn, I saw a chap come out, look both ways, and stand at one end of the veranda to urinate. I made my way over to him and announced that he had been caught, whereupon he turned round and I realized that he was a prefect. I was in a predicament. In law and philosophy, one asks, '*Quis custodiet ipsos custodes?*' ('Who will guard the guardians themselves?'). If the prefect does not obey the rules, how can the students be expected to obey? In effect, the prefect was above the law because he *was* the law, and one prefect was not supposed to report another. But I did not think it fair to avoid reporting the prefect and mark down the fifteen others, so I simply tore up my list and charged no one.

In my final year at Healdtown, an event occurred that for me was like a comet streaking across the night sky. Towards the end of the year, we were informed that the

great Xhosa poet, Krune Mqhayi, was going to visit the
school. Mqhayi was actually an *imbongi*, a praise singer,
a kind of oral historian who marks contemporary
events and history with poetry that is of special meaning to his people.

The day of his visit was declared a holiday by the
school authorities. On the appointed morning, the
entire school, including staff members both black
and white, gathered in the dining hall, which was where
we held school assemblies. There was a stage at one end
of the hall and from it a door led to Dr Wellington's
house. The door itself was nothing special, but we
thought of it as Dr Wellington's door, for no one ever
walked through it except Dr Wellington himself.

Suddenly, the door opened and out walked not
Dr Wellington, but a black man dressed in a leopard-skin kaross and matching hat, who was carrying
a spear in either hand. Dr Wellington followed a
moment later, but the sight of a black man in tribal
dress coming through that door was electrifying. It is
hard to explain the impact it had on us. It seemed to
turn the universe upside down. As Mqhayi sat on the
stage next to Dr Wellington, we were barely able to
contain our excitement.

But when Mqhayi rose to speak, I confess to being
disappointed. I had formed a picture of him in my
mind, and in my youthful imagination I expected a
Xhosa hero like Mqhayi to be tall, fierce and intelli-
gent-looking. But he was not terribly distinguished and,
except for his clothing, seemed entirely ordinary.
When he spoke in Xhosa, he did so slowly and halt-
ingly, frequently pausing to search for the right word
and then stumbling over it when he found it.

At one point, he raised his assegai into the air for emphasis, and accidentally hit the curtain wire above him, which made a sharp noise and caused the curtain to sway. The poet looked at the point of his spear and then the curtain wire and, deep in thought, walked back and forth across the stage. After a minute, he stopped walking, faced us, and newly energized, exclaimed that this incident – the assegai striking the wire – symbolized the clash between the culture of Africa and that of Europe. His voice rose and he said, 'The assegai stands for what is glorious and true in African history; it is a symbol of the African as warrior and the African as artist. This metal wire,' he said, pointing above, 'is an example of Western manufacturing, which is skilful but cold, clever but soulless.'

'What I am talking about,' he continued, 'is not a piece of bone touching a piece of metal, or even the overlapping of one culture and another, what I am talking to you about is the brutal clash between what is indigenous and good, and what is foreign and bad. We cannot allow these foreigners who do not care for our culture to take over our nation. I predict that, one day, the forces of African society will achieve a momentous victory over the interloper. For too long we have succumbed to the false gods of the white man. But we shall emerge and cast off these foreign notions.'

I could hardly believe my ears. His boldness in speaking of such delicate matters in the presence of Dr Wellington and other whites seemed utterly astonishing to us. Yet at the same time it aroused and motivated us, and began to alter my perception of men like Dr Wellington, whom I had automatically considered my benefactor.

Mqhayi then began to recite his well-known poem in which he apportions the stars in the heavens to the various nations of the world. I had never before heard it. Roving the stage and gesturing with his assegai towards the sky, he said that to the people of Europe – the French, the Germans, the English – 'I give you the Milky Way, the largest constellation, for you are a strange people, full of greed and envy, who quarrel over plenty.' He allocated certain stars to the Asian nations, and to North and South America. He then discussed Africa and separated the continent into different nations, giving specific constellations to different tribes. He had been dancing about the stage, waving his spear, modulating his voice, and now, suddenly, he became still, and lowered his voice.

'Now, come you, O House of Xhosa,' he said, and slowly began to lower himself so that he was on one knee. 'I give unto you the most important and transcendent star, the Morning Star, for you are a proud and powerful people. It is the star for counting the years – the years of manhood.' When he spoke this last word, he dropped his head to his chest. We rose to our feet, clapping and cheering. I did not want ever to stop applauding. I felt such intense pride at that point, not as an African, but as a Xhosa; I felt like one of the chosen people.

I was galvanized, but also confused by Mqhayi's performance. He had moved from a more nationalistic, all-encompassing theme of African unity to a more parochial one addressed to the Xhosa people, of whom he was one. As my time at Healdtown was coming to an end, I had many new and sometimes conflicting ideas floating in my head. I was beginning to see that

Africans of all tribes had much in common, yet here was the great Mqhayi praising the Xhosa above all; I saw that an African might stand his ground with a white man, yet I was still eagerly seeking benefits from whites, which often required subservience. In a sense, Mqhayi's shift in focus was a mirror of my own mind because I went back and forth between pride in myself as a Xhosa and a feeling of kinship with other Africans. But as I left Healdtown at the end of the year, I saw myself as a Xhosa first and an African second.

7

Until 1960, the University College of Fort Hare in the municipality of Alice, about twenty miles due east from Healdtown, was the only residential centre of higher education for blacks in South Africa. Fort Hare was more than that: it was a beacon for African scholars from all over Southern, Central and Eastern Africa. For young black South Africans like myself, it was Oxford and Cambridge, Harvard and Yale, all rolled into one.

The regent was anxious for me to attend Fort Hare and I was pleased to be accepted there. Before I went up to the university, the regent bought me my first suit. Double-breasted and grey, the suit made me feel grown-up and sophisticated; I was twenty-one years old and could not imagine anyone at Fort Hare smarter than I.

I felt that I was being groomed for success in the world. I was pleased that the regent would now have a member of his clan with a university degree. Justice had remained at Healdtown to work for his junior certificate. He enjoyed playing more than studying, and was an indifferent scholar.

Fort Hare had been founded in 1916 by Scottish missionaries on the site of what was the largest nineteenth-century frontier fort in the eastern Cape. Built on a rocky platform and moated by the winding arc of the Tyume River, Fort Hare was perfectly situated to enable the British to fight the gallant Xhosa warrior

Sandile, the last Rharhabe king, who was defeated by the British in one of the final frontier battles in the 1800s.

Fort Hare had only 150 students, and I already knew a dozen or so of them from Clarkebury and Healdtown. One of them, who I was meeting for the first time, was K.D. Matanzima. Though K.D. was my nephew according to tribal hierarchy, I was younger and far less senior to him. Tall and slender and extremely confident, K.D. was a third-year student and he took me under his wing. I looked up to him as I had to Justice.

We were both Methodists, and I was assigned to his hostel, known as Wesley House, a pleasant two-storey building on the edge of the campus. Under his tutelage, I attended church services with him at nearby Loveday, took up soccer (in which he excelled), and generally followed his advice. The regent did not believe in sending money to his children at school, and I would have had empty pockets had not K.D. shared his allowance with me. Like the regent, he saw my future role as counsellor to Sabata, and he encouraged me to study law.

Fort Hare, like Clarkebury and Healdtown, was a missionary college. We were exhorted to obey God, respect the political authorities and be grateful for the educational opportunities afforded to us by the Church and the government. These schools have often been criticized for being colonialist in their attitudes and practices. Yet, even with such attitudes, I believe their benefits outweighed their disadvantages. The missionaries built and ran schools when the government was unwilling or unable to do so. The learning environment of the missionary schools, while often morally rigid, was far more open than the racist principles underlying government schools.

Fort Hare was both home and incubator of some of the greatest African scholars the continent has ever known. Professor Z.K. Matthews was the very model of the intellectual. A child of a miner, Z.K. had been influenced by Booker Washington's autobiography, *Up from Slavery*, which preached success through hard work and moderation. He taught social anthropology and African law and spoke out bluntly against the government's social policies.

Fort Hare and Professor D.D.T. Jabavu are virtually synonymous. He was the first member of staff when the university opened in 1916. Professor Jabavu had been awarded a degree in English from the University of London, which seemed an impossibly rare feat. Professor Jabavu taught Xhosa, as well as Latin, history and anthropology. He was an encyclopedia when it came to Xhosa genealogy and told me facts about my father that I had never known. He was also a persuasive spokesman for African rights, becoming the founding president of the All-African Convention in 1936, which opposed legislation in Parliament designed to end the common voters' roll in the Cape.

I recall once travelling from Fort Hare to Umtata by train, riding in the African compartment, in which were the only seats open to blacks. The white train inspector came to check our tickets. When he saw that I had got on at Alice, he said, 'Are you from Jabavu's school?' I nodded yes, whereupon the conductor cheerfully punched my ticket and mumbled something about Jabavu being a fine man.

In my first year, I studied English, anthropology, politics, native administration and Roman Dutch law. Native administration dealt with the laws relating to Africans and was advisable for anyone who wanted to work in the Native Affairs Department. Although K.D. was counselling me to study law, I had my heart set on being an interpreter or a clerk in the Native Affairs Department. At that time, a career as a civil servant was a glittering prize for an African, the highest that a black man could aspire to. In the rural areas, an interpreter in the magistrate's office was considered second only in importance to the magistrate himself. When, in my second year, Fort Hare introduced an interpreting course taught by a distinguished retired court interpreter, Tyamzashe, I was one of the first students to sign up.

Fort Hare could be a rather elitist place, and was not without the problems common to many institutions of higher learning. Seniors treated the juniors with haughtiness and disdain. When I first arrived on campus, I spotted Gamaliel Vabaza across the central courtyard. He was several years older and I had been with him at Clarkebury. I greeted him warmly, but his response was exceedingly cool and superior, and he made a disparaging remark about the fact that I would be staying in the freshman dormitory. Vabaza then informed me that he was on the House Committee of my dormitory even though, as a senior, he no longer shared the dormitory. I found this odd and undemocratic, but it was the accepted practice.

One night, not long after that, a group of us discussed the fact that no residents or freshmen were represented on the House Committee. We decided that we should depart from tradition and elect a House Committee made up of these two groups. We held discussions and lobbied all the residents of the house, and within weeks elected our own House Committee, defeating the seniors. I myself was one of the organizers and was elected to this newly constituted committee.

But the seniors were not so easily subdued. They held a meeting at which one of them, Rex Tatane, an eloquent English-speaker, said, 'This behaviour on the part of freshers is unacceptable. How can we seniors be overthrown by a backward fellow from the countryside like Mandela, a fellow who cannot even speak English properly!' Then he proceeded to mimic the way I spoke, giving me what he perceived to be a Gcaleka accent, at which his own claque laughed heartily. Tatane's sneering speech made us all more resolute. We freshers now constituted the official House Committee and we assigned the seniors the most unpleasant tasks, which was a great indignity for them.

The warden of the college, Reverend A.J. Cook, learned of this dispute and called us into his office. We felt we had right on our side and were not prepared to yield. Tatane appealed to the warden to overrule us, and in the midst of his speech, broke down and wept. The warden asked us to modify our stand, but we would not bend. Like most bullies, Tatane had a brittle but fragile exterior. We informed the warden that if he overruled us we would all resign from the House Committee, depriving the committee itself of any integrity or authority. In the end, the warden decided not to intervene. We had remained firm, and we had won. This was one of my first battles with authority, and I felt the sense of power that comes from having right and justice on one's side. I would not be so lucky in the future in my fight against the authorities at the college.

My education at Fort Hare was as much outside as inside the classroom. I was a more active sportsman than I had been at Healdtown. This was due to two factors: I had grown taller and stronger but, more important, Fort Hare was so much smaller than Healdtown that I had less competition. I was able to compete in both soccer and cross-country running. Running taught me valuable lessons. In cross-country competition, training counted more than intrinsic ability, and I could compensate for a lack of natural aptitude with diligence and discipline. I applied this in everything I did. Even as a student, I saw many young men who had great natural ability, but who did not have the self-discipline and patience to build on their endowment.

I also joined the drama society and acted in a play about Abraham Lincoln that was adapted by my classmate Lincoln Mkentane. Mkentane came from a distinguished Transkeian family, and was another fellow whom I looked up to. This was literally true, as he was the only student at Fort Hare taller than I was. Mkentane portrayed his namesake, while I played John Wilkes Booth, Lincoln's assassin. Mkentane's depiction of Lincoln was stately and formal, and his recitation of one of the greatest of all speeches, the Gettysburg Address, won a standing ovation. My part was the smaller one, though I was the engine of the play's moral, which was that men who take great risks often suffer great consequences.

I became a member of the Students Christian Association and taught Bible classes on Sundays in neighbouring villages. One of my comrades on these expeditions was a serious young science scholar whom I had met on the soccer field. He came from Pondoland, in the Transkei, and his name was Oliver Tambo. From the start, I saw that Oliver's intelligence was diamond-edged; he was a keen debater and did not accept the platitudes that so many of us automatically subscribed to. Oliver lived in Beda Hall, the Anglican hostel, and though I did not have much contact with him at Fort Hare, it was easy to see that he was destined for great things.

On Sundays a group of us would sometimes walk into Alice, to have a meal at one of the restaurants in town. The restaurant was run by whites, and in those days it was inconceivable for a black man to walk in at the front door, much less take a meal in the dining room. Instead, we would pool our resources, go round to the kitchen, and order what we wanted.

I learned not only about physics at Fort Hare, but another precise physical science: ballroom dancing. To a crackly old phonograph in the dining hall, we spent hours practising fox-trots and waltzes, each of us taking turns leading and following. Our idol was Victor Sylvester, the world champion of ballroom dancing, and our tutor was a fellow student, Smallie Siwundla, who seemed a younger version of the master.

In a neighbouring village, there was an African dance-hall known as Ntselamanzi, which catered to the cream of local black society and was off-limits to undergraduates. But one night, desperate to practise our steps with the gentler sex, we put on our suits, stole out of our dormitory, and made it to the dance-hall. It was a sumptuous place, and we felt very daring. I noticed a lovely young woman across the floor and politely asked her to dance. A moment later, she was in my arms. We moved well together and I imagined what a striking figure I was cutting on the floor. After a few minutes, I asked her her name. 'Mrs Bokwe,' she said softly. I almost dropped her on the spot and scampered off the floor. I glanced across the floor and saw Dr Roseberry Bokwe, one of the most respected African leaders and scholars of the time, chatting with his brother-in-law and my professor Z.K. Matthews. I apologized to Mrs Bokwe and then sheepishly escorted her to the side under the curious eyes of Dr Bokwe and Professor Matthews. I wanted to sink beneath the floorboards. I had violated any number of university regulations. But Professor Matthews, who was in charge of discipline at Fort Hare, never said a word to me. He was willing to tolerate what he considered high spirits as long as it was balanced by hard work. I don't think I ever studied more diligently than in the weeks after our evening at Ntselamanzi.

Fort Hare was characterized by a level of sophistication, both intellectual and social, that was new and strange to me. By Western standards, Fort Hare's worldliness may not seem much, but to a country boy like myself, it was a revelation. I wore pyjamas for the first time, finding them uncomfortable in the beginning, but gradually growing used to them. I had never used a toothbrush and toothpaste before; at home, we used ash to whiten our teeth and toothpicks to clean them. The water-flush toilets and hot-water showers were also a novelty to me. I used toilet soap for the first time, not the blue detergent that I had washed with for so many years at home.

Perhaps as a result of all this unfamiliarity, I yearned for some of the simple pleasures that I had known as a boy. I was not alone in this feeling, and I joined a group of young men who engaged in secret evening expeditions to the university's farmland, where we built a fire and roasted mealies. We would then sit around, eating the ears of corn and telling tall tales. We did not do this because we were hungry, but out of a need to recapture what was most homelike to us. We boasted about our conquests, our athletic prowess and how much money we were going to make once we had graduated. Although I felt myself to be a sophisticated young fellow, I was still a country boy who missed country pleasures.

While Fort Hare was a sanctuary removed from the world, we were keenly interested in the progress of the Second World War. Like my classmates, I was an ardent supporter of Great Britain, and I was enormously excited to learn that the speaker at the university's graduation ceremony at the end of my first year would be England's great advocate in South Africa, the former prime minister Jan Smuts. It was a great honour for Fort Hare to play host to a man acclaimed as a world statesman. Smuts, then deputy prime minister, was campaigning around the country for South Africa to declare war on Germany while the prime minister, J.B. Hertzog, advocated neutrality. I was extremely curious to see a world leader like Smuts up close.

While Hertzog had, three years earlier, led the drive to remove the last African voters from the common voters' roll in the Cape, I found Smuts a sympathetic figure. I cared more that he had helped to found the League of Nations, promoting freedom around the world, than the fact that he had repressed freedom at home.

Smuts spoke about the importance of supporting Great Britain against the Germans and the idea that England stood for the same Western values that we, as South Africans, stood for. I remember thinking that his accent in English was almost as poor as mine! Along with my fellow classmates, I heartily applauded him, cheering Smuts's call to do battle for the freedom of Europe, forgetting that we did not have that freedom here in our own land.

Smuts was preaching to the converted at Fort Hare. Each evening the warden of Wesley House used to review the military situation in Europe, and late at night we would huddle around an old radio and listen to BBC broadcasts of Winston Churchill's stirring speeches. But even though we supported Smuts's position, his visit provoked much discussion. During one session, a contemporary of mine, Nyathi Khongisa, who was considered an extremely clever fellow, condemned Smuts as a racist. He said that we might consider ourselves 'black Englishmen', but the English had oppressed us at the same time that they tried to 'civilize' us. Whatever the mutual antagonism between Boer and British, he said, the two white groups would unite to confront the black threat. Khongisa's views stunned us and seemed dangerously radical. A fellow student whispered to me that Nyathi was a member of the African National Congress, an organization that I had vaguely heard of but knew very little about. Following South Africa's declaration of war against Germany, Hertzog resigned and Smuts became prime minister.

During my second year at Fort Hare, I invited my friend Paul Mahabane to spend the winter holidays with me in the Transkei. Paul was from Bloemfontein and was well known on campus because his father, the Reverend Zaccheus Mahabane, had twice been president-general of the African National Congress. His connection with this organization, about which I still knew very little, gave him the reputation of a rebel.

One day during the holiday, Paul and I went to Umtata, the capital of the Transkei, which then consisted of a few paved streets and some government buildings. We were standing outside the post office when the local magistrate, a white man in his sixties, approached Paul and asked him to go inside to buy him some postage stamps. It was quite common for any white person to call on any black person to perform a chore. The magistrate attempted to hand Paul some change, but Paul would not take it. The magistrate was offended. 'Do you know who I am?' he said, his face turning red with irritation. 'It is not necessary to know who you are,' Mahabane said. 'I know what you are.' The magistrate asked him exactly what he meant by that. 'I mean that you are a rogue!' Paul said heatedly. The magistrate boiled over and exclaimed, 'You'll pay dearly for this!' and then walked away.

I was extremely uncomfortable with Paul's behaviour. While I respected his courage, I also found it disturbing. The magistrate knew precisely who I was and I knew that if he had asked me rather than Paul, I would have simply performed the errand and forgotten about it. But I admired Paul for what he had done, even though I was not yet ready to do the same myself. I was beginning to realize that a black man did not have to accept the dozens of petty indignities directed at him each day.

After my holiday, I returned to school early in the new year feeling strong and renewed. I concentrated on my studies, leading to examinations in October. In a year's time, I imagined that I would have a BA, just like clever Gertrude Ntlabathi. A university degree, I believed, was a passport not only to community leadership but to financial success. We had been told over and over again by the principal, Dr Alexander Kerr, and Professors Jabavu and Matthews how, as graduates of Fort Hare, we were the African elite. I believed that the world would be at my feet.

As a BA, I would finally be able to restore to my mother the wealth and prestige that she had lost after my father's death. I would build her a proper home in Qunu, with a garden and modern furniture and fittings. I would support her and my sisters so that they could afford the things that they had so long been denied. This was my dream and it seemed within reach.

During that year, I was nominated to stand for the Student Representative Council, which was the highest student organization at Fort Hare. I did not know at the time that the events surrounding a student election would create difficulties that would change the course of my life. The SRC elections were held in the final term of the year, while we were in the midst of examination preparations. According to the Fort Hare constitution, the entire student body elected the six members of the SRC. Shortly before the election, a meeting of all students was held to discuss problems and voice our grievances. The students unanimously felt that the diet at Fort Hare was unsatisfactory and that the powers of the SRC needed to be increased so that it would be more than a rubber stamp for the administration. I agreed with both motions, and when a majority of students voted to boycott the elections unless the authorities accepted our demands, I voted with them.

Shortly after this meeting, the scheduled voting took place. The majority of the students boycotted the election, but twenty-five, about one-sixth of the student body, showed up and elected six representatives, one of whom was myself. That same day, the six elected *in absentia* met to discuss these events. We unanimously decided to tender our resignations on the ground that we supported the boycott and did not enjoy the support of the majority of the students. We then drafted a letter, which we handed to Dr Kerr.

But Dr Kerr was clever. He accepted our resignations and then announced that new elections were to be held the next day in the dining hall at suppertime. This would ensure that all the students would be present and that there would be no excuse that the SRC did not have the support of the entire student body. That evening the election was held, as the principal ordered, but only the same twenty-five voted, returning the same six SRC members. It would seem that we were back where we started.

Only this time, when the six of us met to consider our position, the voting was very different. My five colleagues held to the technical view that we had been elected at a meeting at which all the students were present and therefore we could no longer argue that we did not represent the student body. The five believed we should now accept office. I countered that nothing in fact had changed; while all the students had been there, a majority of them had not voted, and it would be morally incorrect to say that we enjoyed their confidence. Since our initial goal was to boycott the election, an action that had the confidence of the student body, our duty was still to abide by that resolution, and not be deterred by some trickery on the part of the principal. Unable to persuade my colleagues, I resigned for the second time, the only one of the six to do so.

The following day I was called in to see the principal. Dr Kerr, a graduate of Edinburgh University, was virtually the founder of Fort Hare and was a greatly respected man. He calmly reviewed the events of the past few days and then asked me to reconsider my decision to resign. I told him I could not. He told me to sleep on it and give him my final decision the following day. He did warn me, however, that he could not allow his students to act irresponsibly, and he said that if I insisted on resigning, he would be compelled to expel me from Fort Hare.

I was shaken by what he had said and spent a restless night. I had never had to make such a weighty decision before. That evening I consulted with my friend and mentor, K.D., who felt that as a matter of principle I was correct to resign, and should not capitulate. I think at the time I feared K.D. even more than I did Dr Kerr. I thanked K.D. and returned to my room.

Even though I thought what I was doing was morally

right, I was still uncertain as to whether it was the correct course. Was I sabotaging my academic career over an abstract moral principle that mattered very little? I found it difficult to swallow the idea that I would sacrifice what I regarded as my obligation to the students for my own selfish interests. I had taken a stand, and I did not want to appear to be a fraud in the eyes of my fellow students. At the same time, I did not want to throw away my career at Fort Hare.

I was in a state of indecision when I reached Dr Kerr's office the next morning. It was only when he asked me if I had reached a decision that I actually made up my mind. I told him that I had and that I could not in good conscience serve on the SRC. Dr Kerr seemed a bit taken aback by my response. He thought for a moment or two before speaking. 'Very well,' he said. 'It is your decision, of course. But I have also given the matter some thought, and I propose to you the following: you may return to Fort Hare next year provided you join the SRC. You have all summer to consider it, Mr Mandela.'

I was, in a way, as surprised by my response as Dr Kerr. I knew it was foolhardy for me to leave Fort Hare, but at the moment when I needed to compromise, I simply could not do so. Something inside me would not let me. While I appreciated Dr Kerr's position and his willingness to give me another chance, I resented his absolute power over my fate. I should have had every right to resign from the SRC if I wished. This injustice rankled, and at that moment I saw Dr Kerr less as a benefactor than as a not-altogether-benign dictator. When I left Fort Hare at the end of the year, I was in an unpleasant state of limbo.

8

Usually when I returned to Mqhekezweni I did so with a sense of ease and completion. But not this time. After passing my exams and returning home, I told the regent what had transpired. He was furious, and could not comprehend the reasons for my actions. He thought it utterly senseless. Without even hearing my full explanation, he bluntly informed me that I would obey the principal's instructions and return to Fort Hare in the autumn. His tone invited no discussion. It would have been pointless as well as disrespectful for me to argue with my benefactor. I resolved to let the matter rest awhile.

Justice had also returned to Mqhekezweni and we were mightily glad to see one another. No matter how long Justice and I were apart, the brotherly bonds that united us were instantly renewed. Justice had left school the year before and was living in Cape Town.

Within a few days, I resumed my old life at home. I looked after matters for the regent, including his herd and his relations with other chiefs. I did not dwell on the situation at Fort Hare, but life has a way of forcing decisions on those who vacillate. It was an entirely different matter unrelated to my studies that forced my hand.

A few weeks after my homecoming, the regent summoned Justice and me to a meeting. 'My children,' he said in a very sombre tone, 'I fear that I am not much longer for this world, and before I journey to the land of the ancestors, it is my duty to see my two sons properly married. I have, accordingly, arranged unions for both of you.'

This announcement took us both by surprise, and Justice and I looked at each other with a mixture of shock and helplessness. The two girls came from very good families, the regent said. Justice was to marry the daughter of Khalipa, a prominent Thembu nobleman, and Rolihlahla, as the regent always called me, was to marry the daughter of the local Thembu priest. The marriages, he said, were to take place immediately. *Lobola*, the brideprice or dowry, is normally paid in the form of cattle by the groom's father, and would be paid by the community in Justice's case and in my own by the regent himself.

Justice and I said little. It was not our place to question the regent, and as far as he was concerned, the matter was settled. The regent brooked no discussion: the bride had already been selected and *lobola* paid. It was final.

Justice and I walked out of our interview with our heads down, dazed and dejected. The regent was acting in accordance with Thembu law and custom, and his own motives could not be impugned: he wanted us to be settled during his lifetime. We had always known that the regent had the right to arrange marriages for us, but now it was no longer an abstract possibility. The brides were not fantasies, but flesh-and-blood women whom we actually knew.

With all due respect to the young woman's family, I would be dishonest if I said that the girl the regent had selected for me was my dream bride. Her family was prominent and respected and she was attractive in a rather dignified way, but this young lady, I am afraid, had long been in love with Justice. The regent would not have known this, as parents rarely know the romantic side of their children's lives. My intended partner was undoubtedly no more eager to be burdened with me than I was with her.

At that time, I was more advanced socially than politically. While I would not have considered fighting the political system of the white man, I was quite prepared to rebel against the social system of my own people. Ironically, it was the regent himself who was indirectly to blame for this, for it was the education he had afforded me that had caused me to reject such traditional customs. I had attended college and university with women for years, and had had a small handful of love affairs. I was a romantic, and I was not prepared to have anyone, even the regent, select a bride for me.

I made an appointment with the queen, the regent's wife, and put my case to her. I could not tell her that I did not want the regent to arrange a bride for me under any circumstances, as she would naturally have been unsympathetic. Instead, I devised an alternative plan, and told her that I preferred to marry a girl who was a relative of the queen's, whom I found desirable as a prospective partner. This young lady was in fact very attractive, but I had no idea as to what she thought of me. I said I would marry her as soon as I completed my studies. This was half a ruse, but it was a better option than the regent's plan. The queen took my side in the matter, but the regent could not be dissuaded. He had made his decision and he was not going to alter it.

I felt as though he had left me no choice. I could not go through with this marriage, which I considered unfair and ill-advised. At the same time, I believed that I could no longer remain under the regent's guidance if I rejected his plan for me. Justice agreed, and the two of us decided that the only choice remaining was to run away, and the only place to run to was Johannesburg.

In retrospect, I realize that we did not exhaust all the options available to us. I could have attempted to discuss the matter with the regent through inter-mediaries and perhaps come to some settlement within the framework of our tribe and family. I could have appealed to the regent's cousin, Chief Zilindlovu, one of the most enlightened and influential chiefs at the court of Mqhekezweni. But I was young and impatient, and did not see any virtue in waiting. Escape seemed the only course.

We kept our plot secret while we worked out its details. First, we needed an opportunity. The regent believed Justice and I brought out the worst in each other, or at least Justice's penchant for adventures and high-jinks influenced my more conservative disposition. As a result, he took pains to keep us separate as much as possible. When the regent was travelling, he generally asked one of us to accompany him so that we would not be alone together in his absence. More often than not, he took Justice with him, as he liked me to remain in Mqhekezweni to look after his affairs. But we learned that the regent was preparing to leave for a full week to attend a session of the Bungha, the Transkeian legislative assembly, without either of us, and we decided this was the ideal time to steal away. We resolved that we would depart for Johannesburg shortly after the regent left for the Bungha.

I had few clothes, and we managed to fit whatever we had into a single suitcase. The regent left early on Monday, and by late morning we were ready to go. But just as we were preparing to leave, he unexpectedly returned. We saw his car drive in and we ran into the garden and hid among the mealie stalks. The regent came into the house and his first question was 'Where are those boys?' Someone replied, 'Oh, they are around.' But the regent was suspicious, and was not content with that reply. He had returned, he said, because he had forgotten to take his Epsom salts. He looked around a bit, and then seemed satisfied. I realized that he must have had some kind of premonition because he could easily buy Epsom salts in town. When his car disappeared behind the hills, we were on our way.

We had almost no money between us, but that morning we went to see a local trader and made a deal to sell him two of the regent's prize oxen. The trader assumed that we were selling the animals at the regent's behest, and we did not correct him. He paid us a very good price, and with that money we hired a car to take us to the local station where we would catch a train to Johannesburg.

All seemed to be going smoothly, but unbeknown to us, the regent had driven to the station and instructed the manager that if two boys fitting our description came to buy tickets for Johannesburg, the manager must turn them away because they were not to leave the Transkei. We arrived at the station only to find that the manager would not sell us tickets. We asked him why, and he said, 'Your father has been here and says you are trying to run away.' We were stunned by this, and dashed back to our hired car and told the driver to go to the next station. It was nearly fifty miles away, and it took us more than an hour to get there.

We managed to get a train, but it went only as far as Queenstown. In the 1940s, travelling for an African was a complicated process. All Africans over the age of sixteen were compelled to carry 'Native passes' issued by the Native Affairs Department, and were required to show that pass to any white policeman, civil servant or employer. Failure to do so could mean arrest, trial, a jail sentence or fine. The pass stated where the bearer lived, who his chief was, and whether he had paid the annual poll tax, which was a tax levied only on Africans. Later, the pass took the form of a booklet or 'Reference Book', as it was known, containing detailed information that had to be signed by one's employer every month.

Justice and I had our passes in order, but for an African to leave his magisterial district and enter that of another for the purpose of working or living, he needed travel documents, a permit and a letter from his employer or, as in our case, his guardian – none of which we had. Even at the best of times, when one had all these documents, a police officer might harass you because one of them was missing a signature or had an incorrect date. Not having any was extremely risky. Our plan was to disembark in Queenstown, make our way to the house of a relative, and then arrange the necessary documents. This was also an ill-considered plan, but we came in for a bit of luck because at the house in Queenstown we accidentally met Chief Mpondombini, a brother of the regent, who was fond of Justice and myself.

Chief Mpondombini greeted us warmly, and we

explained that we needed the requisite travel documents from the local magistrate. We lied about why we required them, claiming that we were on an errand for the regent. Chief Mpondombini was a retired interpreter from the Native Affairs Department and knew the chief magistrate well. He had no reason to doubt our story and not only escorted us to the magistrate, but vouched for us and explained our predicament. After listening to the chief, the magistrate rapidly made out the necessary travel documents and affixed the official stamp. Justice and I looked at each other and smiled in complicity. But just as the magistrate was handing over the documents to us, he recalled something and said that, as a matter of courtesy, he ought to inform the chief magistrate of Umtata, in whose jurisdiction we fell. This made us uneasy, but we stayed seated in his office. The magistrate used his telephone to reach his colleague in Umtata. As luck would have it, the regent was just then paying a call on the chief magistrate of Umtata and was in his very office.

As our magistrate was explaining our situation to the chief magistrate of Umtata, the latter gentleman said something like, 'Oh, their father just happens to be right here,' and then put the regent on the line. When the magistrate informed the regent what we were requesting, the regent exploded. 'Arrest those boys!' he shouted, loud enough for us to hear his voice through the receiver. 'Arrest them and bring them back here immediately!' The chief magistrate put down the phone. He regarded us angrily. 'You boys are thieves and liars,' he told us. 'You have presumed upon my good offices and then deceived me. Now I am going to have you arrested.'

I immediately rose to our defence. From my studies at Fort Hare I had a little knowledge of law, and I put it to use. I said that we had told him lies, that was true. But we had committed no offence and violated no laws, and we could not be arrested simply on the recommendation of a chief, even if he happened to be our father. The magistrate backed down and did not arrest us, but told us to leave his office and never to darken his door again.

Chief Mpondombini was also annoyed, and left us to our own devices. Justice remembered that he had a friend in Queenstown named Sidney Nxu who was working in the office of a white attorney. We went to see this man and explained our situation; he told us that the mother of the attorney he worked for was driving into Johannesburg and he would see if she would offer us a lift. He told us that his mother would give us a ride if we paid a fee of £15 sterling. This was a vast sum, far more than the cost of a train ticket. The fee virtually depleted our savings, but we had no choice. We decided to risk getting our passes stamped and to obtain the correct travel documents once we were in Johannesburg.

We left early the following morning. In those days, it was customary for blacks to ride in the back seat of the car if a white was driving. The two of us sat in that fashion, with Justice directly behind the woman. Justice was a friendly, exuberant person and immediately began chatting to me. This made the old woman extremely uncomfortable. She had obviously never been in the company of a black who had no inhibitions about whites. After only a few miles, she told Justice that she wanted him to switch seats with me, so that she could keep an eye on him, and for the rest of the journey she watched him like a hawk. But, after a while, Justice's charm worked on her and she would occasionally laugh at something he said.

At about ten o'clock that evening, we saw before us, glinting in the distance, a maze of lights that seemed to stretch in all directions. Electricity, to me, had always been a novelty and a luxury, and here was a vast landscape of electricity, a city of light. I was terribly excited to see the city I had been hearing about since I was a child. Johannesburg had always been depicted as a city of dreams, a place where one could transform oneself from a poor peasant into a wealthy sophisticate, a city of danger and of opportunity. I remembered the stories that Banabakhe had told us at circumcision school, of buildings so tall you could not see the tops, of crowds of people speaking languages you had never heard of, of sleek motor cars and beautiful women and dashing gangsters. It was eGoli, the city of gold, where I would soon be making my home.

On the outskirts of the city the traffic became denser. I had never seen so many cars on the road at one time – even in Umtata, there were never more than a handful of cars and here there were thousands. We drove around the city, rather than through it, but I could see the silhouette of the tall blocks of buildings, even darker against the dark night sky. I looked at great billboards by the side of the road advertising cigarettes and candy and beer. It all seemed tremendously glamorous.

Soon we were in an area of stately mansions, even the smallest of which was bigger than the regent's palace, with grand front lawns and tall iron gates. This was the suburb where the old lady's daughter lived, and we pulled into the long driveway of one of these beautiful homes. Justice and I were dispatched to the servants' wing, where we were to spend the night. We thanked the old lady, and then crawled off to sleep on the floor. But the prospect of Johannesburg was so exciting to me that I felt as though I slept on a beautiful feather bed that night. The possibilities seemed infinite. I had reached the end of what seemed like a long journey, but it was actually the very beginning of a much longer and more trying journey that would test me in ways that I could not then have imagined.

PART TWO

Johannesburg

9

It was dawn when we reached the offices of Crown Mines, which were located on the plateau of a great hill overlooking the still, dark metropolis. Johannesburg had been built up around the discovery of gold on the Witwatersrand in 1886, and Crown Mines was the largest gold mine in the city of gold. I expected to see a grand building like the government offices in Umtata, but the Crown Mine offices were rusted tin shanties on the face of the mine.

There is nothing magical about a gold mine. Barren and pockmarked, all dirt and no trees, fenced in on all sides, a gold mine resembles a war-torn battlefield. The noise was harsh and ubiquitous: the rasp of shaft-lifts, the jangling power drills, the distant rumble of dynamite, the barked orders. Everywhere I looked I saw black men in dusty overalls looking tired and bent. They lived on the grounds in bleak, single-sex barracks that contained hundreds of concrete bunks separated from each other by only a few inches.

Gold-mining on the Witwatersrand was costly because the ore was low grade and deep under the earth. Only the presence of cheap labour in the form of thousands of Africans working long hours for little pay with no rights made gold-mining profitable for the mining houses – white-owned companies that became wealthy beyond the dreams of Croesus on the backs of the African people. I had never seen such enterprise before, such great machines, such methodical organization and such backbreaking work. It was my first sight of South African capitalism at work, and I knew I was in for a new kind of education.

We went straight to the chief *induna*, or headman. Piliso was a tough old fellow who had seen life at its most pitiless. He knew about Justice, as the regent had sent a letter months before making arrangements for him to get a clerical job, the most coveted and respected job in the mine compound. I, however, was unknown to him. Justice explained that I was his brother.

'I was expecting only Justice,' Piliso responded. 'Your father's letter mentions nothing about a brother.' He looked me over rather sceptically. But Justice pleaded with him, saying it had simply been an oversight, and that the regent had already posted a letter about me. Piliso's crusty exterior hid a sympathetic side, and he took me on as a mine policeman, saying that if I worked well, he would give me a clerical post in three months' time.

The regent's word carried weight at Crown Mines. This was true of all chiefs in South Africa. Mining officials were eager to recruit labour in the countryside, and the chiefs had authority over the men they needed. They wanted the chiefs to encourage their subjects to come to the Reef. The chiefs were treated with great deference; the mining houses provided special lodgings for them whenever they came to visit. One letter from the regent was enough to secure a man a good job, and Justice and I were treated with extra care because of our connection. We were to be given free rations, sleeping quarters and a small salary. We did not stay in the barracks that first night. For our first few days, Piliso, out of courtesy to the regent, invited Justice and me to stay with him.

Many of the miners, especially those from Thembuland, treated Justice as a chief and greeted him with gifts of cash, the custom when a chief visited a mine. Most of these men were in the same hostel; miners were normally housed according to tribe. The mining companies preferred such segregation because it prevented different ethnic groups from uniting around a common grievance and it reinforced the power of the chiefs. The separation often resulted in factional fights between different ethnic groups and clans, which the companies did not effectively discourage.

Justice shared some of his booty with me and gave me a few extra pounds as a bonus. For those first few days, my pockets jingling with newfound riches, I felt like a millionaire. I was beginning to think I was a child of fortune, that luck was shining on me, and that if I had not wasted precious time studying at college I could have been a wealthy man by then. Once again, I did not see that fate was busy setting snares around me.

I started work immediately as a night watchman. I was given a uniform, a new pair of boots, a helmet, a flashlight, a whistle and a knobkerrie, which is a long wooden stick with a heavy ball of wood at one end. The job was a simple one: I waited at the compound entrance next to the sign that read, 'BEWARE: NATIVES CROSSING HERE', and checked the credentials of all those entering and leaving. For the first few nights, I patrolled the grounds of the compound without incident. I did challenge a rather drunken miner late one evening, but he meekly showed his pass and retired to his hostel.

Flushed with our success, Justice and I boasted of our cleverness to a friend of ours whom we knew from home, who was also working at the mines. We explained how we had run away and tricked the regent into the bargain. Although we swore this fellow to secrecy, he went straight away to the *induna* and revealed our secret. A day later, Piliso called us in and the first question he asked Justice was, 'Where is the permission from the regent for your brother?' Justice said that he had already explained that the regent had posted it. Piliso was not mollified by this, and we sensed that something was wrong. He then reached inside his desk and produced a telegram. 'I have had a communication from the regent,' he said in a serious tone of voice, and handed it to us. It contained a single sentence: 'SEND BOYS HOME AT ONCE.'

Piliso then vented his anger on us, accusing us of lying to him. He said we had presumed on his hospitality and the good name of the regent. He told us that he was taking up a collection among the miners to put us on a train back to the Transkei. Justice protested against going home, saying that we simply wanted to work at the mine, and that we could make decisions for ourselves. But Piliso turned a deaf ear. We felt ashamed and humiliated, but we left his office determined not to return to the Transkei.

We rapidly hatched another plan. We went to see Dr A.B. Xuma, an old friend of the regent's who was the president-general of the African National Congress. Dr Xuma was from the Transkei, and was an extremely well-respected physician.

Dr Xuma was pleased to see us, and politely questioned us about family matters in Mqhekezweni. We told him a series of half-truths about why we were in Johannesburg, and that we greatly desired jobs in the mines. Dr Xuma said he would be glad to assist us, and immediately telephoned a Mr Wellbeloved at the Chamber of Mines, a powerful organization representing the mining houses and exerting monopoly control over the hiring of mine labour. Dr Xuma told Mr Wellbeloved what splendid fellows we were and that he should find places for us. We thanked Dr Xuma and went off to see Mr Wellbeloved.

Mr Wellbeloved was a white man whose office was grander than any I had ever seen; his desk seemed as wide as a football field. We met him in the company of a mine boss named Festile, and we told him the same fabrications that we had told Dr Xuma. Mr Wellbeloved was impressed with my not-entirely-truthful explanation that I had come to Johannesburg to continue my studies at the University of the Witwatersrand. 'Well, boys,' he said, 'I will put you in touch with the manager of Crown Mines, a Mr Piliso, and I will tell him to give you jobs as clerks.' He said he had worked with Mr Piliso for thirty years and in all that time Piliso had never lied to him. Justice and I squirmed at this but said nothing. Despite some misgivings, we naively felt we had the upper hand with Mr Piliso now that we had his boss, Mr Wellbeloved, on our side.

We returned to the Crown Mine offices, where the white compound manager was considerate to us because of the letter we presented from Mr Wellbeloved. Just then, Mr Piliso passed by the office, saw us, and then stormed in. 'You boys! You've come back!' he said with irritation. 'What are you doing here?'

Justice was calm. 'We've been sent by Mr Well-beloved,' he replied, his tone bordering on defiance. Mr Piliso considered this for a moment. 'Did you tell him that you ran away from your father?' Piliso then countered. Justice was silent.

'You'll never be employed in any mine that I run!' he yelled. 'Now get out of my sight!' Justice waved Well-beloved's letter. 'I don't give a damn about a letter!' Piliso said. I looked to the white manager, hoping that he might overrule Piliso, but he was as still as a statue and seemed as intimidated as we were. We had no rejoinder for Piliso, and we sheepishly walked out of the office, feeling even more humbled than we had on the first occasion.

Our fortunes were now reversed. We were without jobs, without prospects and without a place to stay. Justice knew various people in Johannesburg, and he went into town to investigate a place for us to stay. In the meantime, I was to fetch our suitcase, which was still at Piliso's, and then meet Justice at George Goch, a small township in southern Johannesburg, later that day.

I prevailed upon a fellow named Bikitsha, whom I knew from home, to help me carry the suitcase to the front gate. A watchman at the gate stopped us both and said he needed to search the bag. Bikitsha protested, asserting there was no contraband in the suitcase. The watchman replied that a search was routine, and he looked through the bag in a cursory way, not even disturbing the clothing. As the watchman was closing it, Bikitsha, who was a cocky fellow, said, 'Why do you make trouble? I told you there was nothing there.' These words irked the watchman, who then decided to search the case with a fine-toothed comb. I became increasingly nervous as he opened every compartment and probed every pocket. He then reached all the way to the bottom of the case and found the very thing I prayed he would not: a loaded revolver wrapped inside some of my clothing.

He turned to my friend and said, 'You are under arrest.' He then blew his whistle, which brought a team of guards over to us. My friend looked at me with a mixture of consternation and confusion as they led him away to the local police station. I followed them at a distance, considering my options. The gun, an old revolver, had been my father's and he had left it to me when he died. I had never used it, but as a precaution, I had brought it with me to the city.

I could not let my friend take the blame in my stead. Not long after he had entered the police station, I went inside and asked to see the officer in charge. I was taken to him and spoke as directly and forthrightly as I could: 'Sir, that is my gun that was found in my friend's suitcase. I inherited it from my father in the Transkei and I brought it here because I was afraid of gangsters.' I explained that I was a student from Fort Hare, and that I was only in Johannesburg temporarily. The officer in charge softened a bit as I spoke, and said that he would release my friend at once. He said he would have to charge me for possession of the gun, though he would not arrest me, and that I should appear in court first thing on Monday morning to answer the charge. I was grateful, and told him that I would certainly appear in court on Monday. I did go to court that Monday, and received only a nominal fine.

In the meantime I had arranged to stay with one of

my cousins, Garlick Mbekeni, in George Goch township. Garlick was a hawker who sold clothing, and had a small box-like house. He was a friendly, solicitous man, and after I had been there a short while, I told him that my real aspiration was to be a lawyer. He commended me for my ambition and said he would think about what I had said.

A few days later, Garlick told me that he was taking me to see 'one of our best people in Johannesburg'. We took the train to the office of an estate agent in Market Street, a dense and rollicking thoroughfare with trams groaning with passengers, pavement vendors on every street, and a sense that wealth and riches were just around the next corner.

Johannesburg in those days was a combination frontier town and modern city. Butchers cut meat on the street next to office buildings. Tents were pitched beside bustling shops, and women hung out their washing next door to high-rise buildings. Industry was energized due to the war effort. In 1939 South Africa, a member of the British Commonwealth, had declared war on Nazi Germany. The country was supplying men and goods to the war effort. Demand for labour was high, and Johannesburg became a magnet for Africans from the countryside seeking work. Between 1941, when I arrived, and 1946, the number of Africans in the city would double. Every morning, the township felt larger than it had the day before. Men found jobs in factories and housing in the 'non-European townships' of Newclare, Martindale, George Goch, Alexandra, Sophiatown and the Western Native Township, a prison-like compound of a few thousand matchbox houses on treeless ground.

Garlick and I sat in the estate agent's waiting room while a pretty African receptionist announced our presence to her boss in the inner office. After she relayed the message, her nimble fingers danced across the keyboard as she typed a letter. I had never in my life seen an African typist before, much less a female one. In the few public and business offices that I had visited in Umtata and Fort Hare, the typists had always been white and male. I was particularly impressed with this young woman because those white male typists had only used two slow-moving fingers to peck out their letters.

She soon ushered us into the inner office, where I was introduced to a man who looked to be in his late twenties, with an intelligent and kindly face, light in complexion, and dressed in a double-breasted suit. Despite his youth, he seemed to me an experienced man of the world. He was from the Transkei, but spoke English with a rapid urban fluency. To judge from his well-populated waiting room and his desk piled high with papers, he was a busy and successful man. But he did not rush us and seemed genuinely interested in our errand. His name was Walter Sisulu.

Sisulu's office specialized in properties for Africans. In the 1940s, there were still quite a few areas where freehold properties could be purchased by Africans, smallholdings located in such places as Alexandra and Sophiatown. In some of these areas, Africans had owned their own homes for several generations. The rest of the African areas were municipal townships containing matchbox houses for which the residents paid rent to the Johannesburg City Council.

Sisulu's name was becoming prominent as both a

businessman and a local leader. He was already a force in the community. He paid close attention as I explained my difficulties at Fort Hare, my ambition to be a lawyer, and how I intended to register at the University of South Africa to finish my degree by correspondence course. I neglected to tell him the circumstances of my arrival in Johannesburg. When I had finished, he leaned back in his chair and pondered what I had said. Then he looked me over one more time, and said that there was a white lawyer with whom he worked named Lazar Sidelsky, whom he believed to be a decent and progressive fellow. Sidelsky, he said, was interested in African education. He would talk to him about taking me on as an articled clerk.

In those days, I believed that proficiency in English and success in business were the direct result of high academic achievements and I assumed as a matter of course that Sisulu was a university graduate. I was greatly surprised to learn from my cousin after I left the office that Walter Sisulu had never gone beyond Standard VI. It was another lesson from Fort Hare that I had to unlearn in Johannesburg. I had been taught that to have a BA meant to be a leader, and to be a leader one needed a BA. But in Johannesburg I found that many of the most outstanding leaders had never been to university at all. Even though I had done all the courses in English that were required for a BA, my English was neither as fluent nor as eloquent as that of many of the men I met in Johannesburg who had not even received a school certificate.

After a brief time staying with my cousin, I arranged to move in with the Reverend J. Mabutho of the Anglican Church at his home in Eighth Avenue in Alexandra township. Reverend Mabutho was a fellow Thembu, a friend of my family, and a generous, God-fearing man. His wife, whom we called Gogo, was warm, affectionate, and a splendid cook who was liberal with her helpings. As a Thembu who knew my family, Reverend Mabutho felt responsible for me. 'Our ancestors have taught us to share,' he once told me.

But I had not learned from my experience at Crown Mines, for I did not tell Reverend Mabutho about the circumstances of my leaving the Transkei. My omission had unhappy consequences. A few days after I had moved in with the Mabuthos, I was having tea with them when a visitor arrived. Unfortunately their friend was Mr Festile, the *induna* at the Chamber of Mines who had been present when Justice and I met Mr Wellbeloved. Mr Festile and I greeted each other in a way that suggested we knew one another, and though nothing was said of our previous meeting, the next day Reverend Mabutho took me aside and made it clear that I could no longer remain under their roof.

I cursed myself for not having told the whole truth. I had become so used to my deceptions that I lied even when I did not have to. I am sure that Reverend Mabutho would not have minded, but when he learned of my circumstances from Festile, he felt deceived. In my brief stay in Johannesburg, I had left a trail of mistruths and, in each case, the falsehood had come back to haunt me. At the time, I felt that I had no alternative. I was frightened and inexperienced, and I knew that I had not got off on the right foot in my new life. In this instance, Reverend Mabutho took pity on me and found me accommodation with his next-door neighbours, the Xhoma family.

Mr Xhoma was one of an elite handful of African landowners in Alexandra. His house – 46 Seventh Avenue – was small, particularly as he had six children, but it was pleasant, with a veranda and a tiny garden. In order to make ends meet, Mr Xhoma, like so many other residents of Alexandra, rented rooms to boarders. He had built a tin-roofed room at the back of his property, no more than a shack, with a dirt floor, no heat, no electricity, no running water. But it was a place of my own and I was happy to have it.

In the meantime, on Walter's recommendation, Lazar Sidelsky had agreed to take me on as a clerk while I completed my BA degree. The firm of Witkin, Sidelsky and Eidelman, one of the largest law firms in the city, handled business from blacks as well as whites. In addition to studying law and passing certain exams, in order to qualify as an attorney in South Africa one had to undergo several years of apprenticeship to a practising lawyer, which is known as serving articles. But in order for me to become articled, I first had to complete my BA degree. To that end, I was studying at night with UNISA, short for the University of South Africa, a respected educational institution that offered credits and degrees by correspondence.

In addition to trying conventional law cases, Witkin, Sidelsky and Eidelman oversaw property transactions for African customers. Walter brought the firm clients who needed a mortgage. The firm would handle their loan applications, and then take a commission, which it would split with the estate agent. In fact, the law firm would take the lion's share of the money, leaving only a pittance for the African estate agent. Blacks were given the crumbs from the table, and had no option but to accept them.

Even so, the law firm was far more liberal than most. It was a Jewish firm, and in my experience I have found Jews to be more broad-minded than most whites on issues of race and politics, perhaps because they themselves have historically been victims of prejudice. The fact that Lazar Sidelsky, one of the firm's partners, would take on a young African as an articled clerk – something almost unheard-of in those days – was evidence of that liberalism.

Mr Sidelsky, whom I came to respect greatly and who treated me with enormous kindness, was a graduate of the University of the Witwatersrand and was in his mid-thirties when I joined the firm. He was involved in African education, donating money and time to African schools. A slender, courtly man, with a pencil moustache, he took a genuine interest in my welfare and future, preaching the value and importance of education – for me individually and for Africans in general. Only mass education, he used to say, would free my people, arguing that an educated man could not be oppressed because he could think for himself. He told me over and over again that becoming a successful attorney and thereby a model of achievement for my people was the most worthwhile path I could follow.

I met most of the firm's staff on my first day in the office, including the one other African employee, Gaur Radebe, with whom I shared an office. Ten years my senior, Gaur was a clerk, interpreter and messenger. He was a short, stocky, muscular man, fluent in English, Sotho and Zulu, and expressing himself in all of them with precision, humour and confidence. He had strong opinions and even stronger arguments to back them up and was a well-known figure in black Johannesburg.

That first morning at the firm, a pleasant young white secretary, Miss Lieberman, took me aside and said, 'Nelson, we have no colour bar here at the law firm.' She explained that at midmorning, the tea-man arrived in the front parlour with tea on a tray and a number of cups. 'In honour of your arrival, we have purchased two new cups for you and Gaur,' she said. 'The secretaries take cups of tea to the principals but you and Gaur will take your own tea, just as we do. I will call you when the tea comes, and then you can take your tea in the new cups.' She added that I should convey this message to Gaur. I was grateful for her ministrations, but I knew that the 'two new cups' she was so careful to mention were evidence of the colour bar that she said did not exist. The secretaries might share tea with two Africans, but not the cups with which to drink it.

When I told Gaur what Miss Lieberman had said, I noticed his expression change as he listened, just as you can see a mischievous idea enter the head of a child. 'Nelson,' he said, 'at teatime, don't worry about anything. Just do as I do.' At 11 o'clock, Miss Lieberman informed us that tea had arrived. In front of the secretaries and some of the other members of the firm, Gaur went over to the tea tray and ostentatiously ignored the two new cups, selecting instead one of the old ones, and proceeded to put in generous portions of sugar, milk and then tea. He stirred his cup slowly, and then stood there drinking it in a very self-satisfied way. The secretaries stared at Gaur and then Gaur nodded to me, as if to say, 'It is your turn, Nelson.'

For a moment I was in a quandary. I neither wanted

to offend the secretaries nor alienate my new colleague, so I settled on what seemed to me the most prudent course of action: I declined to have any tea at all. I said I was not thirsty. I was then just twenty-three years old, and just finding my feet as a man, as a resident of Johannesburg and as an employee of a white firm, and I saw the middle path as the best and most reasonable one. Thereafter, at teatime, I would go to the small kitchen in the office and take my tea there in solitude.

The secretaries were not always so thoughtful. Some time later, when I was more experienced at the firm, I was dictating some information to a white secretary when a white client whom she knew came into the office. She was embarrassed, and to demonstrate that she was not taking dictation from an African, she took a sixpence from her purse and said stiffly, 'Nelson, please go out and get me some shampoo from the chemist.' I left the room and got her shampoo.

In the beginning, my work at the firm was quite rudimentary. As a combination of a clerk and a messenger, I would find, arrange and file documents and serve or deliver papers around Johannesburg. Later, I would draw up contracts for some of the firm's African clients. Yet, no matter how small the job, Mr Sidelsky would explain to me what it was for and why I was doing it. He was a patient and generous teacher, and sought to impart not only the details of the law but the philosophy behind it. His view of the law was broad rather than narrow, for he believed that it was a tool that could be used to change society.

While Mr Sidelsky imparted his views of the law, he warned me against politics. Politics, he said, brings out the worst in men. It was the source of trouble and corruption, and should be avoided at all costs. He painted a frightening picture of what would happen to me if I drifted into politics, and counselled me to avoid the company of men he regarded as trouble-makers and rabble-rousers, specifically Gaur Radebe and Walter Sisulu. While Mr Sidelsky respected their abilities, he abhorred their politics.

Gaur was indeed a 'troublemaker', in the best sense of that term, and was an influential man in the African community in ways that Mr Sidelsky did not know or suspect. He was a member of the Advisory Board in the Western Native Township, an elected body of four local people who dealt with the authorities on matters relating to the townships. While it had little power, the board had great prestige among the people. Gaur was also, as I soon discovered, a prominent member of both the ANC and the Communist Party.

Gaur was his own man. He did not treat our employers with exaggerated courtesy, and often chided them for their treatment of Africans. 'You people stole our land from us,' he would say, 'and enslaved us. Now you are making us pay through the nose to get the worst pieces of it back.' One day, after I returned from doing an errand and entered Mr Sidelsky's office, Gaur turned to him and said, 'Look, you sit there like a lord whilst my chief runs around doing errands for you. The situation should be reversed, and one day it will, and we will dump all of you into the sea.' Gaur then left the room, and Mr Sidelsky just shook his head ruefully.

Gaur was an example of a man without a BA who seemed infinitely better educated than the fellows who left Fort Hare with glittering degrees. Not only was he more knowledgeable, he was bolder and more confident. Although I intended to finish my degree and enter law school, I learned from Gaur that a degree was not in itself a guarantee of leadership and that it meant nothing unless one went out into the community to prove oneself.

I was not the only articled clerk at Witkin, Sidelsky and Eidelman. A fellow about my age named Nat Bregman had started work shortly before I had. Nat was bright, pleasant, and thoughtful. He seemed entirely colour-blind and became my first white friend. He was a deft mimic, and could do fine imitations of the voices of Jan Smuts, Franklin Roosevelt and Winston Churchill. I often sought his counsel on matters of law and office procedure, and he was unfailingly helpful.

One day, at lunchtime, we were sitting in the office and Nat took out a packet of sandwiches. He removed one sandwich and said, 'Nelson, take hold of the other side of the sandwich.' I was not sure why he asked me to do this, but as I was hungry, I decided to oblige. 'Now, pull,' he said. I did so, and the sandwich split roughly in two.

'Now, eat,' he said. As I was chewing, Nat said, 'Nelson, what we have just done symbolizes the philosophy of the Communist Party: to share everything we have.' He told me he was a member of the party and explained the rudiments of what it stood for. I knew that Gaur was a member of the party, but he had never canvassed for it. I listened to Nat that day, and on many subsequent occasions when he preached the virtues of communism and tried to persuade me to join the party. I heard him out, asked questions, but did not join. I was not inclined to join any political organization, and the advice of Mr Sidelsky was still ringing in my ears. I was also quite religious, and the party's antipathy to religion put me off. But I appreciated half that sandwich.

I enjoyed Nat's company and we often went about together, including to a number of lectures and CP meetings. I went primarily out of intellectual curiosity. I was just becoming aware of the history of racial oppression in my own country, and saw the struggle in South Africa as purely racial. But the party saw South Africa's problems through the lens of the class struggle. To them, it was a matter of the Haves oppressing the Have-nots. This was intriguing to me, but did not seem particularly relevant to present-day South Africa. It might have been applicable to Germany or England, or Russia, but it did not seem appropriate for the country that I knew. Even so, I listened and learned.

Nat invited me to a number of parties where there was a mixture of whites, Africans, Indians and Coloureds. The get-togethers were arranged by the party and most of the guests were party members. I remember being anxious the first time I went, mainly because I did not think I had the proper attire. At Fort Hare, we were taught to wear a tie and jacket to a social function of any kind. Though my wardrobe was severely limited, I managed to find a tie to wear to the party.

I discovered a lively and gregarious group of people who did not seem to pay attention to colour at all. It was one of the first mixed gatherings I had ever attended, and I was far more of an observer than a participant. I felt extremely shy, wary of committing a *faux pas*, and unequipped to participate in the high-flown and rapid-fire conversations. My thoughts seemed undeveloped by comparison to the sophisticated dialogue around me.

At one point in the evening I was introduced to Michael Harmel, whom I was told had a master's degree in English from Rhodes University. I was impressed with his degree, but when I met him, I thought to myself, 'This chap has an MA, and he is not even wearing a tie!' I just could not reconcile this discrepancy. Later, Michael and I became friends, and I came to admire him greatly, in no small measure because he rejected so many of the rather foolish conventions I once embraced. He was not only a brilliant writer, but was so committed to communism that he lived in the same manner as an African, though he could have lived on a grander scale.

10

Life in Alexandra was exhilarating and precarious. Its atmosphere was alive, its spirit adventurous, its people resourceful. Although the township did boast some handsome buildings, it could fairly be described as a slum, living testimony to the neglect of the authorities. The roads were unpaved and dirty, and filled with hungry, undernourished children scampering around half-naked. The air was thick with the smoke from coal fires in tin braziers and stoves. A single water tap served several houses. Pools of stinking, stagnant water full of maggots collected by the side of the road. Alexandra was known as 'Dark City' for its complete absence of electricity. Walking home at night was perilous, for there were no lights, the silence pierced by yells, laughter and occasional gunfire. So different from the darkness of the Transkei, which seemed to envelop one in a welcome embrace.

The township was desperately overcrowded; every square foot was occupied by either a ramshackle house or a tin-roofed shack. As so often happens in desperately poor places, the worst elements came to the fore. Life was cheap; the gun and the knife ruled at night. Gangsters – known as *tsotsis* – carrying flick-knives or switchblades were plentiful and prominent; in those days they emulated American movie stars and wore fedoras and double-breasted suits and wide, colourful ties. Police raids were a regular feature of life in

Alexandra. The police routinely arrested masses of people for pass violations, possession of liquor and failure to pay the poll tax. On almost every corner there were shebeens, illegal saloons that were shacks where home-brewed beer was served.

In spite of the hellish aspects of life in Alexandra, the township was also a kind of heaven. As one of the few areas of the country where Africans could acquire freehold property and run their own affairs, where people did not have to kowtow to the tyranny of white municipal authorities, Alexandra was an urban Promised Land, evidence that a section of our people had broken their ties with the rural areas and become permanent city-dwellers. The government, in order to keep Africans in the countryside or working in the mines, maintained that Africans were by nature a rural people, ill suited to city life. Alexandra, despite its problems and flaws, gave the lie to that argument. Its population, drawn from all African language groups, was well adapted to city life and politically conscious. Urban life tended to abrade tribal and ethnic distinctions, and instead of being Xhosas, or Sothos, or Zulus or Shangaans, we were Alexandrans. This created a sense of solidarity, which caused great concern among the white authorities. The government had always utilized divide-and-rule tactics when dealing with Africans and depended on the strength of ethnic divisions between the people. But in places like Alexandra, these differences were being erased.

Alexandra occupies a treasured place in my heart. It was the first place I ever lived away from home. Even though I was later to live in Orlando, a small section of Soweto, for a far longer period than I did in Alexandra,

I always regarded Alexandra Township as a home where I had no specific house, and Orlando as a place where I had a house but no home.

In that first year, I learned more about poverty than I did in all my childhood days in Qunu. I never seemed to have money and I managed to survive on the meagrest of resources. The law firm paid me a salary of £2 per week, having generously waived the premium the articled clerks normally paid the firm. Out of that £2, I paid 13s. 4d. a month for my room at the Xhomas'. The cheapest means of transport to and from Alexandra was the 'Native' bus – for Africans only – which at £1 10s. a month made a considerable dent in my income. I was also paying fees to the University of South Africa in order to complete my degree by correspondence. I spent another pound or so on food. Part of my salary was spent on an even more vital item – candles – for without them I could not study. I could not afford a paraffin lamp; candles allowed me to read late into the night.

I was inevitably short of more than a few pence each month. On many days I walked the six miles to town in the morning and the six back in the evening in order to save the bus fare. I often went days without more than a mouthful of food and without a change of clothing. Mr Sidelsky, who was my height, once gave me an old suit of his and, assisted by considerable stitching and patching, I wore that suit every day for almost five years. In the end, there were more patches than suit.

One afternoon I was returning to Alexandra by bus and took a seat next to another fellow about my age. He was one of those young men who affected a style of dress that mimicked the well-tailored gangsters in

American movies. I realized that my suit was just touching the hem of his jacket. He noticed it also and very carefully moved away so that my jacket would not sully his. It was a tiny gesture, comical in retrospect, but painful at the time.

There is little to be said in favour of poverty, but it was often an incubator of true friendship. Many people will appear to befriend you when you are wealthy, but precious few will do the same when you are poor. If wealth is a magnet, poverty is a kind of repellent. Yet poverty often brings out the true generosity in others. One morning I decided to walk to town to save money and spotted a young lady who had been with me at Fort Hare. Her name was Phyllis Maseko and she was walking towards me on the same side of the street. I was embarrassed by my threadbare clothing and crossed to the other side, hoping she would not recognize me. But I heard her call out, 'Nelson . . . Nelson!' I stopped and crossed over, pretending that I had not noticed her until that moment. She was pleased to see me, but I could tell that she observed how shabby I looked. 'Nelson,' she said, 'here is my address, 234 Orlando East. Come and visit me.' I resolved not to humiliate myself again, but one day I was in need of a proper meal and dropped in. She fed me without alluding to my poverty, and from then on I continued to visit her.

My landlord, Mr Xhoma, was not wealthy, but he was a kind of philanthropist. Every Sunday, for all the time I lived on his property, he and his wife gave me lunch, and those steaming plates of pork and vegetables were often my only hot meal of the week. No matter where I was or what I was doing, I would never fail to be at the

Xhomas' on Sunday. For the rest of the week I would sustain myself on bread, and sometimes the secretaries at the firm would bring me some food.

I was very backward in those days and the combination of poverty and provincialism made for some amusing incidents. One day, not long after I had moved in with the Xhomas, I was on my way home from Johannesburg and very hungry. I had some money that I had saved and decided to splurge on some fresh meat, which I had not had in a long time. I did not see a proper butcher around, so I went into a delicatessen, a type of shop I had never encountered until I came to Johannesburg. Through the glass I saw a large and appetizing piece of meat and asked the man behind the counter to carve off a piece. He wrapped it up, and I put it under my arm and headed home, dreaming of the dinner that awaited me.

When I returned to my room in Alexandra, I called to one of the young daughters in the main house. She was only seven, but a clever girl. I said to her, 'Would you take this piece of meat to one of your older sisters and ask her to cook it for me?' I could see her trying to suppress a smile, but she was too respectful of her elders to laugh. With some irritation, I asked her whether something was wrong. Very softly she said, 'This meat is cooked.' I asked her what she was talking about. She explained that I had bought a piece of smoked ham, and that it was meant to be eaten just as it was. This was entirely new to me, and rather than confess complete ignorance, I told her that I knew it was smoked ham but that I wanted it warmed up. She knew I was bluffing, but ran off anyway. The meat was very tasty.

In Alexandra I rekindled a friendship with the lively,
ever-cheerful Ellen Nkabinde, whom I knew from
Healdtown, and who was then teaching at one of
the township schools. In fact, Ellen and I fell in love.
I had known her only slightly at Healdtown, and it was
not until I saw her again in Alexandra that our relationship blossomed. What little spare time I had in those
months I spent with her. Courtship was difficult: we
were always surrounded by people, and there were few
places to go. The only place we could be alone was
outside under the sun or the stars. So Ellen and I
wandered together in the veld and hills surrounding
the township. Mostly, we would just walk, and when we
both had the time, we might have a picnic.

Ellen was a Swazi, and though tribalism was fading in
the township, a close friend of mine condemned our
relationship on purely tribal grounds. I categorically
rejected this. But our different backgrounds posed
certain problems. Mrs Mabutho, the minister's wife,
did not care for Ellen, largely because she was a Swazi.
One day, while I was at the Mabuthos', Mrs Mabutho
answered a knock at the door. It was Ellen, who was
looking for me, and Mrs Mabutho told her I was not
inside. Only later did she say to me, 'Oh, Nelson, some
girl was here looking for you.' Mrs Mabutho then said
to me, 'Is that girl a Shangaan?' Although the Shangaans are a proud and noble tribe, at the time Shangaan
was considered a derogatory term. I took offence at this
and said, 'No, she is not a Shangaan, she is a Swazi.'
Mrs Mabutho felt strongly that I should take out only
Xhosa girls.

Such advice did not deter me. I loved and respected
Ellen, and felt not a little bit noble in discarding the

counsel of those who disapproved. The relationship was to me a novelty, and I felt daring in having a friendship with a woman who was not a Xhosa. I was young and rather lost in the city, and Ellen played the role not only of romantic partner but of a mother, supporting me, giving me confidence and endowing me with strength and hope. But within a few months Ellen moved away and, sadly, we lost touch with one another.

The Xhoma family had five daughters, each of them lovely, but the loveliest of all was named Didi. Didi, about my age, spent most of the week working as a domestic worker in a white suburb of Johannesburg. When I first moved to the house, I saw her only seldom and fleetingly. But later, when I made her acquaintance properly, I also fell in love with her. But Didi barely took any notice of me, and what she did notice was the fact that I owned only one patched-up suit and a single shirt, and that I did not present a figure much different from a tramp.

Every weekend Didi returned to Alexandra. She was brought home by a young man whom I assumed was her boyfriend, a flashy, well-to-do fellow who had a car, something that was most unusual. He wore expensive double-breasted American suits and wide-brimmed hats, and paid a great deal of attention to his appearance. He must have been a gangster of some sort, but I cannot be sure. He would stand outside in the yard and put his hands in his waistcoat and look altogether superior. He greeted me politely, but I could see that he did not regard me as much competition.

I yearned to tell Didi I loved her, but I was afraid that my advances would be unwanted. I was hardly a Don

Juan. Awkward and hesitant around girls, I did not know or understand the romantic games that others seemed to play effortlessly. At weekends, Didi's mother would sometimes ask her to bring out a plate of food to me. Didi would arrive on my doorstep with the plate and I could tell that she simply wanted to perform her errand as quickly as possible, but I would do my best to delay her. I would ask her opinion on things, all sorts of questions. 'Now, what standard did you attain in school?' I would say. 'Standard V,' she replied. 'Why did you leave?' I asked. She was bored, she replied. 'Ah, well, you must go back to school,' I said. 'You are about the same age as I am,' I continued, 'and there is nothing wrong with returning to school at this age. Otherwise you will regret it when you are old. You must think seriously about your future. It is nice for you now because you are young and beautiful and have many admirers, but you need to have an independent profession.'

I realize that these are not the most romantic words that have ever been uttered by a young man to a young woman with whom he was in love, but I did not know what else to talk to her about. She listened seriously, but I could tell that she was not interested, that in fact she felt a bit superior to me.

I wanted to propose to her but I was unwilling to do so unless I was certain she would say yes. Although I loved her, I did not want to give her the satisfaction of rejecting me. I kept up my pursuit, but I was timid and hesitant. In love, unlike politics, caution is not usually a virtue. I was neither confident enough to think that I might succeed nor secure enough to bear the sense of failure if I did not.

I stayed at that house for about a year and, in the end, I uttered nothing about my feelings. Didi did not show any less interest in her boyfriend or any more interest in me. I bade my good-bye with expressions of gratitude for her friendliness and the hospitality of the family. I did not see Didi again for many years. One day, much later, when I was practising law in Johannesburg, a young woman and her mother walked into my office. The woman had had a child, and her boyfriend did not want to marry her; she was seeking to institute an action against him. That young woman was Didi, only now she looked haggard and wore a faded dress. I was distressed to see her, and thought how things might have turned out differently. In the end, she did not bring a suit against her boyfriend, and I never saw her again.

Despite my romantic deficiencies, I gradually adjusted to township life and began to develop a sense of inner strength, a belief that I could do well outside the world in which I had grown up. I slowly discovered that I did not have to depend on my royal connections or the support of family in order to advance, and I forged relationships with people who did not know or care about my link to the Thembu royal house. I had my own home, humble though it was, and I was developing the confidence and self-reliance necessary to stand on my own two feet.

At the end of 1941 I received word that the regent was visiting Johannesburg and wanted to see me. I was nervous, but knew that I was obliged to see him, and indeed wanted to do so. He was staying at the WNLA compound, the headquarters of the Witwatersrand Native Labour Association, the recruiting agency for mine workers along the Reef.

The regent seemed greatly changed, or perhaps it was I who had changed. He never once mentioned the fact that I had run away, Fort Hare, or the arranged marriage that was not to be. He was courteous and solicitous, questioning me in a fatherly way about my studies and future plans. He recognized that my life was starting in earnest and would take a different course from the one he had envisaged and planned for me. He did not try to dissuade me from my course, and I was grateful for this implicit acknowledgement that I was no longer his charge.

My meeting with the regent had a double effect. I had rehabilitated myself and at the same time restored my own regard for him and the Thembu royal house. I had become indifferent to my old connections, an attitude I had adopted in part to justify my flight and somehow alleviate the pain of my separation from a world I loved and valued. It was reassuring to be back in the regent's warm embrace.

While the regent seemed satisfied with me, he was vexed with Justice, who he said must return to Mqhekezweni. Justice had formed a liaison with a young woman, and I knew he had no intention of going home. After the regent departed, Bangindawo, one of his headmen, instituted proceedings against Justice, and I agreed to help Justice when he was called before the native commissioner. At the hearing, I pointed out that Justice was an adult, and he did not have to return to Mqhekezweni merely because his father ordered it. When Bangindawo spoke, he did not reply to my argument but played on my own loyalties. He addressed me as Madiba, my clan name, something that was well calculated to remind me of my Thembu heritage. 'Madiba,' he said, 'the regent has cared for you, educated you, and treated you like his own son. Now you want to keep his true son from him. This is contrary to the wishes of the man who has been your faithful guardian, and contrary to the path that has been laid out for Justice.'

Bangindawo's speech hit me hard. Justice did have a different destiny from that of myself. He was the son of a chief, and a future chief in his own right. After the hearing, I told Justice that I had changed my mind, and I thought he should return. He was mystified by my reaction and refused to listen to me. He resolved to stay, and must have informed his girlfriend of my advice, for she never thereafter spoke to me.

At the beginning of 1942, in order to save money and be closer to downtown Johannesburg, I moved from the room at the back of the Xhomas' to the WNLA compound. I was assisted by Mr Festile, the *induna* at the Chamber of Mines, who was once again playing a fateful role in my life. On his own initiative he had decided to offer me free accommodation in the mining compound.

The WNLA compound was a multi-ethnic, polyglot community of modern, urban South Africa. There were Sothos, Tswanas, Vendas, Zulus, Pedis, Shangaans, Namibians, Mozambicans, Swazis and Xhosas. Few spoke English, and the lingua franca was an amalgam of many tongues known as Fanagalo. There, I saw not only flare-ups of ethnic animosity, but the comity that was also possible among men of different backgrounds. Yet I was a fish out of water. Instead of spending my days underground, I was studying or working in a law office where the only physical activity was running errands or putting files in a cabinet.

Because the WNLA was a way-station for visiting chiefs, I had the privilege of meeting tribal leaders from all over southern Africa. I recall on one occasion meeting the queen regent of Basutoland, or what is now Lesotho, Mantsebo Moshweshwe. She was accompanied by two chiefs, both of whom knew Sabata's father, Jongilizwe. I asked them about Jongilizwe, and for an hour I seemed to be back in Thembuland as they told colourful tales about his early years.

The queen took special notice of me and at one point addressed me directly, but she spoke in Sesotho, a language in which I knew few words. Sesotho is the language of the Sotho people as well as the Tswana, a large number of whom live in the Transvaal and the Orange Free State. She looked at me with incredulity, and then said in English, 'What kind of lawyer and leader will you be who cannot speak the language of your own people?' I had no response. The question embarrassed and sobered me; it made me realize my parochialism and just how unprepared I was for the task of serving my people. I had unconsciously succumbed to the ethnic divisions fostered by the white government and I did not know how to speak to my own kith and kin. Without language, one cannot talk to people and understand them; one cannot share their hopes and aspirations, grasp their history, appreciate their poetry or savour their songs. I again realized that we were not different people with separate languages; we were one people, with different tongues.

Less than six months after the regent's visit, Justice and I learned of his father's death in the winter of 1942. He had seemed weary when last I saw him and his death did not come as a great surprise. We read of the death in the newspaper because the telegram that had been sent to Justice had gone astray. We hastened down to the Transkei, arriving the day after the regent's funeral.

Though I was disappointed to miss the burial, I was inwardly glad that I had become reconciled with him before his death. But I was not without stabs of guilt. I always knew, even when I was estranged from the regent, that all my friends might desert me, all my plans might founder, all my hopes be dashed, but the regent would never abandon me. Yet I had spurned him, and I wondered whether my desertion might have hastened his death.

The passing of the regent removed from the scene an enlightened and tolerant man who achieved the goal that marks the reign of all great leaders: he kept his people united. Liberals and conservatives, traditionalists and reformers, white-collar officials and blue-collar miners, all remained loyal to him, not because they always agreed with him, but because the regent listened to and respected different opinions.

I spent nearly a week in Mqhekezweni after the funeral and it was a time of retrospection and rediscovery. There is nothing like returning to a place that remains unchanged to find the ways in which you yourself have altered. The Great Place went on as before, no different from when I had grown up there. But I realized that my own outlook and world views had evolved. I was no longer attracted by a career in the civil service, or being an interpreter in the Native Affairs Department. I no longer saw my future bound up with Thembuland and the Transkei. I was even informed that my Xhosa was no longer pure and was now influenced by Zulu, one of the dominant languages in the Reef. My life in Johannesburg, my exposure to men like Gaur Radebe, my experiences at the law firm had radically altered my beliefs. I looked back on that young man who had left Mqhekezweni as a naive and countrified fellow who had seen very little of the world. I now believed I was seeing things as they were. That too, of course, was an illusion.

I still felt an inner conflict between my head and my heart. My heart told me that I was a Thembu, that I had been raised and sent to school so that I could play a special role in perpetuating the kingship. Had I no obligations to the dead? To my father, who had put me in the care of the regent? To the regent himself, who had cared for me like a father? But my head told me that it was the right of every man to plan his own future as he pleased and choose his role in life. Was I not permitted to make my own choices?

Justice's circumstances were different from my own, and after the regent's death he had important new responsibilities thrust upon him. He was to succeed the regent as chief and had decided to remain in Mqhekezweni and take up his birthright. I had to return to Johannesburg, and could not even stay to attend his installation. In my language there is a saying: '*Ndiwelimilambo enamagama*' ('I have crossed famous rivers'). It means that one has travelled a great distance, that one has had wide experience and gained some wisdom from it. I thought of this as I returned to Johannesburg alone. I had, since 1934, crossed many important rivers in my own land: the Mbashe and the Great Kei, on my way to Healdtown;

and the Orange and the Vaal, on my way to Johannesburg. But I had many rivers yet to cross.

At the end of 1942 I passed the final examination for my BA degree. I had now achieved the rank I once considered so exalted. I was proud to have achieved my BA, but I also knew that the degree itself was neither a talisman nor a passport to easy success.

At the firm, I had become closer to Gaur, much to Mr Sidelsky's exasperation. Education, Gaur argued, was essential to our advancement, but he pointed out that no people or nation had ever freed itself through education alone. 'Education is all well and good,' Gaur said, 'but if we are to depend on education, we will wait a thousand years for our freedom. We are poor, we have few teachers and even fewer schools. We do not even have the power to educate ourselves.'

Gaur believed in finding solutions rather than in spouting theory. For Africans, he asserted, the engine of change was the African National Congress; its policies were the best way to pursue power in South Africa. He stressed the ANC's long history of advocating change, noting that the ANC was the oldest national African organization in the country, having been founded in 1912. Its constitution denounced racialism, its presidents had been from different tribal groups, and it preached the goal of Africans as full citizens of South Africa.

Despite Gaur's lack of formal education, he was my superior in virtually every sphere of knowledge. During lunch breaks he would often give impromptu lectures; he lent me books to read, recommended people for me to talk to, meetings for me to attend. I had taken two courses in modern history at Fort Hare, and while I knew many facts, Gaur was able to explain the causes for particular actions, the reasons that men and nations had acted as they did. I felt as though I was learning history afresh.

What made the deepest impression on me was Gaur's total commitment to the freedom struggle. He lived and breathed the quest for liberation. Gaur sometimes attended several meetings a day where he featured prominently as a speaker. He seemed to think of nothing but revolution.

I went along with Gaur to meetings of both the Township Advisory Board and the ANC. I went as an observer, not a participant, for I do not think I ever spoke. I wanted to understand the issues under discussion, evaluate the arguments, see the calibre of the men involved. The Advisory Board meetings were perfunctory and bureaucratic, but the ANC meetings were lively with debate and discussion about Parliament, the pass laws, rents, bus fares – any subject under the sun that affected Africans.

In August 1943 I marched with Gaur and ten thousand others in support of the Alexandra bus boycott, a protest against the raising of fares from four pence to five. Gaur was one of the leaders, and I watched him in action. This campaign had a great effect on me. In a small way, I had departed from my role as an observer and become a participant. I found that to march with one's people was exhilarating and inspiring. But I was also impressed by the boycott's effectiveness: after nine days, during which the buses ran empty, the company reinstated the fare to four pence.

Gaur's views were not the only ones I paid attention to at the firm. Hans Muller, a white estate agent who did business with Mr Sidelsky, would engage me in discussion. He was the prototypical businessman who saw the world through the prism of supply and demand. One day, Mr Muller pointed out of the window. 'Look out there, Nelson,' he said. 'Do you see those men and women scurrying up and down the street? What is it that they are pursuing? What is it they are working for so feverishly? I'll tell you: all of them, without exception, are after wealth and money. Because wealth and money equal happiness. That is what you must struggle for: money, and nothing but money. Once you have enough cash, there is nothing else you will want in life.'

William Smith was a Coloured man involved in the African property business who was often around the office. Smith was a veteran of the ICU (the Industrial and Commercial Workers Union), South Africa's first black trade union founded by Clements Kadalie, but his views had shifted dramatically since those days. 'Nelson,' he said, 'I have been involved in politics for a long time, and I regret every minute of it. I wasted the best years of my life in futile efforts serving vain and selfish men who placed their interests above those of the people they pretended to serve. Politics, in my experience, is nothing but a racket to steal money from the poor.'

Mr Sidelsky did not join these discussions. He seemed to regard discussing politics as almost as much of a waste of time as participating in it. Again and again he would counsel me to avoid politics. He warned me about Gaur and Walter Sisulu. 'These men will poison your mind,' he said. 'Nelson,' he asked, 'you want to be a lawyer, don't you?' I said yes. 'And if you are a lawyer, you want to be a successful lawyer, do you not?' Again, I said yes. 'Well, if you get into politics,' he said, 'your practice will suffer. You will get into trouble with the authorities who are often your allies in your work. You will lose all your clients, you will go bankrupt, you will break up your family and you will end up in jail. That is what will happen if you go into politics.'

I listened to these men and weighed their views carefully. All of the arguments had some merit. I was already leaning towards some type of political involvement, but I did not know what or how, and I lingered on the sidelines, uncertain what to do.

As far as my profession was concerned, it was Gaur who did more than offer advice. One day in early 1943, when I had been at the firm for less than two years, he took me aside and said, 'My boy, as long as I am here at the firm, they will never article you, whether or not you have a degree.' I was startled, and told Gaur that it could not be true, as he was not even in training to be a lawyer. 'That does not make a difference, Nelson,' he continued. 'They will say, "We have Gaur, he can speak law to our people, why do we need someone else? Gaur is already bringing in clients to the firm." But they will not tell you this to your face; they will just postpone and delay. It is important to the future of our struggle in this country for you to become a lawyer, and so I am going to leave the firm and start my own estate agency. When I am gone, they will have no choice but to article you.'

I pleaded with him not to resign, but he was immovable. Within a few days, he handed Mr Sidelsky his resignation, and Mr Sidelsky eventually articled me as promised. I cannot say whether Gaur's absence had anything to do with it, but his resignation was another example of his generosity.

Early in 1943, after passing my examination through UNISA, I returned to Fort Hare for my graduation. Before leaving for the university, I decided to treat myself to a proper suit. In order to do so, I had to borrow the money from Walter Sisulu. I had had a new suit when I went up to Fort Hare, purchased for me by the regent, and now I would have a new suit when I went down. I borrowed academic dress from Randall Peteni, a friend and fellow alumnus.

My nephew, K.D. Matanzima, who had graduated several years before, drove my mother and No-England, the regent's widow, to the ceremony. I was gratified to have my mother there, but the fact that No-England came made it seem as though the regent himself had blessed the event.

After the graduation I spent a few days with Dali-wonga (K.D.'s clan name, which is what I called him), at his home in Qamata. Daliwonga had already chosen the path of traditional leadership. He was in the line of succession to become the head of Emigrant Thembu-land, which lies in the westernmost part of the Trans-kei, and while I was staying with him he pressed me to return to Umtata after qualifying as an attorney. 'Why do you stay in Johannesburg?' he said. 'You are needed more here.'

It was a fair point: there were certainly more profes-sional Africans in the Transvaal than in the Transkei. I told Daliwonga that his suggestion was premature. But in my heart I knew I was moving towards a different commitment. Through my friendship with Gaur and

Walter, I was beginning to see that my duty was to my people as a whole, not just to a particular section or branch. I felt that all the currents in my life were taking me away from the Transkei and towards what seemed like the centre, a place where regional and ethnic loyalties gave way to a common purpose.

The graduation at Fort Hare offered a moment of introspection and reflection. I was struck most forcefully by the discrepancy between my old assumptions and my actual experience. I had discarded my presumptions that graduates automatically became leaders and that my connection to the Thembu royal house guaranteed me respect. Having a successful career and a comfortable salary were no longer my ultimate goals. I found myself being drawn into the world of politics because I was not content with my old beliefs.

In Johannesburg, I moved in circles where common sense and practical experience were more important than high academic qualifications. Even as I was receiving my degree, I realized that hardly anything I had learned at university seemed relevant in my new environment. At the university, teachers had shied away from topics like racial oppression, lack of opportunities for Africans and the nest of laws and regulations that subjugate the black man. But in my life in Johannesburg, I confronted these things every day. No one had ever suggested to me how to go about removing the evils of racial prejudice, and I had to learn by trial and error.

When I returned to Johannesburg at the beginning of 1943 I enrolled at the University of the Witwatersrand for a bachelor of law degree, the preparatory academic training for a lawyer. The University of the Witwatersrand, known to all as 'Wits', is located in Braamfontein in north-central Johannesburg, and is considered by many to be the premier English-speaking university in South Africa.

While working at the law firm brought me into regular contact with whites for the first time, the university introduced me to a group of whites of my own age. At Fort Hare we had occasional contacts with white students from Rhodes University in Grahamstown, but at Wits I was attending classes with white students. This was as new to them as it was to me, for I was the only African student in the law faculty.

The English-speaking universities of South Africa were great incubators of liberal values. It was a tribute to these institutions that they allowed black students. For the Afrikaans universities, such a thing was unthinkable.

Despite the university's liberal values, I never felt entirely comfortable there. Always to be the only African, except for menial workers, to be regarded at best as a curiosity and at worst as an interloper, is not a congenial experience. My manner was always guarded, and I met both generosity and animosity. Although I was to discover a core of sympathetic whites who became friends and later colleagues, most of the whites at Wits were not liberal or colour-blind. I recall getting to a lecture a few minutes late one day and taking a seat next to Sarel Tighy, a classmate who later became a Member of Parliament for the United Party. Though the lecture had already started and there were only a few empty seats, he ostentatiously collected his things and moved to a seat away from me. This type of behaviour was the rule rather than the exception. No one uttered the word 'kaffir'; their hostility was more muted, but I felt it just the same.

Our law professor, Mr Hahlo, was a strict, cerebral sort, who did not tolerate much independence on the part of his students. He held a curious view of the law when it came to women and Africans: neither group, he said, was meant to be lawyers. His view was that law was a social science and that women and Africans were not disciplined enough to master its intricacies. He once told me that I should not be at Wits but studying for my degree through UNISA. Although I disagreed with his views, I did little to disprove them. My performance as a law student was dismal.

At Wits, I met many people who were to share with me the ups and downs of the liberation struggle, and without whom I would have accomplished very little. Many white students went out of their way to make me feel welcome. During my first term at Wits I met Joe Slovo and his future wife, Ruth First. Then as now, Joe had one of the sharpest, most incisive minds I have ever encountered. He was an ardent communist, and was known for his high-spirited parties. Ruth had an outgoing personality and was a gifted writer. Both were the children of Jewish immigrants to South Africa. I began lifelong friendships with George Bizos and Bram Fischer. George, the child of Greek immigrants, was a man who combined a sympathetic nature with an incisive mind. Bram Fischer, a part-time lecturer, was the scion of a distinguished Afrikaner family: his grandfather had been prime minister of the Orange River Colony and his father was judge-president of the

Orange Free State. Although he could have been prime minister of South Africa, he became one of the bravest and staunchest friends of the freedom struggle that I have ever known. I befriended Tony O'Dowd and Harold Wolpe, who were political radicals and members of the Communist Party, and Jules Browde and his wife, who were liberal champions of the anti-apartheid cause.

I also formed close friendships with a number of Indian students. Although there had been a handful of Indian students at Fort Hare, they stayed in a separate hostel and I seldom had contact with them. At Wits I met and became friends with Ismail Meer, J.N. Singh, Ahmed Bhoola and Ramlal Bhoolia. The centre of this tight-knit community was Ismail's apartment, Flat 13, Kholvad House, four rooms in a residential building in the centre of the city. There we studied, talked and even danced until the early hours of the morning, and it became a kind of headquarters for young freedom fighters. I sometimes slept there when it was too late to catch the last train back to Orlando.

Bright and serious, Ismail Meer was born in Natal, and while at law school at Wits he became a key member of the Transvaal Indian Congress. J.N. Singh was a popular, handsome fellow, who was at ease with all colours and also a member of the Communist Party. One day, Ismail, J.N. and myself were in a rush to get to Kholvad House, and we boarded the tram despite the fact that while Indians could use them, Africans could not. We had not been travelling long when the conductor turned to Ismail and J.N. and said in Afrikaans that their 'kaffir friend' was not allowed on. Ismail and J.N. exploded at the conductor, telling him that he did not even understand the word 'kaffir' and that it was offensive to call me that name. The conductor promptly stopped the tram and hailed a policeman, who arrested us, took us down to the station and charged us. We were ordered to appear in court the following day. That night, Ismail and J.N. arranged for Bram Fischer to defend us. The next day, the magistrate seemed in awe of Bram's family connections. We were promptly acquitted, and I saw at first hand that justice was not at all blind.

Wits opened a new world to me, a world of ideas and political beliefs and debates, a world where people were passionate about politics. I was among white and Indian intellectuals of my own generation, young men who would form the vanguard of the most important political movements of the next few years. I discovered for the first time people of my own age firmly aligned with the liberation struggle, who were prepared, despite their relative privilege, to sacrifice themselves for the cause of the oppressed.

PART THREE

———

Birth of a Freedom Fighter

11

I cannot pinpoint a moment when I became politicized, when I knew that I would spend my life in the liberation struggle. To be an African in South Africa means that one is politicized from the moment of one's birth, whether one acknowledges it or not. An African child is born in an Africans Only hospital, taken home in an Africans Only bus, lives in an Africans Only area and attends Africans Only schools, if he attends school at all.

When he grows up, he can hold Africans Only jobs, rent a house in Africans Only townships, ride Africans Only trains and be stopped at any time of the day or night and be ordered to produce a pass, without which he can be arrested and thrown in jail. His life is circumscribed by racist laws and regulations that cripple his growth, dim his potential and stunt his life. This was the reality, and one could deal with it in a myriad of ways.

I had no epiphany, no singular revelation, no moment of truth, but a steady accumulation of a thousand slights, a thousand indignities and a thousand unremembered moments produced in me an anger, a rebelliousness, a desire to fight the system that imprisoned my people. There was no particular day on which I said, Henceforth I will devote myself to the liberation of my people; instead, I simply found myself doing so, and could not do otherwise.

I have mentioned many of the people who influenced me, but more and more I had come under the wise tutelage of Walter Sisulu. Walter was strong, reasonable, practical and dedicated. He never lost his head in a crisis; he was often silent when others were shouting. He believed that the African National Congress was the means to effect change in South Africa, the repository of black hopes and aspirations. Sometimes one can judge an organization by the people who belong to it, and I knew that I would be proud to belong to any organization of which Walter was a member. At the time, there were few options. The ANC was the one organization that welcomed everyone, that saw itself as a great umbrella under which all Africans could find shelter.

Change was in the air in the 1940s. The Atlantic Charter of 1941, signed by Roosevelt and Churchill, reaffirmed faith in the dignity of each human being and propagated a host of democratic principles. Some in the West saw the charter as empty promises, but not those of us in Africa. Inspired by the Atlantic Charter and the fight of the Allies against tyranny and oppression, the ANC created its own charter, called African Claims, which called for full citizenship for all Africans, the right to buy land and the repeal of all discriminatory legislation. We hoped that the government and ordinary South Africans would see that the principles they were fighting for in Europe were the same ones we were advocating at home.

Walter's house in Orlando was a mecca for activists and ANC members. It was a warm, welcoming place and I was often there to sample either a political discussion or Ma Sisulu's cooking. One night in 1943 I met Anton Lembede, who held Master of Arts and Bachelor of Law degrees, and A.P. Mda. From the moment I heard Lembede speak, I knew I was seeing a magnetic personality who thought in original and often startling ways. He was then one of a handful of African lawyers in the whole of South Africa and was the legal partner of the venerable Dr Pixley ka Seme, one of the founders of the ANC.

Lembede said that Africa was a black man's continent, and it was up to Africans to reassert themselves and reclaim what was rightfully theirs. He hated the idea of the black inferiority complex and castigated what he called the worship and idolization of the West and its ideas. The inferiority complex, he affirmed, was the greatest barrier to liberation. He noted that wherever the African had been given the opportunity, he was capable of developing to the same extent as the white man, citing such African heroes as Marcus Garvey, W.E.B. Du Bois and Haile Selassie. 'The colour of my skin is beautiful,' he said, 'like the black soil of Mother Africa.' He believed blacks had to improve their own self-image before they could initiate successful mass action. He preached self-reliance and self-determination, and called his philosophy Africanism. We took it for granted that one day he would lead the ANC.

Lembede declared that a new spirit was stirring among the people, that ethnic differences were melting away, that young men and women thought of themselves as Africans first and foremost, not as Xhosas or Ndebeles or Tswanas. Lembede, whose father was an illiterate Zulu peasant from Natal, had trained as a teacher at Adam's College, an American Board of

Missions institution. He had taught for years in the Orange Free State, learned Afrikaans, and had come to see Afrikaner nationalism as a prototype of African nationalism.

As Lembede later wrote in the newspaper *Inkundla ya Bantu*, an African newspaper in Natal:

> The history of modern times is the history of nationalism. Nationalism has been tested in the people's struggles and the fires of battle and found to be the only antidote against foreign rule and modern imperialism. It is for that reason that the great imperialistic powers feverishly endeavour with all their might to discourage and eradicate all nationalistic tendencies among their alien subjects; for that purpose huge and enormous sums of money are lavishly expended on propaganda against nationalism which is dismissed as 'narrow', 'barbarous', 'uncultured', 'devilish', etc. Some alien subjects become dupes of this sinister propaganda and consequently become tools or instruments of imperialism, for which great service they are highly praised by the imperialistic power and showered with such epithets as 'culture', 'liberal', 'progressive', 'broadminded', etc.

Lembede's views struck a chord in me. I, too, had been susceptible to paternalistic British colonialism and the appeal of being perceived by whites as 'cultured' and 'progressive' and 'civilized'. I was already on my way to being drawn into the black elite that Britain sought to create in Africa. That is what everyone from the regent to Mr Sidelsky had wanted for me. But it was an illusion.

Like Lembede, I came to see the antidote as militant African nationalism.

Lembede's friend and partner was Peter Mda, better known as A.P. While Lembede tended to imprecision and was inclined to be verbose, Mda was controlled and exact. Lembede could be vague and mystical; Mda was specific and scientific. Mda's practicality was a perfect foil for Lembede's idealism.

Other young men were thinking along the same lines and we would all meet to discuss these ideas. In addition to Lembede and Mda, these men included Walter Sisulu; Oliver Tambo; Dr Lionel Majombozi; Victor Mbobo, my former teacher at Healdtown; William Nkomo, a medical student who was a member of the CP; Jordan Ngubane, a journalist from Natal who worked for *Inkundla* as well as *Bantu World*, the largest-selling African newspaper, David Bopape, secretary of the ANC in the Transvaal and a member of the Communist Party and many others. Many felt, perhaps unfairly, that the ANC as a whole had become the preserve of a tired, unmilitant, privileged African elite more concerned with protecting their own rights than those of the masses. The general consensus was that some action must be taken, and Dr Majombozi proposed forming a Youth League as a way of lighting a fire under the leadership of the ANC.

In 1943 a delegation including Lembede, Mda, Sisulu, Tambo, Nkomo and I went to see Dr Xuma, who was head of the ANC, at his rather grand house in Sophiatown. Dr Xuma had a surgery at his home in addition to a small farm. He had performed a great service to the ANC. He had roused it from its slumbering state under Dr Seme, when the organization had shrunk in size and importance. When he assumed the presidency, the ANC had 17s. 6d. in its treasury, and he had boosted the amount to £4,000. He was admired by traditional leaders, had relationships with cabinet ministers and exuded a sense of security and confidence. But he also carried himself with an air of superciliousness that did not befit the leader of a mass organization. Devoted as he was to the ANC, his medical practice took precedence. Xuma presided over the era of delegations, deputations, letters and telegrams. Everything was done in the English manner, the idea being that despite our disagreements we were all gentlemen. He enjoyed the relationships he had formed with the white establishment and did not want to jeopardize them with political action.

At our meeting, we told him that we intended to organize a Youth League and a campaign of action designed to mobilize mass support. We had brought a copy of the draft constitution and manifesto with us. We told Dr Xuma that the ANC was in danger of becoming marginalized unless it stirred itself and took up new methods. Dr Xuma felt threatened by our delegation and strongly objected to a Youth League constitution. He thought the league should be a more loosely organized group and act mainly as a recruiting committee for the ANC. In a paternalistic way, Dr Xuma went on to tell us that Africans as a group were too unorganized and undisciplined to participate in a mass campaign and that such a campaign would be rash and dangerous.

Shortly after the meeting with Dr Xuma, a provisional committee of the Youth League was formed under the leadership of William Nkomo. The members of the committee journeyed to the ANC annual conference in Bloemfontein in December 1943, where they proposed the formation of a Youth League to help recruit new members to the organization. The proposal was accepted.

The actual formation of the Youth League took place on Easter Sunday 1944 at the Bantu Men's Social Centre in Eloff Street. There were about a hundred men there, some coming from as far away as Pretoria. It was a select group, an elite group, a great number of us being Fort Hare graduates; we were far from a mass movement. Lembede gave a lecture on the history of nations, a tour of the horizon from ancient Greece to medieval Europe to the age of colonization. He emphasized the historical achievements of Africa and Africans, and noted how foolish it was for whites to see themselves as a chosen people and an intrinsically superior race.

Jordan Ngubane, A.P. Mda and William Nkomo all spoke, and emphasized the emerging spirit of African nationalism. Lembede was elected president, Oliver Tambo secretary, and Walter Sisulu became treasurer. A.P. Mda, Jordan Ngubane, Lionel Majombozi, Congress Mbata, David Bopape and I were elected to the Executive Committee. We were later joined by prominent young men such as Godfrey Pitje, a student (later teacher then lawyer); Arthur Letele, Wilson Conco, Diliza Mji and Nthato Motlana, all medical doctors; Dan Tloome, a trade unionist; and Joe Matthews, Duma Nokwe and Robert Sobukwe, all students. Branches were soon established in all the provinces.

The basic policy of the league did not differ from the ANC's first constitution in 1912. But we were reaffirming and underscoring those original concerns, many of which had gone by the wayside. African nationalism was our battle cry, and our creed was the creation of one nation out of many tribes, the overthrow of white supremacy, and the establishment of a truly democratic form of government. Our manifesto stated: 'We believe that the national liberation of Africans will be achieved by Africans themselves . . . The Congress Youth League must be the brains-trust and power-station of the spirit of African nationalism.'

The manifesto utterly rejected the notion of trusteeship, the idea that the white government somehow had African interests at heart. We cited the crippling anti-African legislation of the past forty years, beginning with the 1913 Land Act, which ultimately deprived blacks of 87 per cent of the territory in the land of their birth; the Urban Areas Act of 1923, which created teeming African slums, politely called 'native locations', in order to supply cheap labour to white industry; the Colour Bar Act of 1926, which banned Africans from practising skilled trades; the Native Administration Act of 1927, which made the British Crown, rather than the Paramount Chiefs, the supreme chief over all African areas; and finally, in 1936, the Representation of Natives Act, which removed Africans from the common voters' roll in the Cape, thereby shattering any illusion that whites would allow Africans to have control over their own destiny.

We were extremely wary of communism. The document stated: 'We may borrow . . . from foreign ideologies, but we reject the wholesale importation of foreign ideologies into Africa.' This was an implicit rebuke to the Communist Party, which Lembede and many others, including myself, considered a 'foreign' ideology unsuited to the African situation. Lembede felt that the Communist Party was dominated by whites, which undermined African self-confidence and initiative.

A number of committees were formed that day, but the primary purpose of the Youth League was to give direction to the ANC in its quest for political freedom. Although I agreed with this, I was nervous about joining the league and still had doubts about the extent of my political commitment. I was then working full-time and studying part-time, and had little time outside those two activities. I also possessed a certain insecurity, feeling politically backward compared to Walter, Lembede and Mda. They were men who knew their minds, and I was, as yet, unformed. I still lacked confidence as a speaker, and was intimidated by the eloquence of so many of those in the league.

Lembede's Africanism was not universally supported because his ideas were characterized by a racial exclusivity that disturbed some of the other Youth Leaguers. Some of the members felt that a nationalism that would include sympathetic whites was a more desirable course. Others, including myself, countered that if blacks were offered a multiracial form of struggle, they would remain enamoured of white culture and prey to a continuing sense of inferiority. At the time, I was firmly opposed to allowing communists or whites to join the league.

Walter's house was my home from home. For several months in the early 1940s, it actually was my home when I had no other place to stay. The house was always full, and it seemed there was a perpetual discussion going on about politics. Albertina, Walter's wife, was a wise and wonderful presence, and a strong supporter of Walter's political work. (At their wedding, Anton Lembede said: 'Albertina, you have married a married man: Walter married politics long before he met you.')

It was in the lounge of the Sisulus' home that I met Evelyn Mase, my first wife. She was a quiet, pretty girl from the countryside who did not seem overawed by the coming and goings at the Sisulus'. She was then training as a nurse with Albertina and Peter Mda's wife, Rose, at the Johannesburg non-European General Hospital.

Evelyn was from Engcobo, in the Transkei, some distance west of Umtata. Her father, a mineworker, had died when she was an infant, and her mother when she was twelve. After completing primary school, Evelyn was sent to Johannesburg to attend high school.

She stayed with her brother, Sam Mase, who was then living at the Sisulus' house. Ma Sisulu, Walter's mother, was the sister of Evelyn's mother. The Sisulus treated Evelyn as if she was a favourite daughter, and was much loved by them.

I asked Evelyn out very soon after our first meeting. Almost as quickly, we fell in love. Within a few months I had asked her to marry me, and she accepted. We were married in a civil ceremony requiring only signatures and a witness at the Native Commissioner's Court in Johannesburg, for we could not afford a traditional wedding or feast. Our most immediate problem was finding a place to live. We first went to stay with her brother in Orlando East and later with Evelyn's sister at City Deep Mines, where her sister's husband, Msunguli Mgudlwa, worked as a clerk.

12

In 1946 a number of critical events occurred that shaped my political development and the directions of the struggle. The mineworkers' strike, in which 70,000 African miners along the Reef went on strike, affected me greatly. At the initiative of J.B. Marks, Dan Tloome, Gaur Radebe and a number of ANC labour activists, the African Mine Workers' Union (AMWU) had been created in the early 1940s. There were as many as 400,000 African miners working on the Reef, most of them making no more than two shillings a day. The union leadership had repeatedly pressed the Chamber of Mines for a minimum wage of ten shillings a day, as well as family housing and two weeks' paid leave. The chamber ignored the union's demands.

In one of the largest such actions in South African history, the miners went on strike for a week and maintained their solidarity. The state's retaliation was ruthless. The leaders were arrested, the compounds surrounded by police, and the AMWU offices ransacked. A march was brutally repulsed by police; twelve miners died. The Natives' Representative Council adjourned in protest. I had a number of relations who were mineworkers, and during the week of the strike I visited them, discussed the issues and expressed my support.

J.B. Marks, a longtime member of the ANC and the Communist Party, was then president of the African

Mine Workers' Union. Born in the Transvaal of mixed parentage, Marks was a charismatic figure with a distinctive sense of humour. He was a tall man with a light complexion. During the strike I sometimes went with him from mine to mine, talking to workers and planning strategy. From morning to night, he displayed cool and reasoned leadership, with his humour leavening even the most difficult crisis. I was impressed by the organization of the union and its ability to control its membership, even in the face of such savage opposition.

In the end, the state prevailed: the strike was suppressed and the union crushed. The strike was the beginning of my close relationship with Marks. I visited him often at his house, and we discussed my opposition to communism at great length. Marks was a stalwart member of the party, but he never took my objections personally, and felt that it was natural for a young man to embrace nationalism, but that as I grew older and more experienced, my views would broaden. I had these same discussions with Moses Kotane and Yusuf Dadoo, both of whom believed, like Marks, that communism had to be adapted to the African situation. Other communist members of the ANC condemned me and the other Youth Leaguers, but Marks, Kotane and Dadoo never did.

After the strike, fifty-two men, including Kotane and Marks, and many other communists, were arrested and prosecuted, first for incitement, then for sedition. It was a political trial, an effort by the state to show that it was not soft on the Red Menace.

That same year, another event forced me to recast my whole approach to political work. In 1946 the Smuts government passed the Asiatic Land Tenure Act, which curtailed the free movement of Indians, circumscribed the areas where Indians could reside and trade, and severely restricted their right to buy property. In return, they were provided with representation in Parliament by token white surrogates. Dr Dadoo, president of the Transvaal Indian Congress, castigated the restrictions and dismissed the offer of parliamentary representation as 'a spurious offer of a sham franchise'. This law – known as the Ghetto Act – was a grave insult to the Indian community and anticipated the Group Areas Act, which would eventually circumscribe the freedom of all South Africans of colour.

The Indian community was outraged and launched a concerted two-year campaign of passive resistance to oppose the measures. Led by Dr Dadoo and Dr G.M. Naicker, president of the Natal Indian Congress (NIC), the Indian community conducted a mass campaign that impressed us with its organization and dedication. Housewives, priests, doctors, lawyers, traders, students and workers took their place in the front lines of the protest. For two years, people suspended their lives to take up the battle. Mass rallies were held; land reserved for whites was occupied and picketed. No fewer than 2,000 volunteers went to jail, and Dr Dadoo and Dr Naicker were sentenced to six months' hard labour.

The campaign was confined to the Indian community, and the participation of other groups was not encouraged. Even so, Dr Xuma and other African leaders spoke at several meetings, and along with the Youth League gave full moral support to the struggle of the Indian people. The government crippled the rebellion with harsh laws and intimidation, but we in the

Youth League and the ANC had witnessed the Indian people register an extraordinary protest against colour oppression in a way that Africans and the ANC had not.

Ismail Meer and J.N. Singh suspended their studies, said good-bye to their families and went to prison. Ahmed Kathrada, who was still a high-school student, did the same thing. I often visited the home of Amina Pahad for lunch, and then, suddenly, this charming woman put aside her apron and went to jail for her beliefs. If I had once questioned the willingness of the Indian community to protest against oppression, I no longer could.

The Indian campaign became a model for the type of protest that we in the Youth League were calling for. It instilled a spirit of defiance and radicalism among the people, broke the fear of prison, and boosted the popularity and influence of the NIC and TIC. They reminded us that the freedom struggle was not merely a question of making speeches, holding meetings, passing resolutions and sending deputations, but of meticulous organization, militant mass action and, above all, the willingness to suffer and sacrifice. The Indians' campaign harkened back to the 1913 passive resistance campaign in which Mahatma Gandhi led a tumultuous procession of Indians crossing illegally from Natal to the Transvaal. That was history; this campaign was taking place before my own eyes.

Early in 1946, Evelyn and I moved to a two-room municipal house of our own in Orlando East and thereafter to a slightly larger house at No. 8115 Orlando West. Orlando West was a dusty, spartan area of boxy municipal houses that would later became part of Greater Soweto, Soweto being an acronym for South-Western Townships. Our house was situated in an area nicknamed Westcliff by its residents after the fancy white suburb to the north.

The rent of our new home was 17s. 6d. per month. The house itself was identical to hundreds of others built on postage-stamp-size plots on dirt roads. It had the same standard tin roof, the same cement floor, a narrow kitchen, and a bucket toilet at the back. Although there were streetlamps outside, we used paraffin lamps inside as the homes were not yet elec-trified. The bedroom was so small that a double bed took up almost the entire floor space. These houses were built by the municipal authorities for workers who needed to be near town. To relieve the monotony, some people planted small gardens or painted their doors in bright colours. It was the very opposite of grand, but it was my first true home of my own and I was mightily proud. A man is not a man until he has a house of his own. I did not know then that it would be the only residence that would be entirely mine for many, many years.

The state had allocated the house to Evelyn and me because we were no longer just two, but three. That year our first son, Madiba Thembekile, was born. He was given my clan name of Madiba, but was known by the nickname Thembi. He was a solid, happy little boy who most people said resembled his mother more than his father. I had now produced an heir, though I had little as yet to bequeath to him. But I had perpetuated the Mandela name and the Madiba clan, which is one of the basic responsibilities of a Xhosa male.

I finally had a stable base, and I went from being a guest in other people's homes to having guests in my own. My sister Leabie joined us and I took her across the railway line to enrol her at Orlando High School. In my culture, all the members of one's family have a claim to the hospitality of any other member of the family; the combination of my large extended family and my new house meant a great number of guests.

I enjoyed domesticity, even though I had little time for it. I delighted in playing with Thembi, bathing him and feeding him, and putting him to bed with a little story. In fact, I love playing with children and chatting with them; it has always been one of the things that makes me feel most at peace. I enjoyed relaxing at home, reading quietly, taking in the sweet and savoury smells emanating from pots boiling in the kitchen. But I was rarely at home to enjoy these things.

During the latter part of that year, the Reverend Michael Scott came to stay with us. Scott was an Anglican clergyman and a great fighter for African rights. He had been approached by a man named Komo, who was representing a squatter camp outside Johannesburg that the government was seeking to relocate. Komo wanted Scott to protest against the removal. Scott said, 'If I am going to help you I must be one of you,' and he proceeded to move to the squatter camp and start a congregation there. Scott's shanty-town for the homeless was built near a rocky knoll, and the residents christened it Tobruk, after the battle in the North Africa campaign of the war. It was a place I sometimes took Thembi on Sunday morning, as he liked to play hide-and-seek among the rocks. After Scott had set up his congregation, he found that Komo was embezzling money from people who were contributing to the fight against the removal. When Scott confronted Komo, Komo drove Scott out of the camp and threatened his life.

Scott took refuge with us in Orlando and brought along an African priest named Dlamini, who also had a wife and children. Our house was tiny, and Scott slept in the sitting-room, Dlamini and his wife slept in another room, and we put all the children in the kitchen. Michael Scott was a modest, unassuming man, but Dlamini was a bit hard to take. At mealtimes, he would complain about the food. 'Look here,' he would say, 'this meat of yours, it's very lean and hard, not properly cooked at all. I'm not used to meals like this.' Scott was appalled by this, and admonished Dlamini, but Dlamini took no heed. The next night he might say, 'Well, this is a bit better than yesterday, but far from well prepared. Mandela, you know your wife just cannot cook.'

Dlamini indirectly caused the situation to be resolved because I was so eager to have him out of the house that I went to the squatter camp myself and explained that Scott was a true friend of theirs, unlike Komo, and that they had to choose between the two. They then organized an election in which Scott triumphed, and he moved back to the squatter camp, taking Father Dlamini with him.

Early in 1947 I completed the requisite period of three years for articles and my time at Witkin, Sidelsky and Eidelman came to an end. I resolved to become a full-time student in order to gain my LL B so that I could go out on my own and practise as an attorney. The loss of the £8 10s. 1d. per month that I earned at Sidelsky was devastating. I applied to the Bantu Welfare Trust at the South African Institute of Race Relations in Johannesburg for a loan of £250 sterling to help finance my law studies, which included university fees, textbooks and a monthly allowance. I was given a loan of £150.

Three months later, I wrote to them again, noting that my wife was about to take maternity leave, and we would lose her salary of £17 per month, which was absolutely necessary to our survival. I did receive the additional money, for which I was grateful, but the circumstances which warranted it were unfortunate. Our daughter Makaziwe's birth was not difficult, yet she was frail and sickly. From the start, we feared the worst. Many nights, Evelyn and I took turns looking after her. We did not know the name of whatever was consuming this tiny girl and the doctors could not explain the nature of the problem. Evelyn monitored the baby with the combination of a mother's tirelessness and a nurse's professional efficiency. When she was nine months old, Makaziwe passed away. Evelyn was distraught, and the only thing that helped to temper my own grief was trying to alleviate hers.

In politics, no matter how much one plans, circumstances often dictate events. In July 1947, during an informal discussion with Lembede about Youth League business, he complained to me of a sudden pain in his stomach and an accompanying chill. When the pain worsened we drove him to Coronation Hospital, and that same night he was dead at the age of thirty-three. Many were deeply affected by his death. Walter Sisulu seemed almost prostrate with grief. His passing was a setback to the movement, for Lembede was a fount of ideas and attracted others to the organization.

Lembede was succeeded by Peter Mda, whose analytical approach, ability to express himself clearly and simply and tactical experience made him an excellent politician and an outstanding leader of the Youth League. Mda was a lean fellow with no excess weight, just as he used no excess words. In his broad-minded tolerance of different views, his own thinking was more mature and advanced than that of Lembede. It took Mda's leadership to advance Lembede's cause.

Mda believed the Youth League should function as an internal pressure group, a militant nationalistic wing within the ANC as a whole that would propel the organization into a new era. At the time, the ANC did not have a single full-time employee, and was generally poorly organized, operating in a haphazard way. (Later, Walter became the first and only full-time ANC staff member at an extremely meagre salary.)

Mda quickly established a branch of the Youth League at Fort Hare under the guidance of Z.K. Matthews and Godfrey Pitje, a lecturer in anthropology. They recruited outstanding students, bringing in fresh blood and new ideas. Among the most outstanding were Professor Matthews's brilliant son Joe, and Robert Sobukwe, a dazzling orator and incisive thinker.

Mda was more moderate in his nationalism than Lembede, and his thinking was without the racial tinge that characterized Lembede's. He hated white oppression and white domination, not white people themselves. He was also less extreme in his opposition to the Communist Party than Lembede – or myself. I was among the Youth Leaguers who were suspicious of the white left. Even though I had befriended many white communists, I was wary of white influence in the ANC, and I opposed joint campaigns with the party. I was concerned that the communists were intent on taking over our movement under the guise of joint action. I believed that it was an undiluted African nationalism, not Marxism or multi-racialism, that would liberate us. With a few of my colleagues in the league, I even went so far as breaking up CP meetings by storming the stage, tearing up signs and capturing the microphone. At the national conference of the ANC in December, the Youth League introduced a motion demanding the expulsion of all members of the Communist Party, but we were soundly defeated. Despite the influence the Indian passive resistance campaign of 1946 had on me, I felt about the Indians the same way I did about the communists: that they would tend to dominate the ANC, in part because of their superior education, experience and training.

In 1947 I was elected to the Executive Committee of the Transvaal ANC and served under C.S. Ramohanoe, president of the Transvaal region. This was my first position in the ANC proper, and it represented a milestone in my commitment to the organization. Until that time, the sacrifices I had made had not gone much further than being absent from my wife and family during weekends and returning home late in the evening. I had not been directly involved in any major campaign, and I did not yet understand the hazards and unending difficulties of the life of a free-dom fighter. I had coasted along without having to pay a price for my commitment. From the time I was elected to the Executive Committee of the Transvaal region, I came to identify myself with the Congress as a whole, with its hopes and despairs, its success and failures; I was now bound heart and soul.

Ramohanoe was another one of those from whom I learned. He was a staunch nationalist and a skilful organizer who was able to balance divergent views and come forward with a suitable compromise. While Ramohanoe was unsympathetic to the communists, he worked well with them. He believed that the ANC was a national organization that should welcome all those who supported our cause.

In 1947, in the wake of the Indian passive resistance campaign, Dr Xuma, Dr Dadoo and Dr Naicker, presidents respectively of the ANC, the Transvaal Indian Congress and the Natal Indian Congress, signed the Doctors' Pact agreeing to join forces against a common enemy. This was a significant step towards the unity of the African and Indian movements. Rather than creating a central political body to direct all the various movements, they agreed to cooperate on matters of common interest. Later, they were joined by the African People's Organization (APO), a Coloured organization.

But such an agreement was at best tentative, for each national group faced problems peculiar to itself. The pass system, for example, barely affected Indians or Coloureds. The Ghetto Act, which had prompted the Indian protests, barely affected Africans. Coloured groups at the time were more concerned about the race classification and job reservation, issues that did not affect Africans and Indians to the same degree.

The Doctors' Pact laid a foundation for the future cooperation of Africans, Indians and Coloureds, since it respected the independence of each individual group, but acknowledged the achievements that could be realized from acting in concert. The Doctors' Pact precipitated a series of nonracial, antigovernment campaigns around the country, which sought to bring together Africans and Indians in the freedom struggle. The first of these campaigns was the First Transvaal and Orange Free State People's Assembly for Votes for All, a campaign for the extension of the franchise to all black South Africans. Dr Xuma announced ANC participation at a press conference over which I presided. At the time, we believed the campaign would be run by the ANC, but when we learned that the ANC would not be leading the campaign, the Transvaal Executive Committee decided that the ANC should withdraw. My idea at the time was that the ANC should be involved only in campaigns that the ANC itself led. I was more concerned with who got the credit than whether the campaign would be successful.

Even after the withdrawal, Ramohanoe, president of the Transvaal region of the ANC, issued a press statement calling on Africans in the province to take part in the Votes for All campaign in clear contravention of the decision of the Transvaal Executive Committee. This was an act of disobedience the Executive could not tolerate. At a conference called to resolve this dispute, I was asked to move a no-confidence motion against Ramohanoe for his disobedience. I felt an acute conflict between duty and personal loyalty, between my obligations to my organization and to my friend. I well knew that I would be condemning the action of a man whose integrity and devotion I never questioned, a man whose sacrifice in the liberation struggle was far greater than my own. I knew that the action that he had called for was in fact a noble one; he believed that Africans should help their Indian brothers.

But the seriousness of Ramohanoe's disobedience was too strong. While an organization like the ANC is made up of individuals, it is greater than any of its individual parts, and loyalty to the organization takes precedence over loyalty to an individual. I agreed to lead the attack and proposed the motion condemning him, which was seconded by Oliver Tambo. This caused an uproar in the house, with verbal battles between those in the region who supported their president and those who were on the side of the Executive. The meeting broke up in disorder.

13

Africans could not vote, but that did not mean that we did not care who won elections. In the white general election of 1948, the ruling United Party, led by General Smuts, then at the height of his international regard, opposed the revived National Party. While Smuts had enlisted South Africa on the side of the Allies in the Second World War, the National Party refused to support Great Britain and publicly sympathized with Nazi Germany. The National Party's campaign centred on the '*swart gevaar*' (the 'black danger'), and they fought the election on the twin slogans of '*Die kaffer op sy plek*' ('the nigger in his place') and '*Die koelies uit die land*' ('the coolies out of the country') – coolies being the Afrikaner's derogatory term for Indians.

The Nationalists, led by Dr Daniel Malan, a former minister of the Dutch Reformed Church and a newspaper editor, were a party animated by bitterness – bitterness towards the English, who had treated them as inferiors for decades, and bitterness towards the African, who the Nationalists believed was threatening the prosperity and purity of Afrikaner culture. Africans had no loyalty to General Smuts, but we had even less for the National Party.

Malan's platform was known as apartheid. *Apartheid* was a new term but an old idea. It literally means 'apartness', and it represented the codification in one oppressive system of all the laws and regulations that had kept Africans in an inferior position to whites for centuries. What had been more or less *de facto* was to become relentlessly *de jure*. The often haphazard segregation of the past three hundred years was to be consolidated into a monolithic system that was diabolical in its detail, inescapable in its reach and overwhelming in its power. The premise of apartheid was that whites were superior to Africans, Coloureds and Indians, and the function of it was to entrench white supremacy for ever. As the Nationalists put it, *'Die wit man moet altyd baas wees'* ('The white man must always remain boss'). Their platform rested on the term: *baasskap*, literally 'boss-ship', a loaded word that stood for white supremacy in all its harshness. The policy was supported by the Dutch Reformed Church, which furnished apartheid with its religious underpinnings by suggesting that Afrikaners were God's chosen people and that blacks were a subservient species. In the Afrikaner's world view, apartheid and the church went hand in hand.

The Nationalists' victory in the Anglo-Boer War was the beginning of the end of the domination of the Afrikaner by the Englishman. English would now take second place to Afrikaans as an official language. The Nationalists' slogan encapsulated their mission: *'Eie volk, eie taal, eie land'* – 'Our own people, our own language, our own land'. In the distorted cosmology of the Afrikaner, the Nationalist victory was like the Israelites' journey to the Promised Land. This was the fulfilment of God's promise, and the justification for their view that South Africa should be a white man's country for ever.

The victory was a shock. The United Party and

General Smuts had beaten the Nazis, and surely they would defeat the National Party. On election day, I attended a meeting in Johannesburg with Oliver Tambo and several others. We barely discussed the question of a Nationalist government because we did not expect one. The meeting went on all night, and we emerged at dawn and found a newspaper stall selling the *Rand Daily Mail*: the Nationalists had triumphed. I was stunned and dismayed, but Oliver took a more considered line. 'I like this,' he said. 'I like this.' I could not imagine why. He explained, 'Now we will know exactly who our enemies are and where we stand.'

Even General Smuts realized the dangers of this harsh ideology, decrying apartheid as 'a crazy concept, born of prejudice and fear'. From the moment of the Nationalists' election, we knew that our land would henceforth be a place of tension and strife. For the first time in South African history, an exclusively Afrikaner party led the government. 'South Africa belongs to us once more,' Malan proclaimed in his victory speech.

That same year, the Youth League outlined its policy in a document written by Mda and issued by the league's Executive Committee. It was a rallying cry to all patriotic youth to overthrow white domination. We rejected the communist notion that Africans were oppressed primarily as an economic class rather than as a race, adding that we needed to create a powerful national liberation movement under the banner of African nationalism and 'led by Africans themselves'.

We advocated the redivision of land on an equitable basis, the abolition of colour bars prohibiting Africans from doing skilled work and the need for free and compulsory education. The document also spotlighted the push-and-pull between two rival theories of African nationalism, between the more extreme, Marcus Garvey-inspired, 'Africa for the Africans' nationalism and the Africanism of the Youth League, which recognized that South Africa was a multiracial country.

I was sympathetic to the ultra-revolutionary stream of African nationalism. I was angry at the white man, not at racism. While I was not prepared to hurl the white man into the sea, I would have been perfectly happy if he had climbed aboard his steamships and left the continent of his own volition.

The Youth League was marginally more friendly to the Indians and the Coloureds, stating that Indians, like Africans, were oppressed, but that Indians had India, a mother country that they could look to. The Coloureds, too, were oppressed, but unlike the Indians had no mother country except Africa. I was prepared to accept Indians and Coloureds provided they accepted our policies; but their interests were not identical with ours, and I doubted whether or not they could truly embrace our cause.

In short order, Malan began to implement his pernicious programme. Within weeks of coming to power, the Nationalist government pardoned Robey Leibbrandt, the wartime traitor who had organized uprisings in support of Nazi Germany. The government announced their intention to curb the trade union movement and do away with the limited franchises of the Indian, Coloured and African peoples. The Separate Representation of Voters Bill eventually robbed the Coloureds of their representation in Parliament. The Prohibition of Mixed

Marriages Act was introduced in 1949 and was followed in rapid succession by the Immorality Act, making sexual relations between white and nonwhite illegal. The Population and Registration Act labelled all South Africans by race, making colour the single most important arbiter of an individual. Malan introduced the Group Areas Act – which he described as 'the very essence of apartheid' – requiring separate urban areas for each racial group. In the past, whites took land by force; now they secured it by legislation.

In response to this new and much more powerful threat from the state, the ANC embarked on an unaccustomed and historic path. In 1949, it launched a landmark effort to turn itself into a truly mass organization. The Youth League drafted a Programme of Action, the cornerstone of which was a campaign of mass mobilization.

At the ANC annual conference in Bloemfontein, the organization adopted the league's Programme of Action, which called for boycotts, strikes, stay-at-homes, passive resistance, protest demonstrations and other forms of mass action. This was a radical change: the ANC's policy had always been to keep its activities within the law. We in the Youth League had seen the failure of legal and constitutional means to strike at racial oppression; now the entire organization was set to enter a more activist stage.

These changes did not come without internal upheaval. A few weeks before the conference, Walter Sisulu, Oliver Tambo and I met Dr Xuma privately at his home in Sophiatown. We explained that we thought the time had come for mass action along the lines of Gandhi's non-violent protests in India and the 1946 passive resistance campaign, asserting that the ANC had become too docile in the face of oppression. The ANC's leaders, we said, had to be willing to violate the law and if necessary go to prison for their beliefs as Gandhi had.

Dr Xuma was adamantly opposed, claiming that such strategies were premature and would merely give the government an excuse to crush the ANC. Such forms of protest, he said, would eventually take place in South Africa, but at the moment such a step would be fatal. He made it clear that he was a doctor with a wide and prosperous practice that he would not jeopardize by going to prison.

We gave Dr Xuma an ultimatum: we would support him for re-election to the presidency of the ANC provided he supported our proposed Programme of Action. If he would not support our programme, we would not support him. Dr Xuma became heated, accusing us of blackmail and laying down the conditions on which we would vote for him. He told us that we were young and arrogant, and treating him without respect. We remonstrated with him, but to no avail. He would not go along with our proposal.

He unceremoniously showed us out of his house at 11 p.m., and closed the gate behind him. There were no streetlights in Sophiatown and it was a moonless night. All forms of public transport had long since ceased and we lived miles away in Orlando. Oliver remarked that Xuma could at the very least have offered us some transport. Walter was friendly with a family that lived nearby, and we prevailed upon them to take us in for the night.

At the conference that December, we in the Youth League knew we had the votes to depose Dr Xuma. As an alternative candidate, we sponsored Dr J.S. Moroka for the presidency. He was not our first choice. Professor Z.K. Matthews was the man we wanted to lead us, but Z.K. considered us too radical and our plan of action too impractical. He called us naive firebrands, adding that we would mellow with age.

Dr Moroka was an unlikely choice. He was a member of the All-African Convention (AAC) which was dominated by Trotskyite elements at that time. When he agreed to stand against Dr Xuma, the Youth League then enrolled him as a member of the ANC. When first approached, he consistently referred to the ANC as the African National 'Council'. He was not very knowledgeable about the ANC, neither was he an experienced activist, but he was respectable, and amenable to our programme. Like Dr Xuma he was a doctor, and one of the wealthiest black men in South Africa. He had studied at Edinburgh and Vienna. His great-grandfather had been a chief in the Orange Free State, and had greeted the Afrikaner *voortrekkers* of the nineteenth century with open arms and gifts of land, and then been betrayed. Dr Xuma was defeated and Dr Moroka became president-general of the ANC. Walter Sisulu was elected the new secretary-general, and Oliver Tambo was elected to the National Executive.

The Programme of Action approved at the annual conference called for the pursuit of political rights through the use of boycotts, strikes, civil disobedience and non-cooperation. In addition, it called for a national day of work stoppage in protest against the racist and reactionary policies of the government. This was a departure from the days of decorous protest, and many of the old stalwarts of the ANC were to fade away in this new era of greater militancy. Youth League members had now graduated to the senior organization. We had now guided the ANC to a more radical and revolutionary path.

I could only celebrate the Youth League's triumph from a distance, for I was unable to attend the conference. I was then working for a new law firm, and they did not give me permission to take two days off to attend the conference in Bloemfontein. The firm was a liberal one, but wanted me to concentrate on my work and forget politics. I would have lost my job if I had attended the conference, and I could not afford to do that.

The spirit of mass action surged, but I remained sceptical of any action undertaken with the communists and Indians. The 'Defend Free Speech Convention' in March 1950 organized by the Transvaal ANC, the Transvaal Indian Congress, the African People's Organization and the District Committee of the Communist Party drew ten thousand people to Johannesburg's Market Square. Dr Moroka, without consulting the Executive, agreed to preside over the convention. The convention was a success, yet I remained wary, as the prime mover behind it was the party.

At the instigation of the Communist Party and the Indian Congress, the convention passed a resolution for a one-day general strike, known as Freedom Day, on 1 May, calling for the abolition of the pass laws and all discriminatory legislation. Although I supported these objectives, I believed that the communists were trying to steal the thunder from the ANC's National Day of

Protest. I opposed the May Day strike on the grounds that the ANC had not originated the campaign, believing that we should concentrate on our own campaign.

Ahmed Kathrada was then barely twenty-one and, like all youths, eager to flex his muscles. He was a key member of the Transvaal Indian Youth Congress and had heard I was opposed to the May Day strike. One day, while walking along Commissioner Street, I met Kathrada and he heatedly confronted me, charging that I and the Youth League did not want to work with Indians or Coloureds. In a challenging tone, he said, 'You are an African leader and I am an Indian youth. But I am convinced of the support of the African masses for the strike and I challenge you to nominate any African township for a meeting and I guarantee the people will support me.' It was a hollow threat, but it angered me all the same. I even complained to a joint meeting of the Executive Committees of the ANC, the South African Indian Congress and the Communist Party, but Ismail Meer calmed me down, saying, 'Nelson, he is young and hotheaded. Don't you be the same.' I consequently felt a bit sheepish about my actions and I withdrew the complaint. Although I disagreed with Kathrada, I admired his fire, and it was an incident we came to laugh about.

The Freedom Day strike went ahead without official ANC support. In anticipation, the government banned all meetings and gatherings on 1 May. More than two-thirds of African workers stayed at home during the one-day strike. That night, Walter and I were in Orlando West on the fringes of a Freedom Day crowd that had gathered despite the government's restrictions. The moon was bright, and as we watched the orderly march of protesters, we could see a group of policemen camped across a stream about five hundred yards away. They must have seen us as well, because all of a sudden they started firing in our direction. We dived to the ground, and remained there as mounted police galloped into the crowd, smashing people with batons. We took refuge in a nearby nurses' dormitory, where we heard bullets smashing into the wall of the building. Eighteen Africans died and many others were wounded in this indiscriminate and unprovoked attack.

Despite protest and criticism, the Nationalist response was to tighten the screws of repression. A few weeks later the government introduced the notorious Suppression of Communism Act, and the ANC called an emergency conference in Johannesburg. The act outlawed the Communist Party of South Africa and made it a crime, punishable by a maximum of ten years' imprisonment, to be a member of the party or to further the aims of communism. But the bill was drafted in such a broad way that it outlawed all but the mildest protest against the state, deeming it a crime to advocate any doctrine that promoted 'political, industrial, social or economic change within the Union by the promotion of disturbance or disorder'. Essentially, the bill permitted the government to outlaw any organization and to restrict any individual opposed to its policies.

The ANC, the SAIC and the APO again met to discuss these new measures, and Dr Dadoo, among others, said that it would be foolish to allow past differences to thwart a united front against the government. I spoke and echoed his sentiments: clearly, the repression of any one liberation group was repression of all liberation groups. It was at that meeting that Oliver uttered prophetic words: 'Today it is the Communist Party. Tomorrow it will be our trade unions, our Indian Congress, our APO, our African National Congress.'

Supported by the SAIC and the APO, the ANC resolved to stage a National Day of Protest on 26 June 1950 against the government's murder of eighteen Africans on 1 May and the passage of the Suppression of Communism Act. The proposal was ratified, and in preparation for the Day of Protest, we closed ranks with the SAIC, the APO and the Communist Party. Here, I believed, was a sufficient threat that compelled us to join hands with our Indian and communist colleagues.

Earlier that year I had been co-opted onto the National Executive Committee of the ANC, taking the place of Dr Xuma, who had resigned after his failure to be re-elected president-general. I was not unmindful of the fact that it had been Dr Xuma who had tried to help me get my first job when I came to Johannesburg ten years before, when I had no thought of entering politics. Now, as a member of the National Executive, I was playing in the first team with the most senior people in the ANC. I had moved from the role of a gadfly within the organization to one of the powers that I had been rebelling against. It was a heady feeling, and not without mixed emotions. In some ways, it is easier to be a dissident, for then one is without responsibility. As a member of the Executive, I had to weigh arguments and make decisions, and expect to be criticized by rebels like myself.

Mass action was perilous in South Africa, where it was a criminal offence for an African to strike, and where the rights of free speech and movement were unmercifully curtailed. By striking, an African worker stood to lose not only his job but his entire livelihood and his right to stay in the area in which he was living. In my experience, a political strike is always riskier than an economic one. A strike based on a political grievance rather than on clear-cut issues such as higher wages or shorter hours is a more precarious form of protest and demands particularly efficient organization. The Day of Protest was a political rather than an economic strike.

In preparation for 26 June, Walter travelled around the country consulting local leaders. In his absence, I took charge of the bustling ANC office, the hub of a complicated national action. Every day, various leaders looked in to see that matters were going according to plan: Moses Kotane, Dr Dadoo, Diliza Mji, J.B. Marks, president of the Transvaal ANC, Yusuf Cachalia and his brother Maulvi, Gaur Radebe, secretary of the Council of Action, Michael Harmel, Peter Raboroko, Nthato Motlana. I was coordinating the actions in different parts of the country, and talking by phone with regional leaders. We had left ourselves little time, and the planning was hastily done.

The Day of Protest was the ANC's first attempt to hold a political strike on a national scale, and it was a moderate success. In the cities, the majority of workers stayed at home and black businesses did not open. In Bethal, Gert Sibande, who later became president of the Transvaal ANC, led a demonstration of five thousand people, which received headlines in the major papers across the country. The Day of Protest boosted our morale, made us realize our strength and sent a warning to the Malan government that we would not remain passive in the face of apartheid. 26 June has since become a landmark day in the freedom struggle, and within the liberation movement it is observed as Freedom Day.

It was the first time I had taken a significant part in a national campaign, and I felt the exhilaration that springs from the success of a well-planned battle against the enemy and the sense of comradeship that is born of fighting against formidable odds.

The struggle, I was learning, was all-consuming. A man involved in the struggle was a man without a home life. It was in the midst of the Day of Protest that my second son, Makgatho Lewanika, was born. I was with Evelyn at the hospital when he came into the world, but it was only a brief respite from my activities. He was named for Sefako Mapogo Makgatho, the second president of the ANC from 1917 until 1924, and Lewanika, a leading chief in Zambia. Makgatho, the son of a Pedi chief, had led volunteers to defy the colour bar that did not permit Africans to walk on the pavements of Pretoria, and his name for me was an emblem of indomitability and courage.

One day, during this same time, my wife informed me that my elder son, Thembi, then five, had asked her, 'Where does Daddy live?' I had been returning home late at night, long after he had gone to sleep, and departing early in the morning before he woke. I did not relish being deprived of the company of my children. I missed them a great deal during those days, long before I had any inkling that I would spend decades apart from them.

I was far more certain in those days of what I was against than what I was for. My long-standing opposition to communism was breaking down. Moses Kotane, the general secretary of the party and a member of the Executive of the ANC, often came to my house late at night and we would debate until morning. Clear-thinking and self-taught, Kotane was the son of peasant farmers in the Transvaal. 'Nelson,' he would say, 'what do you have against us? We are all fighting the same enemy. We do not seek to dominate the ANC; we are working within the context of African nationalism.' In the end, I had no good response to his arguments.

Because of my friendships with Kotane, Ismail Meer and Ruth First, and my observation of their own sacrifices, I was finding it more and more difficult to justify my prejudice against the party. Within the ANC, party members such as J.B. Marks, Edwin Mofutsanyana, Dan Tloome and David Bopape among others were devoted and hard-working, and could not be faulted as freedom fighters. Dr Dadoo, one of the leaders of the 1946 resistance, was a well-known Marxist whose role as a fighter for human rights had made him a hero to all groups. I could not, and no longer did, question the bona fides of such men and women.

If I could not challenge their dedication, I could still question the philosophical and practical underpinnings of Marxism. But I had little knowledge of Marxism, and in political discussions with my communist friends I found myself handicapped by my ignorance of their philosophy. I decided to remedy this.

I acquired the complete works of Marx and Engels, Lenin, Stalin, Mao Tse-tung and others, and probed the philosophy of dialectical and historical materialism. I had little time to study these works properly. While I was stimulated by the *Communist Manifesto*, I was exhausted by *Das Kapital.* But I found myself strongly drawn to the idea of a classless society which, to my mind, was similar to traditional African culture where life was shared and communal. I subscribed to Marx's basic dictum, which has the simplicity and generosity of the Golden Rule: 'From each according to his ability; to each according to his needs.'

Dialectical materialism seemed to offer both a search-light illuminating the dark night of racial oppression and a tool that could be used to end it. It helped me to see the situation other than through the prism of black and white relations, for if our struggle was to succeed, we had to transcend black and white. I was attracted to the scientific underpinnings of dialectical materialism, for I am always inclined to trust what I can verify. Its materi-alistic analysis of economics rang true to me. The idea that the value of goods was based on the amount of labour that went into them seemed particularly appro-priate for South Africa. The ruling class paid African labour a subsistence wage and then added value to the cost of the goods, which they retained for themselves.

Marxism's call to revolutionary action was music to the ears of a freedom fighter. The idea that history progresses through struggle and that change occurs in revolutionary jumps was similarly appealing. In my reading of Marxist works, I found a great deal of information that bore on the types of problems that face a practical politician. Marxists gave serious atten-tion to national liberation movements, and the Soviet Union in particular supported the national struggles of many colonial peoples. This was another reason why I amended my view of communists and accepted the ANC position of welcoming Marxists into its ranks.

A friend once asked me how I could reconcile my creed of African nationalism with a belief in dialectical materialism. For me, there was no contradiction. I was first and foremost an African nationalist fighting for our emancipation from minority rule and the right to control our own destiny. But, at the same time, South Africa and the African continent were part of the larger world. Our problems, while distinctive and special, were not unique, and a philosophy that placed those problems in an international and historical context of the greater world and the course of history was valuable. I was prepared to use whatever means necessary to speed up the erasure of human prejudice and the end of chauvinistic and violent nationalism. I did not need to become a communist in order to work with them. I found that African nationalists and African communists generally had far more to unite them than to divide them. The cynical have always suggested that the communists were using us. But who is to say that we were not using them?

14

If we had any hopes or illusions about the National Party before they came into office, we were disabused of them quickly. Their threat to put the kaffir in his place was not an idle one. Apart from the Suppression of Communism Act, two laws passed in 1950 formed the cornerstones of apartheid: the Population Registration Act and the Group Areas Act. As I have mentioned, the Population Registration Act authorized the government officially to classify all South Africans according to race. If it had not already been so, race became the *sine qua non* of South African society. The arbitrary and meaningless tests to decide black from Coloured or Coloured from white often resulted in tragic cases where members of the same family were classified differently, all depending on whether one child had a lighter or darker complexion. Where one was allowed to live and work could rest on such absurd distinctions as the curl of one's hair or the size of one's lips.

The Group Areas Act was the foundation of residential apartheid. Under its regulations, each racial group could own land, occupy premises and trade only in its own separate area. Indians could henceforth only live in Indian areas, Africans in African, Coloureds in Coloured. If whites wanted the land or houses of another group, they could simply declare the land a white area and take it. The Group Areas Act initiated the era of forced removals, when African communities, towns and villages in newly designated 'white' urban areas were violently relocated because the nearby white landowners did not want Africans living near them or simply wanted their land.

At the top of the list for removal was Sophiatown, a vibrant community of more than fifty thousand people, which was one of the oldest black settlements in Johannesburg. Despite its poverty, Sophiatown brimmed with a rich life and was an incubator of so much that was new and valuable in African life and culture. Even before the government's efforts to remove it, Sophiatown held a symbolic importance for Africans disproportionate to its small population.

The following year, the government passed two more laws that directly attacked the rights of Coloureds and Africans. The Separate Representation of Voters Act aimed to transfer Coloureds to a separate voters' roll in the Cape, thereby diluting the franchise rights that they had enjoyed for more than a century. The Bantu Authorities Act abolished the Natives' Representative Council, the one indirect forum of national representation for Africans, and replaced it with a hierarchical system of tribal chiefs appointed by the government. The idea was to restore power to traditional and mainly conservative ethnic leaders in order to perpetuate ethnic differences that were beginning to erode. Both laws epitomized the ethos of the Nationalist government, which pretended to preserve what they were attempting to destroy. Laws stripping people of their rights were inevitably described as laws restoring those rights.

The Coloured people rallied against the Separate Representation of Voters Act, organizing a tremendous demonstration in Cape Town in March 1951 and a strike in April that kept shops closed and schoolchildren at home. It was in the context of this spirit of activism by Indians, Coloureds and Africans that Walter Sisulu first broached the idea to a small group of us of a national civil disobedience campaign. He outlined a plan under which selected volunteers from all groups would deliberately invite imprisonment by defying certain laws.

The idea immediately appealed to me, as it did to the others, but I differed from Walter on the question of who should take part. I had recently become national president of the Youth League, and in my new role I urged that the campaign should be exclusively African. The average African, I said, was still cautious about joint action with Indians and Coloureds. While I had made progress in terms of my opposition to communism, I still feared the influence of Indians. In addition, many of our grassroots African supporters saw Indians as exploiters of black labour in their role as shopkeepers and merchants.

Walter vehemently disagreed, suggesting that the Indians, Coloureds and Africans were inextricably bound together. The issue was taken up at a meeting of the National Executive Committee and my view was voted down, even by those who were considered staunch African nationalists. But I was nevertheless persistent and I raised the matter once more at the national conference in December 1951, where the delegates dismissed my view as emphatically as the National Executive had done. Now that my view had been rejected by the highest levels of the ANC, I fully accepted the agreed-upon position. While my speech advocating a go-it-alone strategy was met with a lukewarm reception, the speech I gave as president of the Youth League after the league pledged its support for the new policy of cooperation was given a resounding ovation.

At the behest of a joint planning council consisting of Dr Moroka, Walter, J.B. Marks, Yusuf Dadoo and Yusuf Cachalia, the ANC conference endorsed a resolution calling upon the government to repeal the Suppression of Communism Act, the Group Areas Act, the Separate Representation of Voters Act, the Bantu Authorities Act, the pass laws and stock limitation laws by 29 February 1952. The law was intended to reduce overgrazing by cattle, but its impact would be to further curtail land for Africans. The council resolved that the ANC would hold demonstrations on 6 April 1952 as a prelude to the launching of the Campaign for the Defiance of Unjust Laws. That same day white South Africans would be celebrating the three-hundredth anniversary of Jan van Riebeeck's arrival at the Cape in 1652. 6 April is the day white South Africans annually commemorate as the founding of their country – and Africans revile as the beginning of three hundred years of enslavement.

The ANC drafted a letter to the prime minister advising him of these resolutions and the deadline for repealing the laws. Because the letter was to go out under the name of Dr Moroka, and Dr Moroka had not participated in the writing of it, I was instructed to take him the letter by driving to his home in Thaba 'Nchu, a town near Bloemfontein in the Orange Free State, a very conservative area of the country. I almost did not make it there to see him.

Only a few weeks before, I had taken my driving test. In those days, a driver's licence was an unusual thing for an African, for very few blacks had cars. On the appointed day, I borrowed a car to use for the test. I was a bit cocky, and decided to drive the car there myself. I was running late and was driving faster than I should, and as I manoeuvred the car along a side street that met a main road, I failed to look both ways and collided with a car coming in another direction. The damage was minimal, but now I would certainly be late. The other driver was a reasonable fellow and we simply agreed to pay our own expenses.

When I reached the testing station, I observed a white woman ahead of me in the middle of her test. She was driving properly and cautiously. When the test was finished, the driving inspector said, 'Thank you. Would you please park the car over there', gesturing to a space nearby. She had performed the test well enough to pass, but as the woman drove over to the parking place, she did not negotiate a corner properly and the back wheel jumped the kerb. The inspector hurried over and said, 'I'm sorry, madam, you've failed the test, please make another appointment.' I felt my confidence ebbing. If this fellow tricks a white woman into failing her test, what hope would I have? But I performed well on the test, and when the inspector told me to park the car at the end of the exam, I drove so carefully that I thought he might penalize me for going too slowly.

Once I could legally drive, I became a one-man taxi service. It was one's obligation to give rides to comrades and friends. I was thus deputized to take the letter to Dr Moroka. This was no hardship to me as I have always found it enjoyable to gaze out of the window while driving. I seemed to have my best ideas while driving through the countryside with the wind whipping through the window.

On my way down to Thaba 'Nchu I passed through Kroonstad, a conservative Free State town about 120 miles south of Johannesburg. I was driving up a hill and saw two white boys ahead of me on bicycles. My driving was still a bit unsteady, and I came too close to them, one of whom suddenly made a turn without signalling, and we collided. He was knocked off his bicycle and was groaning when I got out of the car to help him. He had his arms out, indicating that I should pick him up, but just as I was about to do so, a white truck-driver yelled for me not to touch the boy. The truck-driver scared the child, who then dropped his arms as though he did not want me to pick him up. The boy was not badly hurt, and the truck-driver took him to the police station, which was close by.

The local police arrived a short time later, and the white sergeant took one look at me and said, '*Kaffer, jy sal kak vandag!*' ('Kaffir, you will shit today!') I was shaken by the accident and the violence of his words, but I told him in no uncertain terms that I would shit when I pleased, not when a policeman told me to. At this, the sergeant took out his notebook to record my particulars. Afrikaans policemen were surprised if a black man could speak English, much less answer back.

After I identified myself, he turned to the car, which he proceeded to ransack. From under the floor mat he pulled out a copy of the left-wing weekly, *The Guardian*, which I had hidden immediately after the accident. (I had slipped the letter to Dr Moroka inside my shirt.) He looked at the title and then held it up in the air like a pirate with his booty: '*Wragtig ons het 'n Kommunis gevang!*' he cried. ('My word, we've caught a communist!') Brandishing the newspaper, he hurried off.

The sergeant returned after about four hours, accompanied by another officer. This sergeant, also an

Afrikaner, was intent on doing his duty correctly. He said he would need to take measurements at the site of the accident for police records. I told the sergeant that it was not proper to take measurements at night when the accident had occurred in daylight. I added that I intended to spend the night in Thaba 'Nchu, and that I could not afford to stay in Kroonstad. The sergeant eyed me impatiently and said, 'What is your name?'

'Mandela,' I said.

'No, the first one,' he said. I told him.

'Nelson,' the sergeant said, as if he were talking to a boy, 'I want to help you resume your journey. But if you are going to be difficult with me I will have no alternative but to be difficult with you and lock you up for the night.' That brought me down to earth and I consented to the measurements.

I resumed my journey late that night, and the next morning I was travelling through the district of Excelsior when my car ground to a halt. I had run out of petrol. I walked to a nearby farmhouse and explained in English to an elderly white lady that I would like to buy some petrol. As she was closing the door, she said, 'I don't have any petrol for you.' I tramped two miles to the next farm and, chastened by my unsuccessful first effort, tried a different approach. I asked to see the farmer, and when he appeared I assumed a humble demeanour. 'My *baas* has run out of petrol,' I said. (*Baas*, the Afrikaans word for boss or master, signifies subservience.) Friendly and helpful, the farmer was a relation of Prime Minister Strydom. Yet I believe he would have given me the petrol had I told him the truth and not used the hated word *baas*.

* * *

The meeting with Dr Moroka proved far less eventful than my journey there. He approved of the letter and I made my way back to Johannesburg without incident. The letter to the prime minister noted that the ANC had exhausted every constitutional means at our disposal to achieve our legitimate rights, and that we demanded the repeal of the six 'unjust laws' by 29 February 1952, or else we would take extra-constitutional action. Malan's reply, signed by his private secretary, asserted that whites had an inherent right to take measures to preserve their own identity as a separate community, and ended with the threat that if we pursued our actions the government would not hesitate to make full use of its machinery to quell any disturbances.

We regarded Malan's curt dismissal of our demands as a declaration of war. We now had no alternative but to resort to civil disobedience, and we embarked in earnest on preparations for mass action. The recruitment and training of volunteers was one of the essential tasks of the campaign and would in large part be responsible for its success or failure. On 6 April preliminary demonstrations took place in Johannesburg, Pretoria, Port Elizabeth, Durban and Cape Town. While Dr Moroka addressed a crowd at Freedom Square in Johannesburg, I spoke to a group of potential volunteers at the Garment Workers' Union. I explained to a group of several hundred Africans, Indians and Coloureds that volunteering was a difficult and even dangerous duty as the authorities would seek to intimidate, imprison and perhaps attack the volunteers. No matter what the authorities did, the volunteers could not retaliate, otherwise they would undermine the value of the entire enterprise. They must respond to violence with non-violence; discipline must be maintained at all costs.

On 31 May the Executives of the ANC and the SAIC met in Port Elizabeth and announced that the Defiance Campaign would begin on 26 June, the anniversary of the first National Day of Protest. They also created a National Action Committee to direct the campaign and a National Volunteer Board to recruit and train volunteers. I was appointed national volunteer-in-chief of the campaign and chairman of both the Action Committee and the Volunteer Board. My responsibilities were to organize the campaign, coordinate the regional branches, canvass for volunteers and raise funds.

We also discussed whether the campaign should follow the Gandhian principles of non-violence or what the Mahatma called *satyagraha*, a non-violence that seeks to conquer through conversion. Some argued for non-violence on purely ethical grounds, saying it was morally superior to any other method. This idea was strongly affirmed by Manilal Gandhi, the Mahatma's son and the editor of the newspaper *Indian Opinion*, who was a prominent member of the SAIC. With his gentle demeanour, Gandhi seemed the very personification of non-violence, and he insisted that the campaign be run along identical lines to that of his father's in India.

Others said that we should approach this issue not from the point of view of principles but of tactics, and that we should employ the method demanded by the conditions. If a particular method or tactic enabled us to defeat the enemy, then it should be used. In this case, the state was far more powerful than we, and any attempts at violence by us would be devastatingly crushed. This made non-violence a practical necessity rather than an option. This was my view, and I saw non-violence on the Gandhian model not as an inviolable principle but as a tactic to be used as the situation demanded. The principle was not so important that the strategy should be used even when it was self-defeating, as Gandhi himself believed. I called for non-violent protest for as long as it was effective. This view prevailed, despite Manilal Gandhi's strong objections.

The joint planning council agreed upon an open-ended programme of non-cooperation and non-violence. Two stages of defiance were proposed. In the first stage, a small number of well-trained volunteers would break selected laws in a handful of urban areas. They would enter proscribed areas without permits, use Whites Only facilities such as toilets, Whites Only railway compartments, waiting rooms and post office entrances. They would deliberately remain in town after curfew. Each batch of defiers would have a leader who would inform the police in advance of the act of disobedience so that the arrests could take place with a minimum of disturbance. The second stage was envisioned as mass defiance, accompanied by strikes and industrial actions across the country.

Prior to the inauguration of the Defiance Campaign, a rally, called the Day of the Volunteers, was held in Durban on 22 June. Chief Luthuli, president of the Natal ANC, and Dr Naicker, president of the Natal Indian Congress, both spoke and committed themselves to the campaign. I had driven down the day before and was the main speaker. About ten thousand people were in attendance, and I told the crowd that the Defiance Campaign would be the most powerful action ever undertaken by the oppressed masses in South Africa. I had never addressed such a great crowd before, and it was an exhilarating experience. One cannot speak to a mass of people as one addresses an audience of two dozen. Yet I have always tried to take the same care to explain matters to great audiences as to small ones. I told the people that they would make history and focus the attention of the world on the racist policies of South Africa. I emphasized that unity among the black people – Africans, Coloureds and Indians – in South Africa had at last become a reality.

All across the country, those who defied on 26 June did so with courage, enthusiasm and a sense of history. The campaign began in the early morning hours in Port Elizabeth, where thirty-three defiers, under the leadership of Raymond Mhlaba, entered a railway station through a Whites Only entrance and were arrested. They marched in singing freedom songs, to the accompanying cheers of friends and family. In a call and response, the defiers and the crowd yelled, '*Mayibuye! Afrika!*' ('Let Africa come back!')

On the morning of the twenty-sixth, I was in the ANC office overseeing the day's demonstrations. The Transvaal batch of volunteers was scheduled to go into action at midday at an African township near Boksburg, east of Johannesburg. Led by the Reverend N.B. Tantsi, they were to court arrest by entering the township without permission. Reverend Tantsi was an elderly fellow, a minister in the African Methodist Episcopal Church, and the acting president of the Transvaal ANC.

It was late morning, and as I was waiting for Reverend Tantsi to arrive from Pretoria he telephoned me at the office. With regret in his voice, he told me that his doctor advised him against defying and going to prison. I assured him that we would provide him with warm clothing and that he would spend only a night in jail, but to no avail. This was a grave disappointment, for Reverend Tantsi was a distinguished figure and had been selected in order to show the authorities that we were not just a group of young rabble-rousers.

In place of Reverend Tantsi, we quickly found someone equally venerable: Nana Sita, the president of the Transvaal Indian Congress, who had served a month in jail for his passive resistance during the 1946 protest campaign. Despite his advanced age and acute arthritis, Sita was a fighter and agreed to lead our defiers.

In the afternoon, as we were preparing to go to Boksburg, I realized that the secretary of the Transvaal branch of the ANC was nowhere to be found. He was meant to accompany Nana Sita to Boksburg. This was another crisis, and I turned to Walter and said, 'You must go.' This was our first event in the Transvaal, and it was necessary to have prominent figures to lead the defiers, otherwise the leaders would appear to be hanging back while the masses took the punishment. Even though Walter was one of the organizers and was scheduled to defy later, he readily agreed. My main concern was that he was wearing a suit, impractical dress for prison, but we managed to find him some old clothes instead.

We then left for Boksburg, where Yusuf Cachalia and I planned to deliver a letter to the Boksburg magistrate, advising him that fifty of our volunteers would enter the African township in his area that day without permits. When we arrived at the magistrate's office, we found a large contingent of pressmen and photographers. As I handed the envelope to the magistrate, the photographers went into action. The magistrate shielded himself from the camera flashes and then invited Yusuf and me into his chambers to discuss the matter privately. He was a reasonable man, and said his office was always open to us, but that excessive publicity would only worsen matters.

From the magistrate's office we went straight to the township where the demonstration was taking place, and even from half a mile away we heard the robust singing of our volunteers and the great crowd of supporters who had come to encourage them. At the scene, we found the high metal gates to the township locked and our volunteers waiting patiently outside, demanding entrance. There were fifty-two volunteers in all, both Africans and Indians, and a crowd of several hundred enthusiastic spectators and journalists. Walter was at the head of the defiers; his presence was evidence that we meant business. But the guiding spirit of the demonstrators was Nana Sita who, despite his arthritis, was moving among the demonstrators in high spirits, slapping them on the back and bolstering their confidence with his own.

For the first hour there was a standoff. The police were uncharacteristically restrained and their behaviour baffled us. Was their restraint a strategy to exhaust the volunteers? Were they waiting for the journalists to depart and then planning to stage a massacre under the cover of darkness? Or were they faced with the dilemma that by arresting us – which is what they would have normally done – they would be doing the very thing we wanted? But even while we were wondering, the situation suddenly changed. The police ordered the gates opened. Immediately the volunteers surged through the gate, thus breaking the law. A police lieutenant blew a whistle and seconds later the police had surrounded the volunteers and began arresting them. The campaign was under way. The demonstrators were carted off to the local police station and charged.

That same evening, the leaders of the Action Committee, which included Oliver Tambo, Yusuf Cachalia and myself, attended a meeting in the city to discuss the day's events and to plan for the week ahead. It was near the area where the second batch of defiers, led by Flag Boshielo, chairman of the central branch of the ANC, were courting arrest. Shortly after eleven o'clock, we found them marching in unison in the street; at eleven, curfew regulations went into effect and Africans needed a permit to be outside.

We emerged from our meeting at midnight. I felt exhausted, and was thinking not of defiance but of a hot meal and a night's sleep. At that moment, a policeman approached Yusuf and me. It was obvious that we were going home, not protesting. 'No, Mandela,' the policeman called out. 'You can't escape.' He pointed with his nightstick to the police waggon parked nearby and said, 'Into the van.' I felt like explaining to him that I was in charge of running the campaign on a day-to-day basis and was not scheduled to defy and be arrested until much later, but of course that would have been ridiculous. I watched as he arrested Yusuf, who burst out laughing at the irony of it all. It was a lovely sight to see him smiling as he was led away by the police.

Moments later, Yusuf and I found ourselves among the more than fifty of our volunteers led by Flag Boshielo who were being taken in trucks to the red-brick police station known as Marshall Square. As the leaders of the Action Committee, we were worried that the others would wonder at our absence and I was concerned about who would be running the campaign. But spirits were high. Even on the way to prison, the vans swayed to the rich voices of the defiers singing 'Nkosi Sikelel' iAfrika' ('God Bless Africa'), the hauntingly beautiful African national anthem.

That first night, in the drill yard, one of us was pushed so violently by a white warder that he fell down some steps and broke his ankle. I protested to the warder about his behaviour, and he lashed out by kicking me in the shin. I demanded that the injured man receive medical attention and we initiated a small but vocal demonstration. We were curtly informed that the injured man could make a request for a doctor the next day if he so wished. We were aware throughout the night of his acute pain.

Until then I had spent bits and pieces of time in prison, but this was my first concentrated experience. Marshall Square was squalid, dark and dingy, but we were all together and so impassioned and spirited that I barely noticed my surroundings. The camaraderie of our fellow defiers made the two days pass very quickly.

On that first day of the Defiance Campaign more than 250 volunteers around the country violated various unjust laws and were imprisoned. It was an auspicious beginning. Our troops were orderly, disciplined, and confident.

Over the next five months, 8,500 people took part in the campaign. Doctors, factory workers, lawyers, teachers, students, ministers, defied and went to jail. They sang, 'Hey, Malan! Open the jail doors. We want to enter.' The campaign spread throughout the Witwatersrand, to Durban and to Port Elizabeth, East London and Cape Town, and smaller towns in the eastern and western Cape. Resistance was beginning to percolate even in the rural areas. For the most part, the offences were minor, and the penalties ranged from no more than a few nights in jail to a few weeks, with the option of a fine which rarely exceeded £10. The campaign received an enormous amount of publicity and the membership of the ANC shot up from some 20,000 to 100,000, with the most spectacular increase occurring in the eastern Cape, which contributed half of all new members.

During the six months of the campaign I travelled a great deal throughout the country. I generally went by car, leaving at night or very early in the morning. I toured the Cape, Natal and the Transvaal, explaining the campaign to small groups, sometimes going from house to house in the townships. Often, my task was to iron out differences in areas that were about to launch actions or had recently done so. In those days, when mass communication for Africans was primitive or non-existent, politics were parochial. We had to win people over one by one.

On one occasion I drove to the eastern Cape to resolve a dispute involving Alcott Gwentshe, who was running the campaign in East London. Gwentshe, a successful shopkeeper, had played an important role in organizing East London for the stay-at-home of 26 June two years before. He had briefly gone to jail at the beginning of the Defiance Campaign. He was a strong and able man, but he was an individualist who ignored the advice of the Executive and took decisions unilaterally. He was now at odds with his own executive, which was mainly populated with intellectuals.

Gwentshe knew how to exploit certain issues in order to discredit his opponents. He would speak before local members who were workers, not intellectuals, and say – in Xhosa, never English, for English was the language of the intellectuals – 'Comrades, I think you know that I have suffered for the struggle. I had a good job and then went to jail at the beginning of the Defiance Campaign and I lost that job. Now that I am out of prison, these intellectuals have come along and said, "Gwentshe, we are better educated than you, we are more capable than you, let us run this campaign."'

When I investigated the situation I found that Gwentshe had indeed ignored the advice of the Executive. But the people were behind him, and he had created a disciplined and well-organized group of volunteers who had defied in an orderly fashion even while Gwentshe was in prison. Even though I thought Gwentshe was wrong for disregarding the Executive, he was doing a good job and was so firmly entrenched that he could not easily be dislodged. When I saw the members of the Executive, I explained that it was impractical to do anything about the situation now, but if they wanted to remedy it, they must defeat him at the next election. It was one of the first times that I saw that it was foolhardy to go against the people. It is no use to take an action to which the masses are opposed, for it will then be impossible to enforce.

The government saw the campaign as a threat to its security and its policy of apartheid. They regarded civil disobedience not as a form of protest but as a crime, and were perturbed by the growing partnership between Africans and Indians. Apartheid was designed to divide racial groups, and we showed that different groups could work together. The prospect of a united front between Africans and Indians, between moderates and radicals, greatly worried them. The Nationalists insisted that the campaign was instigated and led by communist agitators. The minister of justice announced that he would soon pass legislation to deal with our defiance, a threat he implemented during the 1953 parliamentary session with the passage of the Public Safety Act, which empowered the government to declare martial law and to detain people without trial, and the Criminal Laws Amendment Act, which authorized corporal punishment for defiers.

The government tried a number of underhanded means to interrupt the campaign. Government propagandists repeatedly claimed that the leaders of the campaign were living it up in comfort while the masses were languishing in jail. This allegation was far from the truth, but it achieved a certain currency. The government also infiltrated spies and *agents provocateurs* into the organization. The ANC welcomed virtually anyone who wanted to join. Although our volunteers were carefully screened before they were selected to defy, the police managed to penetrate not only our local branches but some of the batches of defiers. When I was arrested and sent to Marshall Square, I noticed two fellows among the defiers, one of whom I had never seen before. He wore unusual prison garb: a suit and tie with an overcoat and a silk scarf. What kind of person goes to jail dressed like that? His name was Ramaila, and on the third day when we were due to be released, he simply vanished.

The second man, whose name was Makhanda, stood

out because of his military demeanour. We were out in the courtyard and all in high spirits. The defiers would march in front of Yusuf and me and salute us. Makhanda, who was tall and slender, marched in a soldierly manner and then gave a crisp, graceful salute. A number of the fellows teased him that he must be a policeman to salute so well.

Makhanda had previously worked as a janitor at ANC headquarters. He was very industrious and was popular because he would run out and get fish and chips whenever anyone was hungry. But at a later trial we discovered that both Makhanda and Ramaila were police spies. Ramaila testified that he had infiltrated the ranks of the defiers; the trusty Makhanda was actually Detective Sergeant Motloung.

Africans who worked as spies against their own brothers generally did so for money. Many blacks in South Africa believed that any effort by the black man to challenge the white man was foolhardy and doomed to failure; the white man was too smart and too strong. These spies saw us not as a threat to the white power structure but to black interests, for whites would mistreat all blacks based on the conduct of a few agitators.

Yet there were many black policemen who secretly aided us. They were decent fellows and found themselves in a moral quandary. They were loyal to their employer and needed to keep their jobs to support their families, but they were sympathetic to our cause. We had an understanding with a handful of African officers who were members of the security police that they would inform us when there was going to be a police raid. These men were patriots who risked their lives to help the struggle.

The government was not our only impediment. Others who might have helped us hindered us instead. At the height of the Defiance Campaign, the United Party sent two of its MPs to urge us to halt the campaign. They said that if we abandoned our campaign in response to a call made by J.G.N. Strauss, the United Party leader, it would help the party defeat the Nationalists in the next election. We rejected this and Strauss proceeded to attack us with the same scorn used by the Nationalists.

We also came under attack from a breakaway ANC group called the National Minded Bloc. Led by Selope Thema, a former member of the National Executive, the group split from the ANC when J.B. Marks was elected president of the Transvaal ANC. Thema, who was editor of the newspaper *Bantu World*, fiercely criticized the campaign in his paper, claiming that communists had taken over the ANC and that Indians were exploiting the Africans. He asserted that the communists were more dangerous now that they were working underground, and that Indian economic interests were in conflict with those of Africans. Although he was in a minority in the ANC, his views got a sympathetic hearing among certain radical Youth Leaguers.

In May, during the middle of the Defiance Campaign, J.B. Marks was banned under the 1950 Suppression of Communism Act for 'furthering the aims of communism'. Banning was a legal order by the government, and generally entailed forced resignation from indicated organizations, and restriction from attending gatherings of any kind. It was a kind of walking imprisonment. To ban a person, the government required no proof, offered no charges; the minister of justice simply declared it so. It was a strategy designed to remove the individual from the struggle, allowing him to live a narrowly defined life outside politics. To violate or ignore a banning order was to invite imprisonment.

At the Transvaal conference that year in October, my name was proposed to replace the banned J.B. Marks, who had recommended that I succeed him. I was the national president of the Youth League, and the favourite for Marks's position, but my candidacy was opposed by a group from within the Transvaal ANC that called itself 'Bafabegiya' ('Those Who Die Dancing'). The group consisted mainly of ex-communists turned extreme African nationalists. They sought to cut all links with Indian activists and to move the ANC in the direction of a more confrontational strategy. They were led by MacDonald Maseko, a former communist who had been chairman of the Orlando branch of the ANC during the Defiance Campaign, and Seperepere Marupeng, who had been the chief volunteer for the Defiance Campaign in the Witwatersrand. Both Maseko and Marupeng intended to stand for the presidency of the Transvaal.

Marupeng was considered something of a demagogue. He used to wear a military-style khaki suit adorned with epaulets and gold buttons, and carried a baton like that made famous by Field Marshal Montgomery. He would stand up in front of meetings, his baton clutched underneath his arm, and say: 'I am tired of waiting for freedom. I want freedom now! I will meet Malan at the crossroads and I will show him what I want.' Then, banging his baton on the podium, he would cry, 'I want freedom now!'

Because of speeches like these, Marupeng became extremely popular during the Defiance Campaign, but popularity is only one factor in an election. He thought that because of his newfound prominence he would be a certainty for the presidency. Before the election, when it was known that I would be a candidate, I approached him and said, 'I would like you to stand for election to the Executive so that you can serve with me when I am president.' He regarded this as a slight, that I was in effect demoting him, and he refused, choosing instead to run for the presidency himself. But he had miscalculated, for I won the election with an overwhelming majority.

On 30 July 1952, at the height of the Defiance Campaign, I was at work at my then law firm of H.M. Basner when the police arrived with a warrant for my arrest. The charge was violation of the Suppression of Communism Act. The state made a series of simultaneous arrests of campaign leaders in Johannesburg, Port Elizabeth and Kimberley. Earlier in the month, the police had raided homes and offices of ANC and SAIC officials all over the country and confiscated papers and documents. This type of raid was something new and set a pattern for the pervasive and illegal searches that subsequently became a regular feature of the government's behaviour.

My arrest and those of the others culminated in a trial in September in Johannesburg of twenty-one accused, including the presidents and general secretaries of the ANC, the SAIC, the ANC Youth League and the Transvaal Indian Congress. Among the twenty-one on trial in Johannesburg were Dr Moroka, Walter Sisulu and J.B. Marks. A number of Indian leaders were arrested, including Dr Dadoo, Yusuf Cachalia and Ahmed Kathrada.

Our appearances in court became the occasion for exuberant political rallies. Massive crowds of demonstrators marched through the streets of Johannesburg and converged on the city's magistrates' court. There were white students from the University of the Witwatersrand, old ANC campaigners from Alexandra, Indian schoolchildren from primary and secondary schools, people of all ages and colours. The court had never been deluged with such crowds before. The courtroom itself was packed with people, and shouts of '*Mayibuye Afrika!*' punctuated the proceedings.

The trial should have been an occasion of resolve and solidarity, but it was sullied by a breach of faith by Dr Moroka. Moroka, the president-general of the ANC and the figurehead of the campaign, shocked us all by employing his own attorney. The plan was for all of us to be tried together. My fellow accused appointed me to discuss the matter with Dr Moroka and attempt to persuade him not to separate himself. The day before the trial I went to see Dr Moroka at Village Deep, Johannesburg.

At the outset of our meeting, I suggested alternatives to him, but he was not interested and instead aired a number of grievances. He felt that he had been excluded from the planning of the campaign. Yet Moroka was often quite uninterested in ANC affairs and content to be so. But he said the matter that disturbed him more than any other was that by being defended with the rest of us, he would be associated with men who were communists. Dr Moroka shared the government's animosity to communism. I remonstrated with him and said that it was the tradition of the ANC to work with anyone who was against racial oppression. But Moroka was unmoved.

The greatest jolt came when Moroka tendered a humiliating plea in mitigation to Judge Rumpff and took the witness stand to renounce the very principles on which the ANC had been founded. Asked whether he thought there should be equality between black and white in South Africa, Moroka replied that there would never be such a thing. We felt like slumping in despair in our seats. When his own lawyer asked him whether there were some among the defendants who were communists, Moroka actually began to point his finger at various people, including Dr Dadoo and Walter Sisulu. The judge informed him that that was not necessary.

His performance was a severe blow to the organization, and we all immediately realized that Dr Moroka's days as ANC president were numbered. He had committed the cardinal sin of putting his own interests ahead of those of the organization and the people. He was unwilling to jeopardize his medical career and fortune for his political beliefs, and thereby he had destroyed the image he had built during three years of courageous work on behalf of the ANC and the Defiance Campaign. I regarded this as a tragedy, for Dr Moroka's faintheartedness in court took away some of the glow from the campaign. The man who had gone round the country preaching the importance of the campaign had now forsaken it.

On 2 December we were all found guilty of what Judge Rumpff defined as 'statutory communism' – as opposed to what he said 'is commonly known as communism'. According to the statutes of the Suppression of Communism Act, virtually anyone who opposed the government in any way could be defined as – and therefore convicted of being – a 'statutory communist', even without ever having been a member of the party. The judge, who was fair-minded and reasonable, said that although we had planned acts that ranged from 'open non-compliance of laws to something that equals high treason', he accepted that we had consistently advised our members 'to follow a peaceful course of action and to avoid violence in any shape or form'. We were sentenced to nine months' imprisonment with hard labour, but the sentence was suspended for two years.

We made many mistakes, but the Defiance Campaign marked a new chapter in the struggle. The six laws we singled out were not overturned; but we never had any illusion that they would be. We selected them as the most immediate burden pressing on the lives of the people, and the best way to engage the greatest number of people in the struggle.

Prior to the campaign, the ANC was more talk than action. We had no paid organizers, no staff and a membership that did little more than pay lip-service to our cause. As a result of the campaign, our membership swelled to 100,000. The ANC emerged as a truly mass-based organization with an impressive corps of experienced activists who had braved the police, the courts and the jails. The stigma usually associated with imprisonment had been removed. This was a significant achievement, for fear of prison is a tremendous hindrance to a liberation struggle. From the Defiance Campaign onward, going to prison became a badge of honour among Africans.

We were extremely proud of the fact that during the six months of the campaign, there was not a single act of violence on our side. The discipline of our resisters was exemplary. During the later part of the campaign, riots broke out in Port Elizabeth and East London in which more than forty people were killed. Though these outbreaks had nothing whatsoever to do with the campaign, the government attempted to link us with them. In this, the government was successful, for the riots poisoned the views of some whites who might otherwise have been sympathetic.

Some within the ANC had unrealistic expectations and were convinced that the campaign could topple the government. We reminded them that the idea of the campaign was to focus attention on our grievances, not eradicate them. They argued that we had the government where we wanted it, and that we should continue the campaign indefinitely. I stepped in and said that this government was too strong and too ruthless to be brought down in such a manner. We could embarrass it, but overthrowing it as a result of the Defiance Campaign was impossible.

As it was, we continued the campaign for too long. We should have listened to Dr Xuma. When the planning committee met Dr Xuma during the tail-end of the campaign, he told us that it would soon lose momentum and it would be wise to call it off before it fizzled out altogether. To halt the campaign while it was still on the offensive would be a shrewd move that would capture the headlines. Dr Xuma was right: the campaign soon slackened, but in our enthusiasm and even arrogance, we brushed aside his advice. My heart wanted to keep it going but my head told me that it should stop. I argued for closure but went along with the majority. By the end of the year, the campaign foundered.

The Defiance Campaign never expanded beyond the initial stage of small batches of mostly urban defiers. Mass defiance, especially in the rural areas, was never achieved. The eastern Cape was the only region where we succeeded in reaching the second stage and where a strong resistance movement emerged in the countryside. In general, we did not penetrate the countryside, a historical weakness of the ANC. The campaign was hampered by the fact that we did not have any full-time organizers. I was attempting to organize it and practise as a lawyer at the same time, and that is no way to wage a mass campaign. We were still amateurs.

I nevertheless felt a great sense of accomplishment and satisfaction: I had been engaged in a just cause and had the strength to fight for it and win. The campaign freed me from any lingering sense of doubt or inferiority I might still have felt; it liberated me from the feeling of being overwhelmed by the power and seeming invincibility of the white man and his institutions. But now the white man had felt the power of my punches and I could walk upright like a man, and look everyone in the eye with the dignity that comes from not having succumbed to oppression and fear. I had come of age as a freedom fighter.

PART FOUR

The Struggle Is My Life

15

At the ANC annual conference at the end of 1952, there was a changing of the guard. The ANC designated a new, more vigorous, president for a new, more activist, era: Chief Albert Luthuli. In accordance with the ANC constitution, as provincial president of the Transvaal, I became one of the four deputy presidents. Furthermore, the National Executive Committee appointed me as First Deputy President. Luthuli was one of a handful of ruling chiefs who were active in the ANC and had staunchly resisted the policies of the government.

The son of a Seventh Day Adventist missionary, Luthuli was born in what was then Southern Rhodesia and educated in Natal. He had trained as a teacher at Adam's College near Durban. A fairly tall, heavy-set, dark-skinned man with a great broad smile, he combined an air of humility with deep-seated confidence. He was a man of patience and fortitude, who spoke slowly and clearly as though every word was of equal importance.

I had first met him in the late 1940s when he was a member of the Natives' Representative Council. In September 1952, only a few months before the annual conference, Luthuli had been summoned to Pretoria and given an ultimatum: he must either renounce his membership of the ANC and his support of the Defiance Campaign, or he would be dismissed from his position as an elected and government-paid tribal chief. Luthuli was a teacher, a devout Christian and a proud Zulu chief, but he was even more firmly committed to the struggle against apartheid. Luthuli refused to resign from the ANC and the government dismissed him from his post. In response, he issued a statement of principles called 'The Road to Freedom is via the Cross', in which he reaffirmed his support for non-violent passive resistance and justified his choice with words that still echo plaintively today: 'Who will deny that thirty years of my life have been spent knocking in vain, patiently, moderately and modestly at a closed and barred door?'

I supported Chief Luthuli, but I was unable to attend the national conference. A few days before the conference was to begin, fifty-two leaders around the country were banned from attending any meetings or gatherings for six months. I was among those leaders, and my movements were restricted to the district of Johannesburg for that same period.

My bans extended to meetings of all kinds, not only political ones. I could not, for example, attend my son's birthday party. I was prohibited from talking to more than one person at a time. This was part of a systematic effort by the government to silence, persecute and immobilize the leaders of those fighting apartheid and was the first of a series of bans on me that continued with brief intervals of freedom until the time I was deprived of all freedom some years later.

Banning not only confines one physically, it imprisons one's spirit. It induces a kind of psychological claustrophobia that makes one yearn for not only freedom of movement but spiritual escape. Banning was a dangerous game, for one was not shackled or chained behind bars; the bars were laws and regulations that could easily be violated and often were. One could slip away unseen for short periods of time and have the temporary illusion of freedom. The insidious effect of bans was that at a certain point one began to think that the oppressor was not without but within.

Although I was prevented from attending the 1952 annual conference, I was immediately informed as to what had transpired. One of the most significant decisions was one taken in secret and not publicized at the time.

Along with many others, I had become convinced that the government intended to declare the ANC and the SAIC illegal organizations, just as it had done with the Communist Party. It seemed inevitable that the state would attempt to put us out of business as a legal organization as soon as it could. With this in mind, I approached the National Executive with the idea that we must come up with a contingency plan for just such an eventuality. I said it would be an abdication of our responsibility as leaders of the people if we did not do so. They instructed me to draw up a plan that would enable the organization to operate from underground. This strategy came to be known as the Mandela-Plan or, simply, M-Plan.

The idea was to set up organizational machinery that would allow the ANC to take decisions at the highest level, which could then be swiftly transmitted to the organization as a whole without calling a meeting. In other words, it would allow an illegal organization to continue to function and enable leaders who were banned to continue to lead. The M-Plan was designed to allow the organization to recruit new members, respond to local and national problems and maintain regular contact between the membership and the underground leadership.

I held a number of secret meetings among ANC and SAIC leaders, both banned and not banned, to discuss the parameters of the plan. I worked on it for a number of months and came up with a system that was broad enough to adapt itself to local conditions and not fetter individual initiative, but detailed enough to facilitate order. The smallest unit was the cell, which in urban townships consisted of roughly ten houses on a street. A cell steward would be in charge of each of these units. If a street had more than ten houses, a street steward would take charge and the cell stewards would report to him. A group of streets formed a zone directed by a chief steward, who was in turn responsible to the secretariat of the local branch of the ANC. The secretariat was a subcommittee of the branch executive, which reported to the provincial secretary. My notion was that every cell and street steward should know every person and family in his area, so that he would be trusted by the people and would know whom to trust. The cell steward arranged meetings, organized political classes and collected dues. He was the linchpin of the plan. Although the strategy was primarily created for predominantly urban areas, it could be adapted to rural ones.

The plan was accepted, and was to be implemented immediately. Word went out to the branches to begin to prepare for this covert restructuring. Although it was accepted at most branches, some of the more far-flung outposts felt that the plan was an effort by Johannesburg to centralize control over the regions.

As part of the M-Plan, the ANC introduced an elementary course of political lectures for its members throughout the country. These lectures were meant not only to educate but to hold the organization together. They were given in secret by branch leaders. Those members in attendance would in turn give the same lectures to others in their homes and communities. In the beginning, the lectures were not systematized, but within a number of months there was a set curriculum.

There were three courses, 'The World We Live In', 'How We Are Governed' and 'The Need for Change'. In the first course, we discussed the different types of political and economic systems around the world as well as in South Africa. It was an overview of the growth of capitalism as well as socialism. We discussed, for example, how blacks in South Africa were oppressed both as a race and an economic class. The lecturers were mostly banned members, and I myself frequently gave lectures in the evening. This arrangement had the virtue of keeping banned individuals active as well as keeping the membership in touch with these leaders.

During this time, the banned leadership would often meet secretly and alone, and then arrange to meet the present leaders. The old and the new leadership meshed very well, and the decision-making process was collective as it had been before. Sometimes it felt as if nothing had changed except that we had to meet in secret.

The M-Plan was conceived with the best intentions, but it was instituted with only modest success and its adoption was never widespread. The most impressive results were once again in the eastern Cape and Port Elizabeth. The spirit of the Defiance Campaign continued in the eastern Cape long after it vanished elsewhere, and ANC members there seized on the M-Plan as a way of continuing to defy the government.

The plan faced many problems: it was not always adequately explained to the membership, there were no paid organizers to help implement or administer it and there was often dissension within branches that prevented agreement on imposing the plan. Some provincial leaders resisted it because they believed it undermined their power. To some, the government's crackdown did not seem imminent so they did not take the precautions necessary to lessen its effect. When the government's iron fist did descend, they were not prepared.

16

My life, during the Defiance Campaign, ran on two separate tracks: my work in the struggle and my livelihood as an attorney. I was never a full-time organizer for the ANC; the organization had only one, and that was Thomas Titus Nkobi. The work I did had to be arranged around my schedule as an attorney. In 1951, after I had completed my articles at Witkin, Sidelsky and Eidelman, I went to work for the law firm of Terblanche & Briggish. When I completed my articles, I was not yet a fully fledged attorney, but I was in a position to draw court pleadings, send out summonses and interview witnesses – all of which an attorney must do before a case goes to court.

After leaving Sidelsky, I had investigated a number of white firms – there were, of course, no African law firms. I was particularly interested in the scale of fees charged by these firms and was outraged to discover that many of the most blue-chip law firms charged Africans even higher fees for criminal and civil cases than they did their far wealthier white clients.

After working for Terblanche & Briggish for about one year, I joined the firm of Helman and Michel. It was a liberal firm, and one of the few that charged Africans on a reasonable scale. In addition, it prided itself on its devotion to African education, towards which it donated handsomely. Mr Helman, the firm's senior partner, was involved with African causes long before they became popular or fashionable. The firm's other partner, Rodney Michel, a veteran of the Second World War, was also extremely liberal. He was a pilot, and years later helped fly ANC people out of South Africa during the worst periods of repression. Michel's only discernible vice was that he was a heavy smoker who puffed on one cigarette after another all day long at the office.

I stayed at Helman and Michel for a number of months while I was studying for my qualification exam, which would establish me as a fully fledged attorney. I had given up studying for an LLB degree at the University of the Witwatersrand after failing my exams several times. I opted to take the qualifying exam so that I could practise and begin to earn enough money to support my family. At the time, my sister was living with us and my mother had come to visit, and Evelyn's wages as a trainee nurse plus my own paltry income were not enough to keep everyone warm and fed.

When I passed the qualification exam, I went to work as a fully fledged attorney at the firm of H.M. Basner. Basner had been an Africans' representative in the Senate, an early member of the Communist Party, and a passionate supporter of African rights. As a lawyer, he was a defender of African leaders and trade unionists. For the months that I worked there, I was often in court representing the firm's many African clients. Mr Basner was an excellent boss and as long as I got my work done at the firm he encouraged my political activities. After the experience I gained there, I felt ready to go off on my own.

In August 1952 I opened my own law office. What early success I enjoyed I owed to Zubeida Patel, my secretary. I had met her when she had gone to work at

H.M. Basner as a replacement for an Afrikaans-speaking secretary, Miss Koch, who had refused to take my dictation. Zubeida was the wife of my friend Cassim Patel, a member of the Indian Congress, and she was without any sense of colour bar whatsoever. She had a wide circle of friends, knew many people in the legal world, and when I went out on my own, she agreed to work for me. She brought a great deal of business through the door.

Oliver Tambo was then working for a firm called Kovalsky and Tuch. I often visited him there during his lunch hour, and made a point of sitting in a Whites Only chair in the Whites Only waiting room. Oliver and I were very good friends, and we mainly discussed ANC business during those lunch hours. He had first impressed me at Fort Hare where I noticed his thoughtful intelligence and sharp debating skills. With his cool, logical style he could demolish an opponent's argument – precisely the sort of intelligence that is useful in a courtroom. Before Fort Hare, he had been a brilliant student at St Peter's in Johannesburg. His even-tempered objectivity was an antidote to my more emotional reactions to issues. Oliver was deeply religious and had for a long time considered the ministry to be his calling. He was also a neighbour: he came from Bizana in Pondoland, part of the Transkei, and his face bore the distinctive scars of his tribe. It seemed natural for us to practise together and I asked him to join me. A few months later, when Oliver was able to extricate himself from his firm, we opened our own office in downtown Johannesburg.

'Mandela and Tambo' read the brass plate on our office door in Chancellor House, a small building just across the street from the marble statues of justice standing in front of the magistrates' court in central Johannesburg. Our building, owned by Indians, was one of the few places where Africans could rent offices in the city. From the beginning, Mandela and Tambo was besieged with clients. We were not the only African lawyers in South Africa, but we were the only firm of African lawyers. For Africans, we were the firm of first choice and last resort. To reach our offices each morning, we had to move through a crowd of people in the corridors, on the stairs and in our small waiting room.

Africans were desperate for legal help in government buildings: it was a crime to walk through a Whites Only door, a crime to ride a Whites Only bus, a crime to use a Whites Only drinking fountain, a crime to walk on a Whites Only beach, a crime to be on the streets after 11 p.m., a crime not to have a pass book and a crime to have the wrong signature in that book, a crime to be unemployed and a crime to be employed in the wrong place, a crime to live in certain places and a crime to have no place to live.

Every week we interviewed old men from the countryside who told us that generation after generation of their family had worked a bleak piece of land from which they were now being evicted. Every week we interviewed old women who brewed African beer as a way to supplement their tiny incomes, who now faced jail terms and fines they could not afford to pay. Every week we interviewed people who had lived in the same house for decades only to find that it was now in what was declared a white area and they had to leave without any recompense. Every day we heard and saw the thousands of humiliations that ordinary Africans confronted every day of their lives.

* * *

Oliver had a prodigious capacity for work. He spent a great deal of time with each client, not so much for professional reasons but because he was a man of limitless compassion and patience. He became involved in his clients' cases and in their lives. He was touched by the plight of the masses as a whole and by each and every individual.

I realized quickly what Mandela and Tambo meant to ordinary Africans. It was a place where they could come and find a sympathetic ear and a competent ally, a place where they would not be either turned away or cheated, a place where they might actually feel proud to be represented by men of their own skin colour. This was the reason I had become a lawyer in the first place, and my work often made me feel I had made the right decision.

We often dealt with half a dozen cases in a morning, and were in and out of court all day long. In some courts we were treated with courtesy, in others with contempt. But even as we practised and fought and won cases, we always knew that no matter how well we pursued our careers as attorneys, we could never become a prosecutor, a magistrate, a judge. Although we were dealing with officials whose competence was no greater than our own, their authority was founded on and protected by the colour of their skin.

We frequently encountered prejudice in the court itself. White witnesses often refused to answer questions from a black attorney. Instead of citing them for contempt of court, the magistrate would then pose the questions they would not answer from me. I routinely put policemen on the stand and interrogated them; though I would catch them in discrepancies and lies, they never considered me anything but a 'kaffir lawyer'.

I recall once being asked at the outset of a trial to identify myself. This was customary. I said, 'I am Nelson Mandela and I appear for the accused.' The magistrate said, 'I don't know you. Where is your certificate?' A certificate is the fancy diploma that one frames and hangs on the wall; it is not something that an attorney ever carries with him. It would be like asking a man for his university degree. I requested that the magistrate begin the case, and I would bring in my certificate in due course. But the magistrate refused to hear the case, even going so far as to ask a court officer to evict me.

This was a clear violation of court practice. The matter eventually came before the Supreme Court and my friend, George Bizos, an advocate, appeared on my behalf. At the hearing, the presiding judge criticized the conduct of the magistrate and ordered that a different magistrate must hear the case.

Being a lawyer did not guarantee respect out of court either. One day, near our office, I saw an elderly white woman whose motor car was sandwiched between two cars. I immediately went over and pushed the car, which helped free it. The English-speaking woman turned to me and said, 'Thank you, John' – John being the name whites used to address any African whose name they did not know. She then handed me a sixpence coin, which I politely refused. She pushed it towards me, and again I said no, thank you. She then exclaimed, 'You refuse a sixpence. You must want a shilling, but you shall not have it!' and then threw the coin at me, and drove off.

Within a year, Oliver and I discovered that under the Urban Areas Act we were not permitted to occupy business premises in the city without ministerial consent. Our request was denied, and we received instead a temporary permit under the Group Areas Act, which soon expired. The authorities refused to renew it, insisting that we move our offices to an African location many miles away and virtually unreachable for our clients. We interpreted this as an effort by the authorities to put us out of business, and occupied our premises illegally, with threats of eviction constantly hanging over our heads. Working as a lawyer in South Africa meant operating under a debased system of justice, a code of law that did not enshrine equality but its opposite. One of the most pernicious examples of this was the Population Registration Act, which defined that inequality. I once handled the case of a Coloured man who was inadvertently classified as an African. He had fought for South Africa during the Second World War in North Africa and Italy, but after his return, a white bureaucrat had reclassified him as African. This was the type of case, not at all untypical in South Africa, that offered a moral jigsaw puzzle. I did not support or recognize the principles in the Population Registration Act, but my client needed representation, and he had been classified as something he was not. There were many practical advantages to being classified as Coloured rather than African, such as the fact that Coloured men were not required to carry passes.

On his behalf, I appealed to the Classification Board, which adjudicated cases falling under the Population Registration Act. The board consisted of a magistrate and two other officials, all white. I had formidable documentary evidence to establish my client's case, and the prosecutor formally indicated that he would not oppose our appeal. But the magistrate seemed uninterested in both my evidence and the prosecutor's demurral. He stared at my client and gruffly asked him to turn round so that his back faced the bench. After scrutinizing my client's shoulders, which sloped down sharply, he nodded to the other officials and upheld the appeal. In the view of the white authorities in those days, sloping shoulders were one stereotype of the Coloured physique. And so it came about that the course of this man's life was decided purely on a magistrate's opinion about the structure of his shoulders.

We tried many cases involving police brutality, though our success rate was quite low. Police assaults were always difficult to prove. The police were clever enough to detain a prisoner long enough for the wounds and bruises to heal, and often it was simply the word of a policeman against our client. The magistrates naturally sided with the police. The coroner's verdict on a death in police custody would often read 'Death due to multiple causes' or some vague explanation that let the police off the hook.

Whenever I had a case outside Johannesburg, I applied to have my bans temporarily lifted, and this was often granted. For example, I travelled to the eastern Transvaal, and defended a client in the town of Carolina. My arrival caused quite a sensation, as many of the people had never before seen an African lawyer. I was received warmly by the magistrate and prosecutor, and the case did not begin for quite a while as they asked me numerous questions about my career and how I became a lawyer. The court was similarly crowded with curious townspeople.

In a nearby village I appeared for a local medicine man charged with witchcraft. This case also attracted a large crowd – not to see me, but to find out whether the white man's laws could be applied to a *sangoma*. The medicine man exerted tremendous power in the area, and many people both worshipped and feared him. At one point, my client sneezed violently, causing a virtual stampede in the courtroom; most observers believed he was casting a spell. He was found not guilty, but I suspect that the local people attributed this not to my skill as a lawyer, but to the power of the medicine man's herbs.

As an attorney, I could be rather flamboyant in court. I did not act as though I were a black man in a white man's court, but as if everyone else – white and black – was a guest in my court. When presenting a case, I often made sweeping gestures and used high-flown language. I was punctilious about all court regulations, but I sometimes used unorthodox tactics with witnesses. I enjoyed cross-examinations, and often played on racial tension. The spectators' gallery was usually crowded, because people from the township attended court as a form of entertainment.

I recall once defending an African woman who worked as a domestic worker in town. She was accused of stealing her 'madam's' clothes. The clothing that was allegedly stolen was displayed on a table in court. After the 'madam' had testified, I began my cross-examination by walking over to the table of evidence. I studied the clothing and then, with the tip of my pencil, I picked up an item of ladies' underwear. I slowly turned to the witness box brandishing the panties and simply asked, 'Madam, are these . . . yours?' 'No,' she replied quickly, too embarrassed to admit that they were. Because of this response, and other discrepancies in her evidence, the magistrate dismissed the case.

17

Situated four miles west of Johannesburg's centre, on the face of a rocky outcrop overlooking the city, was the African township of Sophiatown. Father Trevor Huddleston, one of the township's greatest friends, once compared Sophiatown to an Italian hill town, and from a distance the place did indeed have a good deal of charm: the closely packed, red-roofed houses; the smoke curling up into a pink sky; the tall and slender gum trees that hugged the township. Up close one saw the poverty and squalor in which too many of Sophiatown's people lived. The streets were narrow and unpaved, and every plot was filled with dozens of shanties huddled close together.

Sophiatown was part of what was known as the Western Areas townships, along with Martindale and Newclare. The area was originally intended for whites, and a property developer actually built a number of houses there for white buyers. But because of a municipal refuse dump in the area, whites chose to live elsewhere. Reluctantly, the developer sold his houses to Africans. Sophiatown was one of the few places in the Transvaal where Africans had been able to buy stands, or plots, prior to the 1923 Urban Areas Act. Many of these old brick and stone houses, with their tin-roofed verandas, still stood in Sophiatown, giving the township an air of Old World graciousness. As industry in Johannesburg grew, Sophiatown became the home of a rapidly expanding African workforce. It was convenient and close to town. Workers lived in shanties that were erected in the back and front yards of older residences. Several families might all be crowded into a single shanty. Up to forty people could share a single water tap. Despite the poverty, Sophiatown had a special character; for Africans, it was the Left Bank in Paris, Greenwich Village in New York, the home of writers, artists, doctors and lawyers. It was both bohemian and conventional, lively and sedate. It was home to both Dr Xuma, where he had his practice, and assorted *tsotsis* (gangsters) like the Berliners and the Americans who adopted the names of American movie stars like John Wayne and Humphrey Bogart. Sophiatown boasted the only swimming pool for African children in Johannesburg.

In Johannesburg, the Western Areas Removal scheme meant the evacuation of Sophiatown, Martindale and Newclare, with a collective population that was somewhere between 60,000 and 100,000. In 1953, the Nationalist government had purchased a tract of land called Meadowlands, thirteen miles from the city. People were to be resettled there in seven different 'ethnic groups'. The excuse given by the government was slum clearance, a smokescreen for the government policy that regarded all urban areas as white areas where Africans were temporary residents.

The government was under pressure from its supporters in the surrounding areas of Westdene and Newlands, which were comparatively poor white areas. These working-class whites were envious of some of the fine houses owned by blacks in Sophiatown. The government wanted to control the movements of all Africans, and such control was far more difficult in freehold urban townships, where blacks could own property, and people came and went as they pleased. Though the pass system was still in effect, one did not need a special permit to enter a freehold township, as was the case with municipal locations. Africans had lived and owned property in Sophiatown for over fifty years; now the government was callously planning on relocating all Sophiatown's African residents to another black township. So cynical was the government's plan that the removal was to take place even before the houses were built to accommodate the evacuated people. The removal of Sophiatown was the first major test of strength for the ANC and its allies after the Defiance Campaign.

Although the government's removal campaign for Sophiatown had started in 1950, efforts by the ANC to combat it did not begin in earnest until 1953. By the middle of the year, the local branches of the ANC and the TIC and the local Ratepayers Association were mobilizing people to resist. In June 1953 a public meeting was called by the provincial executive of the ANC and the TIC at Sophiatown's Odin cinema to discuss opposition to the removal. It was a lively, exuberant meeting attended by more than twelve hundred people, none of whom seemed intimidated by the presence of dozens of heavily armed policemen.

Only a few days before the meeting, my banning orders, as well as Walter's, had expired. This meant that we were no longer prevented from attending or speaking at gatherings, and arrangements were quickly made for me to speak at the cinema.

Shortly before the meeting was to begin, a police officer saw Walter and me outside the cinema talking with Father Huddleston, one of the leaders of the opposition to the removal. The officer informed the two of us that as banned individuals we had no right to be there, and he then ordered his officers to arrest us. Father Huddleston shouted to the policemen coming towards us, 'No, you must arrest me instead, my dears.' The officer ordered Father Huddleston to stand aside, but he refused. As the policemen moved Father Huddleston out of the way, I said to the officer, 'You must make sure whether we are under a ban or not. Be careful, because it would be a wrongful arrest to take us in if our bans have expired. Now, do you think we would be here tonight talking to you if our bans had not expired?'

The police were notorious for keeping very poor records and were often unaware when bans ended. The officer knew this as well as I did. He pondered what I had said, then told his men to pull back. They stood aside as we entered the hall.

Inside, the police were provocative and contemptuous. Equipped with pistols and rifles, they strutted around the hall pushing people around, making insulting remarks. I was sitting on stage with a number of other leaders and, as the meeting was about to begin, I saw Major Prinsloo come swaggering in through the stage door, accompanied by a number of armed officers. I caught his eye and made a gesture as if to say, 'Me?' and he shook his head. He then walked over to the podium, where Yusuf Cachalia had already begun to speak, and ordered the other officers to arrest him, whereupon they took him by the arms and started to drag him off. Outside, the police had already arrested Robert Resha and Ahmed Kathrada.

The crowd began yelling and booing, and I saw that matters could turn extremely ugly if the crowd did not control itself. I jumped to the podium and started singing a well-known protest song, and as soon as I pronounced the first few words the crowd joined in. I feared that the police might have opened fire if the crowd had become too unruly.

The ANC was then holding meetings every Sunday evening in Freedom Square, in the centre of Sophiatown, to mobilise opposition to the removal. These were vibrant sessions, punctuated by repeated cries of '*Asihambi!*' ('We are not moving!') and the singing of '*Sophiatown likhaya lam asihambi*' ('Sophiatown is my home; we are not moving'). The meetings were addressed by leading ANC members, standholders, tenants, city councillors, and often by Father Huddleston, who ignored police warnings to confine himself to church affairs.

One Sunday evening, not long after the incident at the Odin cinema, I was scheduled to speak in Freedom Square. The crowd that night was passionate, and their emotion undoubtedly influenced mine. There were a great many young people present, and they were angry and eager for action. As usual, policemen were clustered around the perimeter, armed with both guns and pencils, the latter to take notes of who was speaking and what the speaker was saying. We tried to make this into a virtue by being as open with the police as possible to show them that in fact we had nothing to hide, not even our distaste for them.

I began by speaking about the increasing repressiveness of the government in the wake of the Defiance Campaign. I said the government was now scared of the might of the African people. As I spoke, I grew more and more indignant. In those days, I was something of a rabble-rousing speaker. I liked to incite an audience, and I was doing so that evening.

As I condemned the government for its ruthlessness and lawlessness, I overstepped the line: I said that the time for passive resistance had ended, that non-violence was a useless strategy and could never overturn a white minority regime bent on retaining its power at any cost. At the end of the day, I said, violence was the only weapon that would destroy apartheid and we must be prepared, in the near future, to use that weapon.

The crowd was excited; the youth in particular were clapping and cheering. They were ready to act on what I said right then and there. At that point I began to sing a freedom song, the lyrics of which say, 'There are the enemies, let us take our weapons and attack them.' I sang and the crowd joined in, and when it was finished, I pointed to the police and said, 'There, there are our enemies!' The crowd again started cheering and made aggressive gestures in the direction of the police. The police looked nervous, and a number of them pointed back at me as if to say, 'Mandela, we will get you for this.' I did not mind. In the heat of the moment I did not think of the consequences.

But my words that night did not come out of no-where. I had been thinking of the future. The government was busily taking measures to prevent anything like the Defiance Campaign from recurring. I had begun to analyse the struggle in different terms. The ambition of the ANC was to wage a mass struggle, to engage the workers and peasants of South Africa in a campaign so large and powerful that it might overcome the *status quo* of white oppression. But the Nationalist government was making any legal expression of dissent or protest impossible. I saw that it would ruthlessly suppress any legitimate protest on the part of the African majority. A police state did not seem far off.

I began to suspect that both legal and extra-constitutional protests would soon be impossible. In India, Gandhi had been dealing with a foreign power that ultimately was more realistic and far-sighted. That was not the case with the Afrikaners in South Africa. Non-violent passive resistance is effective as long as your opposition adheres to the same rules as you do. But if peaceful protest is met with violence, its efficacy is at an end. For me, non-violence was not a moral principle but a strategy; there is no moral goodness in using an ineffective weapon. But my thoughts on this matter were not yet formed, and I had spoken too soon.

That was certainly the view of the National Executive. When they learned of my speech, I was severely reprimanded for advocating such a radical departure from accepted policy. Although some on the Executive sympathized with my remarks, no one could support the intemperate way that I had made them. They admonished me, noting that the impulsive policy I had called for was not only premature but dangerous. Such speeches could provoke the enemy to crush the organization entirely while the enemy was strong and we were as yet still weak. I accepted the censure, and thereafter faithfully defended the policy of non-violence in public. But, in my heart, I knew that non-violence was not the answer.

In those days I was often in hot water with the Executive. In early 1953, Chief Luthuli, Z.K. Matthews and a handful of other high-ranking ANC leaders were invited to a meeting with a group of whites who were in the process of forming the Liberal Party. A meeting of the ANC Executive took place afterwards at which a few of us asked for a report of the earlier meeting with the white liberals. The participants refused, saying that they had been invited in their private capacity, not as members of the ANC. We continued to pester them, and finally Professor Matthews, who was a lawyer, said that it had been a privileged conversation. In a fit of indignation, I said, 'What kind of leaders are you who can discuss matters with a group of white liberals and then not share that information with your colleagues at the ANC? That's the trouble with you, you are scared and overawed of the white man. You value his company more than that of your African comrades.'

This outburst provoked the wrath of both Professor Matthews and Chief Luthuli. First, Professor Matthews responded: 'Mandela, what do you know about whites? I taught you whatever you know about whites and you are still ignorant. Even now, you are barely out of your student uniform.' Luthuli was burning with a cold fire and said, 'All right, if you are accusing me of being afraid of the white man, I have no other recourse but to resign. If that is what you say, then that is what I intend to do.' I did not know whether Luthuli was bluffing, but his threat frightened me. I had spoken hastily, without thinking, without a sense of responsibility, and I now greatly regretted it. I immediately withdrew my charge and apologized. I was a young man who attempted to make up for his ignorance with militancy.

At the same time as my speech in Sophiatown, Walter Sisulu informed me that he had been invited to attend the World Festival of Youth and Students for Peace and Friendship in Bucharest as a guest of honour. The timing of the invitation gave him virtually no opportunity to consult with the National Executive. I was keen that he should go and encouraged him to do so, whether or not he conferred with the Executive. Walter resolved to go, and I helped him to arrange for a substitute passport, an affidavit stating his identity and citizenship. (The government would never have issued him with a proper passport.) The group, which was headed by Walter Sisulu and Duma Nokwe, travelled on the only airline that would accept such an affidavit: El Al.

I was convinced, despite my reprimand from the Executive, that the policies of the Nationalists would soon make non-violence an even more limited and ineffective policy. Walter was privy to my thoughts and, before he left, I made a suggestion: he should arrange to visit the People's Republic of China and discuss with them the possibility of supplying us with weapons for an armed struggle. Walter liked the idea, and promised to make the attempt.

This action was taken purely on my own and my methods were highly unorthodox. To some extent, they were the actions of a hotheaded revolutionary who had not thought things through and who acted without discipline. They were the actions of a man frustrated with the immorality of apartheid and the ruthlessness of the state in protecting it.

Walter's visit caused a storm within the Executive. I undertook the task of personally conveying his apologies, without mentioning my secret request. Luthuli objected to the flouting of the ANC's code of conduct, and Professor Matthews expressed dismay about Walter visiting socialist countries. The Executive was sceptical about Walter's motives, and questioned my explanation of the circumstances. A few wanted to censure Walter and me formally, but in the end did not.

Walter managed to reach China, where the leadership received him warmly. They conveyed their support of our struggle, but they were wary and cautious when he broached the idea of an armed struggle. They warned him that this was an extremely grave undertaking, and they questioned whether the liberation movement had matured sufficiently to justify such an endeavour. Walter came back with encouragement but no guns.

18

In Johannesburg, I had become a man of the city. I wore smart suits, I drove a colossal Oldsmobile and I knew my way around the back alleys of the city. I commuted daily to a downtown office. But in fact I remained a country boy at heart, and there was nothing that lifted my spirits as much as blue skies, the open veld and green grass. In September, as my banning orders had ended, I decided to take advantage of my freedom and get some respite from the city. I took on a case in the little dorp of Villiers in the Orange Free State.

The drive to the Orange Free State from Johannesburg used to take several hours, and I set out from Orlando at 3 a.m, which has always been my favourite hour for departure. I am an early riser anyway, and at 3 a.m. the roads are empty and quiet, and one can be alone with one's thoughts. I like to see the coming of dawn, the change between day and night, which is always majestic. It was also a convenient hour for departure because the police were usually nowhere to be found.

The province of the Orange Free State has always had a magical effect on me, though some of the most racist elements of the white population call the Free State their home. With its flat dusty landscape as far as the eye can see, the great blue ceiling above, the endless stretches of yellow mealie fields, scrub and bushes, the Free State's landscape gladdens my heart no matter what my mood. When I am there I feel that nothing can shut me in, that my thoughts can roam as far and wide as the horizons.

The landscape bore the imprint of General Christiaan R. de Wet, the gifted Boer commander who outclassed the British in dozens of engagements during the final months of the Anglo-Boer war; fearless, proud and shrewd, he would have been one of my heroes had he been fighting for the rights of all South Africans, not just Afrikaners. He demonstrated the courage and resourcefulness of the underdog, and the power of a less sophisticated but patriotic army against a tested war machine. As I drove, I imagined the hiding places of General de Wet's army and wondered whether they would some day shelter African rebels.

The drive to Villiers cheered me considerably, and I was labouring under a false sense of security when I entered the small courthouse on the morning of 3 September. I found a group of policemen waiting for me. With nary a word, they served me with an order under the Suppression of Communism Act requiring me to resign from the ANC, restricting me to the Johannesburg district and prohibiting me from attending any meetings or gatherings for two years. I knew such measures would come, but I had not expected to receive my bans in the remote village of Villiers.

I was thirty-five, and these new and more severe bans ended a period of nearly a decade of involvement with the ANC, years that had been the time of my political awakening and growth, and my gradual commitment to the struggle that had become my life. Henceforth, all my actions and plans on behalf of the ANC and the liberation struggle would become secret and illegal. Once served, I had to return to Johannesburg immediately.

My bans drove me from the centre of the struggle to the sidelines, from a role that was primary to one that was peripheral. Though I was often consulted and was able to influence the direction of events, I did so at a distance and only when expressly asked. I no longer felt like a vital organ of the body – the heart, lung or backbone – but a severed limb. Even freedom fighters, at least then, had to obey the laws and, at that point, imprisonment for violating my bans would have been useless to the ANC and to myself. We were not yet at the point where we were open revolutionaries, overtly fighting the system no matter what the cost. We believed then that it was better to organize underground than to go to prison. When I was forced to resign from the ANC, the organization had to replace me, and no matter what I might have liked, I could no longer wield the authority I once possessed. While driving back to Johannesburg, the Free State scenery did not have quite the same elevating effect on me as before.

19

When I received my banning, the Transvaal conference of the ANC was due to be held the following month, and I had already completed the draft of my presidential address. It was read to the conference by Andrew Kunene, a member of the Executive. In that speech, which subsequently became known as 'The No Easy Walk to Freedom' speech, a line taken from Jawaharlal Nehru, I said that the masses now had to be prepared for new forms of political struggle. The new laws and tactics of the government had made the old forms of mass protest – public meetings, press statements, stay-aways – extremely dangerous and self-destructive. Newspapers would not publish our statements and printing presses refused to print our leaflets, all for fear of prosecution under the Suppression of Communism Act. 'These developments require the evolution of new forms of political struggle. The old methods,' I said, were now 'suicidal'.

'The oppressed people and the oppressors are at loggerheads. The day of reckoning between the forces of freedom and those of reaction is not very far off. I have not the slightest doubt that when that day comes truth and justice will prevail . . . The feelings of the oppressed people have never been more bitter. The grave plight of the people compels them to resist to the death the stinking policies of the gangsters that rule our country . . . To overthrow oppression has been sanctioned by humanity and is the highest aspiration of every free man.'

In April 1954 the Law Society of the Transvaal applied to the Supreme Court for my name to be struck off the roll of accredited attorneys on the ground that the political activities for which I was convicted in the Defiance case amounted to unprofessional and dishonourable conduct. This occurred at a time when the firm of Mandela and Tambo was flourishing and I was in court dozens of times a week.

The documents were served at my office, and as soon as the application against me had been made and publicized, I began to receive offers of support and help. I received offers of help even from a number of well-known Afrikaner lawyers. Many of these men were supporters of the Nationalist Party, but they believed that the application was biased and unfair. Their response suggested to me that even in racist South Africa professional solidarity can sometimes transcend colour, and that there were still attorneys and judges who refused to be the rubber stamps of an immoral regime.

My case was ably defended by advocate Walter Pollak, Q.C., chairman of the Johannesburg Bar Council. At the time that I retained Walter Pollak, I was advised that I should also retain someone who was not connected with the struggle, as that would positively influence the Transvaal Bar. To that end, we retained William Aaronsohn, as instructing attorney, who was head of one of the oldest law firms in Johannesburg. Both men acted for me without charge. We argued that the application was an affront to the idea of justice and that I had an inherent right to fight for my political beliefs, which was the right of all men in a state where the rule of law applied.

But the argument that had great weight was Pollak's use of the case of a man called Strijdorn, who was detained during the Second World War together with B.J. Vorster (who later became Prime Minister). Both were interned for their pro-Nazi stance. Following a failed escape attempt, Strijdorn had been found guilty of car theft. Later, after he was released, he applied to the Bar for admittance as an advocate. Despite his crimes, Pollak said, 'There are of course differences between Strijdorn and Mandela. Mandela is not a Nationalist and Mandela is not a white.'

Judge Ramsbottom, who heard the case, was an example of a judge who refused to be a mouthpiece for the Nationalists and upheld the independence of the judiciary. His judgment in the case completely upheld our claim that I had a right to campaign for my political beliefs even though they were opposed to the government, and he dismissed the Law Society's application, and, in an unusual move, ordered the Law Society to pay its own costs.

20

The anti-removal campaign in Sophiatown was a long-running battle. We held our ground, as did the state. Throughout 1954 and into 1955, rallies were held twice a week, on Wednesday and Sunday evenings. Speaker after speaker continued to decry the government's plans. The ANC and the Ratepayers Association, under the direction of Dr Xuma, protested to the government in letters and petitions. We ran the anti-removal campaign on the slogan 'Over Our Dead Bodies', a motto often shouted from the platforms and echoed by the audience. One night it even roused the otherwise cautious Dr Xuma to utter the electrifying slogan used to rally African warriors to battle in the previous century: '*Zemk' inkomo magwalandini!*' ('The enemy has captured the cattle, you cowards!')

The government had scheduled the removal for 9 February 1955. As the day approached, Oliver Tambo and I were in the township daily, meeting local leaders, discussing plans and acting in our professional capacity for those being forced out of the area or prosecuted. We sought to prove to the court that the government's documentation was often incorrect and that many orders to leave were therefore illegal. But this was only a temporary measure; the government would not let a few illegalities stand in its way.

Shortly before the scheduled removal, a special mass meeting was planned for Freedom Square. Ten thousand people gathered to hear Chief Luthuli speak. But upon his arrival in Johannesburg he was served with a banning order that forced him to return to Natal.

The night before the removal, Joe Modise, one of the most dedicated of the local ANC leaders, addressed a tense meeting of more than five hundred youthful activists. They expected the ANC to give them an order to defy the police and the army. They were prepared to erect barricades overnight and engage the police with weapons and whatever came to hand the next day. They assumed our slogan meant what it said: that Sophiatown would be removed only over our dead bodies.

But after discussions with the ANC leadership, including myself, Joe told the youth to stand down. They were angry and felt betrayed. But we believed that violence would have been a disaster. We pointed out that an insurrection required careful planning or it would become an act of suicide. We were not yet ready to engage the enemy on its own terms.

In the hazy dawn hours of 9 February, four thousand police and army troops cordoned off the township while workers razed empty houses, and government trucks began moving families from Sophiatown to Meadowlands. The night before, the ANC had evacuated several families to prearranged accommodation with pro-ANC families in the interior of Sophiatown. But our efforts were too little and too late, and could be only a stopgap measure. The army and the police were relentlessly efficient. After a few weeks, our resistance collapsed. Most of our local leaders had been banned or arrested and, in the end, Sophiatown died not to the sound of gunfire but to the sound of rumbling trucks and sledgehammers.

One can always be correct about a political action one is reading about in the next day's newspaper, but when you are in the centre of a heated political fight, you are given little time for reflection. We made a variety of mistakes in the Western Areas anti-removal campaign and learned a number of lessons. 'Over Our Dead Bodies' was a dynamic slogan, but it proved as much a hindrance as a help. A slogan is a vital link between the organization and the masses it seeks to lead. It should synthesize a particular grievance into a succinct and pithy phrase, while mobilizing the people to combat it. Our slogan caught the imagination of the people, but it led them to believe that we would fight to the death to resist the removal. In fact, the ANC was not prepared to do that at all.

We never provided the people with an alternative to moving to Meadowlands. When the people in Sophia-town realized we could neither stop the government nor provide the tenants with housing elsewhere, their own resistance waned and the flow of people to Mea-dowlands increased. Many tenants moved willingly, for they found they would have more space and cleaner housing in Meadowlands. We did not take into account the different situations of landlords and tenants. While the landlords had reasons to stay, many tenants had an incentive to leave. The ANC was criticized by a number of Africanist members who accused the leadership of protecting the interests of the landlords at the expense of the tenants.

The lesson I took away from the campaign was that, in the end, we had no alternative to armed and violent resistance. Over and over again, we had used all the non-violent weapons in our arsenal – speeches, deputations, threats, marches, strikes, stay-aways, voluntary imprisonment – all to no avail, for whatever we did was met by an iron hand. A freedom fighter learns the hard way that it is the oppressor who defines the nature of the struggle, and the oppressed is often left no recourse but to use methods that mirror those of the oppressor. At a certain point, one can only fight fire with fire.

Education is the great engine of personal development. It is through education that the daughter of a peasant can become a doctor, that the son of a mineworker can become the head of the mine, that a child of farmworkers can become the president of a great nation. It is what we make out of what we have, not what we are given, that separates one person from another.

Since the turn of the century, Africans owed their educational opportunities primarily to the foreign churches and missions that created and sponsored schools. Under the United Party, the syllabus for African secondary schools and white secondary schools was essentially the same. The mission schools provided Africans with Western-style English-language education, which I myself received. We were limited by lesser facilities, but not by what we could read or think or dream.

Yet even before the Nationalists came to power, the disparities in funding tell a story of racist education. The government spent about six times as much per white student as per African student. Education was not compulsory for Africans and was free only in the primary grades. Fewer than half of all African children of school age attended any school at all, and only a tiny number of Africans received high school certificates.

Even this amount of education proved distasteful to the Nationalists. The Afrikaner has always been unenthusiastic about education for Africans. To him it was simply a waste, for the African was inherently ignorant and lazy and no amount of education could remedy that. The Afrikaner was traditionally hostile to Africans learning English, for English was a foreign tongue to the Afrikaner and the language of emancipation to us.

In 1953 the Nationalist-dominated Parliament passed the Bantu Education Act, which sought to put apartheid's stamp on African education. The act transferred control of African education from the Department of Education to the much loathed Native Affairs Department. Under the act, African primary and secondary schools operated by Church and mission bodies were given the choice of turning over their schools to the government or receiving gradually diminished subsidies; either the government took over education for Africans or there would be no education for Africans. African teachers were not permitted to criticize the government or any school authority. It was intellectual *baasskap*, a way of institutionalizing inferiority.

Dr Hendrik Verwoerd, the minister of Bantu Education, explained that education 'must train and teach people in accordance with their opportunities in life'. His meaning was that Africans did not and would not have any opportunities; therefore, why educate them?

'There is no place for the Bantu in the European community above the level of certain forms of labour,' he said. In short, Africans should be trained to be menial workers, to be in a position of perpetual subordination to the white man.

To the ANC, the act was a deeply sinister measure designed to retard the progress of African culture as a whole and, if enacted, permanently set back the freedom struggle of the African people. The mental outlook of all future generations of Africans was at stake. As Professor Matthews wrote at the time, 'Education for ignorance and for inferiority in Verwoerd's schools is worse than no education at all.'

The act and Verwoerd's crude exposition of it aroused widespread indignation from both black and white. With the exception of the Dutch Reformed Church, which supported apartheid, and the Lutheran mission, all Christian churches opposed the new measure. But the unity of the opposition extended only to condemning the policy, not resisting it. The Anglicans, the most fearless and consistent critics of the new policy, were divided. Bishop Ambrose Reeves of Johannesburg took the extreme step of closing his schools, which had a total enrolment of ten thousand children. But the archbishop of the church in South Africa, anxious to keep children off the streets, handed over the rest of the schools to the government. Despite their protests, all the other churches did the same with the exception of the Roman Catholics, the Seventh Day Adventists, and the United Jewish Reformed Congregation – who soldiered on without state aid. Even my own Church, the Wesleyan, handed over their two hundred thousand African students to

the government. If all the other Churches had followed the example of those who resisted, the government would have been confronted with a stalemate
that might have forced a compromise. Instead, the
state marched over us.

The transfer of control to the Native Affairs Department was set to take place on 1 April 1955, and the
ANC began to discuss plans for a school boycott that
would begin on that date. Our secret discussions in the
Executive turned on whether we should call on the
people to stage a protest for a limited period or
whether we should proclaim a permanent school boycott to destroy the Bantu Education Act before it could
take root. The discussions were fierce, and both sides
had forceful advocates. The argument for an indefinite
boycott was that Bantu Education was a poison one
could not drink even at the point of death from thirst.
To accept it in any form would cause irreparable
damage. They argued that the country was in an
explosive mood and the people were hungry for something more spectacular than a mere protest.

   Although I had the reputation of being a firebrand, I
always felt that the organization should never promise
to do more than it was able, for the people would then
lose confidence in it. I took the stance that our actions
should be based not on idealistic considerations but on
practical ones. An indefinite boycott would require
massive machinery and vast resources that we did
not possess, and our past campaigns showed no indica-
tion that we were capable of such an undertaking. It
was simply impossible for us to create our own schools
fast enough to accommodate hundreds of thousands of

pupils, and if we did not offer our people an alternative, we were offering next to nothing. Along with others, I urged a week's boycott.

The National Executive resolved that a week-long school boycott should begin on 1 April. This was recommended at the annual conference in Durban in December 1954, but the delegates rejected the recommendation and voted for an indefinite boycott. The conference was the supreme authority, even greater than the Executive, and we found ourselves saddled with a boycott that would be almost impossible to effect. Dr Verwoerd announced that the government would permanently close all schools that were boycotted and that children who stayed away would not be readmitted.

For this boycott to work, the parents and the community would have to step in and take the place of the schools. I spoke to parents and ANC members and told them that every home, every shack, every community structure, must become a centre of learning for our children.

The boycott began on 1 April and had mixed results. It was often sporadic, disorganized and ineffectual. On the east Rand it affected some seven thousand school-children. Pre-dawn marches called on parents to keep their children at home. Women picketed the schools and plucked out children who had wandered into them.

In Germiston, a township southeast of the city, Joshua Makue, chairman of our local branch, ran a school for eight hundred boycotting children that lasted for three years. In Port Elizabeth, Barrett Tyesi gave up a government teaching post and ran a school for boycotting children. In 1956, he presented seventy of these children for the Standard VI exams; all but three passed. In many places, improvised schools (described as 'cultural clubs' in order not to attract the attention of the authorities) taught boycotting students. The government subsequently passed a law that made it an offence punishable by fine or imprisonment to offer unauthorized education. Police harassed these clubs, but many continued to exist underground. In the end, the community schools withered away and parents, faced with a choice between inferior education and no education at all, chose the former. My own children were at the Seventh Day Adventist school, which was private and did not depend on government subsidies.

The campaign should be judged on two levels: whether the immediate objective was achieved, and whether it politicized more people and drew them into the struggle. On the first level, the campaign clearly failed. We did not close down African schools throughout the country, neither did we rid ourselves of the Bantu Education Act. But the government was sufficiently rattled by our protest to modify the act, and at one point Verwoerd was compelled to declare that education should be the same for all. The government's November 1954 draft syllabus was a retreat from the original notion of modelling the school system on tribal foundations. In the end we had no option but to choose between the lesser of two evils, and agree to a diminished education. But the consequences of Bantu Education came back to haunt the government in unforeseen ways. For it was Bantu

Education that produced in the 1970s the angriest, most rebellious generation of black youth the country had ever seen. When these children of Bantu Education entered their late teens and early twenties, they rose with a vehemence.

Several months after Chief Luthuli was elected president of the ANC, Professor Z.K. Matthews returned to South Africa after a year as a visiting professor in the US, armed with an idea that would reshape the liberation struggle. In a speech at the ANC annual conference in the Cape, he said: 'I wonder whether the time has not come for the African National Congress to consider the question of convening a national convention, a congress of the people, representing all the people of this country irrespective of race or colour, to draw up a Freedom Charter for the democratic South Africa of the future.'

Within months the ANC national conference accepted the proposal, and a Council of the Congress of the People was created, with Chief Luthuli as chairman and Walter Sisulu and Yusuf Cachalia as joint secretaries. The Congress of the People was to create a set of principles for the foundation of a new South Africa. Suggestions for a new constitution were to come from the people themselves, and ANC leaders all across the country were authorized to seek ideas in writing from everyone in their area. The charter would be a document born of the people.

The Congress of the People represented one of the two main currents of thought operating within the organization. It seemed inevitable that the government would ban the ANC, and many argued that the organization must be prepared to operate underground and illegally. At the same time, we did not want to give up the important public policies and activities that brought the ANC attention and mass support. The Congress of the People would be a public display of strength.

Our dream for the Congress of the People was that it would be a landmark event in the history of the freedom struggle – a convention uniting all the oppressed and all the progressive forces of South Africa to create a clarion call for change. Our hope was that it would one day be looked upon with the same reverence as the founding convention of the ANC in 1912.

We sought to attract the widest possible sponsorship and invited some two hundred organizations – white, black, Indian and Coloured – to send representatives to a planning conference at Tongaat, near Durban, in March 1954. The National Action Council created there was composed of eight members from each of the four sponsoring organizations. The chairman was Chief Luthuli, and the secretariat consisted of Walter Sisulu (later replaced by Oliver after Walter's banning forced him to resign), Yusuf Cachalia of the SAIC, Stanley Lollan of the South African Coloured People's Organization (SACPO) and Lionel Bernstein of the Congress of Democrats (COD).

Formed in Cape Town in September 1953 by Coloured leaders and trade unionists, SACPO was the belated offspring of the struggle to preserve the Coloured vote in the Cape and it sought to represent Coloured interests. SACPO's founding conference was addressed by Oliver Tambo and Yusuf Cachalia. Inspired by the Defiance Campaign, the COD was formed in late 1952 as a party for radical, left-wing, anti-government whites. The COD, though small and limited mainly to Johannesburg and Cape Town, had an influence disproportionate to its numbers. Its members, such as Michael Harmel, Bram Fischer and Rusty Bernstein, were eloquent advocates of our cause. The COD closely identified itself with the ANC and the SAIC and advocated a universal franchise and full equality between black and white. We saw the COD as a means whereby our views could be put directly to the white public. The COD served an important symbolic function for Africans; blacks who had come into the struggle because they were anti-white discovered that there were indeed whites of goodwill who treated Africans as equals.

The National Action Council invited all participating organizations and their followers to send suggestions for a freedom charter. Circulars were sent out to townships and villages all across the country. 'IF YOU COULD MAKE THE LAWS . . . WHAT WOULD YOU DO?' they said. 'HOW WOULD YOU SET ABOUT MAKING SOUTH AFRICA A HAPPY PLACE FOR ALL THE PEOPLE WHO LIVE IN IT?' Some of the flyers and leaflets were filled with the poetic idealism that characterized the planning:

WE CALL THE PEOPLE OF SOUTH AFRICA BLACK AND WHITE – LET US SPEAK TOGETHER OF FREEDOM! – LET THE VOICES OF ALL THE PEOPLE BE HEARD. AND LET THE DEMANDS OF ALL THE PEOPLE FOR THE THINGS THAT WILL MAKE US FREE BE RECORDED. LET THE DEMANDS BE

GATHERED TOGETHER IN A GREAT CHAR-
TER OF FREEDOM.

The call caught the imagination of the people. Suggestions came in from sports and cultural clubs, church
groups, ratepayers' associations, women's organizations, schools, trade union branches. They came on
serviettes, on paper torn from exercise books, on scraps
of foolscap, on the backs of our own leaflets. It was
humbling to see how the suggestions of ordinary people were often far ahead of those of the leaders. The
most commonly cited demand was for one-man-one-
vote. There was a recognition that the country belongs
to all those who have made it their home.

The ANC branches contributed a great deal to the
process of writing the charter and in fact the two best
drafts came from Durban and Pietermaritzburg. A
combination of these drafts was then circulated to
different regions and committees for comments and
questions. The charter itself was drafted by a small
committee of the National Action Council and reviewed by the ANC's National Executive.

The charter would be presented at the Congress of
the People and each of its elements submitted to the
delegates for approval. In June, a few days before the
Congress was scheduled, a small group of us reviewed
the draft. We made few changes, as there was little time
and the document was already in good shape.

The Congress of the People took place at Kliptown, a
multiracial village on a scrap of veld a few miles southwest of Johannesburg, on two clear, sunny days, 25 and
26 June 1955. More than three thousand delegates

braved police intimidation to assemble and approve the final document. They came by car, bus, truck and foot. Although the overwhelming number of delegates were black, there were more than three hundred Indians, two hundred Coloureds and one hundred whites.

I drove to Kliptown with Walter. We were both under banning orders, so we found a place at the edge of the crowd where we could observe without mixing in or being seen. The crowd was impressive both in size and in its discipline. 'Freedom volunteers' wearing black, green and yellow armbands met the delegates and arranged for their seating. There were old women and young wearing Congress skirts, Congress blouses, Congress *doekies* (scarves); old men and young wearing Congress armbands and Congress hats. Signs everywhere said, 'FREEDOM IN OUR LIFETIME, LONG LIVE THE STRUGGLE'. The platform was a rainbow of colours: white delegates from the COD, Indians from the SAIC, Coloured representatives from SACPO all sat in front of a replica of a four-spoked wheel representing the four organizations in the Congress Alliance. White and African police and members of the Special Branch milled around, taking photographs, writing in notebooks and trying unsuccessfully to intimidate the delegates.

There were dozens of songs and speeches. Meals were served. The atmosphere was both serious and festive. On the afternoon of the first day, the charter was read aloud, section by section, to the people in English, Sesotho and Xhosa. After each section, the crowd shouted its approval with cries of '*Afrika!*' and '*Mayibuye!*' The first day of the Congress was a success.

The second day was much like the first. Each section of the charter had been adopted by acclamation, and at 3.30 the final approval was to be voted when a brigade of police and Special Branch detectives brandishing sten guns swarmed on to the platform. In a gruff Afrikaans-accented voice, one of the police took the microphone and announced that treason was suspected and that no one was to leave the gathering without police permission. The police began pushing people off the platform and confiscating documents and photographs, even signs such as 'SOUP WITH MEAT' and 'SOUP WITHOUT MEAT'. Another group of constables armed with rifles formed a cordon round the crowd. The people responded magnificently by loudly singing '*Nkosi Sikelel' iAfrika*'. The delegates were then allowed to leave one by one, each person interviewed by the police and his or her name taken down. I had been on the outskirts of the crowd when the police raid began, and while my instinct was to stay and help, discretion seemed the wiser course, because I would have immediately been arrested and tossed into jail. An emergency meeting had been called in Johannesburg, and I made my way back there. As I returned to Johannesburg, I knew that this raid signalled a harsh new turn on the part of the government.

Though the Congress of the People had been broken up, the charter itself became a great beacon for the liberation struggle. Like other enduring political documents, such as the American Declaration of Independence, the French Declaration of the Rights of Man and the Communist Manifesto, the Freedom Charter is a mixture of practical goals and poetic language. It extols the abolition of racial discrimination and the achievement of equal rights for all. It welcomes all who embrace freedom to participate in the making of a democratic, non-racial South Africa. It captured the hopes and dreams of the people and acted as a blueprint for the liberation struggle and the future of the nation. The preamble reads:

We, the people of South Africa, declare for all our country and the world to know: –

That South Africa belongs to all who live in it, black and white, and that no government can justly claim authority unless it is based on the will of the people;

That our people have been robbed of their birthright to land, liberty and peace by a form of government founded on injustice and inequality;

That our country will never be prosperous or free until all our people live in brotherhood, enjoying equal rights and opportunities;

That only a democratic state, based on the will of the people, can secure to all their birthright without distinction of colour, race, sex or belief;

And therefore, we, the people of South Africa, black and white, together – equals, countrymen and brothers – adopt this FREEDOM CHARTER. And we pledge ourselves to strive together, sparing nothing of our strength and courage, until the democratic changes here set out have been won.

The charter then lays out the requirements for a free and democratic South Africa.

THE PEOPLE SHALL GOVERN!

Every man and woman shall have the right to vote for and stand as a candidate for all bodies which make laws;

All the people shall be entitled to take part in the administration of the country;

The rights of the people shall be the same regardless of race, colour or sex;

All bodies of minority rule, advisory boards, councils and authorities shall be replaced by democratic organs of self-government.

ALL NATIONAL GROUPS SHALL HAVE EQUAL RIGHTS!

There shall be equal status in the bodies of state, in the courts and in the schools for all national groups and races;

All national groups shall be protected by law against insults to their race and national pride;

All people shall have equal rights to use their own language and to develop their own folk culture and customs;

The preaching and practice of national, race or colour discrimination and contempt shall be a punishable crime;

All apartheid laws and practices shall be set aside.

THE PEOPLE SHALL SHARE IN THE COUNTRY'S WEALTH!

The national wealth of our country, the heritage of all South Africans, shall be restored to the people;

The mineral wealth beneath the soil, the banks and monopoly industry shall be transferred to the ownership of the people as a whole;

All other industries and trade shall be controlled to assist the well-being of the people;

All people shall have equal rights to trade where they choose, to manufacture and to enter all trades, crafts and professions.

THE LAND SHALL BE SHARED AMONG THOSE WHO WORK IT!

Restriction of land ownership on racial basis shall be ended, and all the land re-divided amongst those who work it, to banish famine and land hunger . . .

Some in the ANC, particularly the Africanist contingent who were anti-communist and anti-white, objected to the charter as being a design for a radically different South Africa from the one the ANC had called for throughout its history. They claimed the charter favoured a socialist order and believed the COD and white communists had had a disproportionate influence on its ideology. In June 1956, in the monthly journal *Liberation*, I pointed out that the charter endorsed private enterprise and would allow capitalism to flourish among Africans for the first time. The charter guaranteed that when freedom came, Africans would have the opportunity to own their own businesses in their own names, to own their own houses and property; in short, to prosper as capitalists and entrepreneurs. The charter does not speak about the eradication of classes and private property, or public ownership of the means of production, or promulgate any of the tenets of scientific socialism. The clause discussing the possible nationalization of the mines, the banks and monopoly industries was an action that needed to be taken if the economy was not to be solely owned and operated by white businessmen.

The charter was in fact a revolutionary document precisely because the changes it envisioned could not be achieved without radically altering the economic and political structure of South Africa. It was not meant to be capitalist or socialist but a melding together of the people's demands to end the oppression. In South Africa, merely to achieve fairness, one had to destroy apartheid itself, for it was the very embodiment of injustice.

21

In early September 1955, my bans expired. I had last had a holiday in 1948 when I was an untested light-weight in the ANC with few responsibilities beyond attending meetings of the Transvaal executive and addressing the odd public gathering. Now, at the age of thirty-eight, I had reached the light heavyweight division and carried more pounds and more respon-sibility. I had been confined to Johannesburg for two years, chained to my legal and political work, and had neglected Mandela family affairs in the Transkei. I was keen to visit the countryside again, to be in the open veld and rolling valleys of my childhood. I was anxious to see my family and confer with Sabata and Daliwonga on certain problems involving the Transkei, while the ANC was eager that I confer with them on political matters. I was to have a working holiday, the only kind of holiday I knew how to take.

The night before I left, a number of friends gathered at my home to see me off. Duma Nokwe, the young and good-natured barrister who was then national secretary of the Youth League, was among them. Duma had accompanied Walter on his trip to the Youth Festival in Bucharest, and that night he entertained us with the Russian and Chinese songs he had learned on his trip. At midnight, as my guests were getting ready to leave, my daughter Makaziwe, then two, woke up and asked if she could come along with me. I had been spending insufficient time with my family, and Makaziwe's request provoked pangs of guilt. Suddenly my enthusiasm for my trip vanished. But I carried her back to bed and kissed her good night and, as she dropped off to sleep, I made my final preparations for my journey.

I was embarking on a fact-finding mission, which I would combine with the pleasures of seeing the countryside and old friends and comrades. I had been isolated from developments in other parts of the country and was eager to see for myself what was transpiring in the hinterlands. Although I read a variety of newspapers from around the country, newspapers are only a poor shadow of reality; their information is important to a freedom fighter not because it reveals the truth, but because it discloses the biases and perceptions of both those who produce the paper and those who read it. On this trip I wanted to talk first hand with our people in the field.

I left shortly after midnight and within an hour I was on the highway to Durban. The roads were empty and I was accompanied only by the stars and gentle Transvaal breezes. Though I had not slept, I felt lighthearted and fresh. At daybreak I crossed from Volksrust to Natal, the country of Cetywayo, the last independent king of the Zulus, whose troops had defeated a British column at Isandhlwana in 1879. But the king was unable to withstand the firepower of the British and eventually surrendered his kingdom. Shortly after crossing the river on the Natal border I saw the Majuba Hills, the steep escarpment where a small Boer commando ambushed and defeated a garrison of British redcoats less than two years after the defeat of Cetywayo. At Majuba Hill the Afrikaner had stoutly defended his independence against British imperialism and struck a blow for nationalism. Now the descendants of those same freedom fighters were persecuting my people who were struggling for precisely the same thing the Afrikaners had once fought and died for. I drove through those historic hills, thinking less of the ironies of history by which the oppressed becomes the oppressor than of how the ruthless Afrikaners deserved their own Majuba Hill at the hands of my people.

This harsh reverie was interrupted by the happy music of Radio Bantu on my car radio. While I despised the conservative politics of Radio Bantu served up by the government-run South African Broadcasting Corporation, I revelled in its music. (In South Africa, African artists made the music, but white record companies made the money.) I was listening to a popular programme called 'Rediffusion Service', which featured most of the country's leading African singers: Miriam Makeba, Dolly Rathebe, Dorothy Masuku, Thoko Shukuma and the smooth sound of the Manhattan Brothers. I enjoy all types of music, but the music of my own flesh and blood goes right to my heart. The curious beauty of African music is that it uplifts even as it tells a sad tale. You may be poor, you may have only a ramshackle house, you may have lost your job, but that song gives you hope. African music is often about the aspirations of the African people, and it can ignite the political resolve of those who might otherwise be indifferent to politics. One merely has to witness the infectious singing at African rallies. Politics can be strengthened by music, but music has a potency that defies politics.

I made a number of stops in Natal, secretly meeting

ANC leaders. Nearing Durban, I took the opportunity of stopping in Pietermaritzburg, where I spent the entire night with Dr Chota Motala, Moses Mabhida and others, reviewing the political situation in the country. I then travelled on to Groutville, spending the day with Chief Luthuli. Although he had been confined by banning orders for more than a year, the chief was well informed about ANC activities. He was uneasy about what he saw as the increasing centralization of the ANC in Johannesburg and the declining power of the regions. I reassured him that we wanted the regions to remain strong.

My next stop was a meeting in Durban with Dr Naicker and the Executive Committee of the Natal Indian Congress, where I raised a sensitive issue: the National Executive believed that the Indian Congress had become inactive of late. I was reluctant to do this as Dr Naicker was my senior and a man who had suffered far more than I, but we discussed ways to overcome government restrictions.

From Durban I drove south along the coast past Port Shepstone and Port St Johns, small and lovely colonial towns that dotted the shimmering beaches fronting the Indian Ocean. While mesmerized by the beauty of the area, I was constantly rebuked by the buildings and streets that bear the names of white imperialists who suppressed the very people whose names belonged there. At this point, I turned inland and drove to Umzumkulu to meet with Dr Conco, the treasurer-general of the ANC, for further discussions and consultations.

With excitement mounting, I then set off for Umtata. When I turned into York Road, the main street of

Umtata, I felt the rush of familiarity and fond memories one gets from coming home after a long exile. I had been away for thirteen years, and while there were no banners and fatted calves to greet this prodigal son upon his return, I was tremendously excited to see my mother, my humble home and the friends of my youth. But my trip to the Transkei had a second motive: my arrival coincided with the meeting of a special committee appointed to oversee the transition of the Transkeian Bungha system to that of the Bantu Authorities.

The role of the Bungha, which consisted of 108 members, one-quarter of whom were white and three-quarters African, was to advise the government on legislation affecting Africans in the area and to regulate local matters like taxes and roads. While the Bungha was the most influential political body in the Transkei, its resolutions were advisory and its decisions subject to review by white magistrates. The Bungha was only as powerful as whites permitted it to be. Yet the Bantu Authorities Act would replace it with an even more repressive system: a feudalistic order resting on hereditary and tribal distinctions as decided by the state. The government suggested that Bantu Authorities would free the people from the control of white magistrates, but this was a smokescreen for the state's undermining of democracy and promotion of tribal rivalries. The ANC regarded any acceptance of Bantu Authorities as a capitulation to the government.

On the night of my arrival, I briefly met a number of Transkeian councillors and my nephew, K.D. Matanzima, whom I called Daliwonga. Daliwonga was playing a leading part in persuading the Bungha to accept

Bantu Authorities, for the new order would reinforce and even increase his power as the chief of Emigrant Thembuland. Daliwonga and I were on separate sides of this difficult issue. We had grown apart: he had opted for a traditional leadership role and was cooperating with the system. But it was late and, rather than begin a lengthy discussion, we resolved to meet the following day.

I spent that night in a boarding-house in town, rose early, and was joined for coffee in my room by two local chiefs to discuss their role in the new Bantu Authorities. In the middle of our conversation the owner of the boarding-house nervously ushered a white man into my room. 'Are you Nelson Mandela?' he demanded.

'And who is asking?' I said.

He gave his name and rank as a detective sergeant in the security police.

'May I see your warrant, please?' I asked. It was obvious that the sergeant resented my audacity, but he grudgingly produced an official document. Yes, I was Nelson Mandela, I told him. He informed me that the commanding officer wanted to see me. I replied that if he wanted to see me, he knew where I was. He then ordered me to accompany him to the police station. I asked him whether I was under arrest, and he replied that I was not.

'In that case,' I said, 'I am not going.' He was taken aback by my refusal but knew I was on firm legal ground. He proceeded to fire a succession of questions at me: when had I left Johannesburg? Where had I visited? Whom had I spoken with? Did I have a permit to enter the Transkei and how long would I be staying?

I informed him that the Transkei was my home and that I did not need a permit to enter it. The sergeant stomped out of the room.

The chiefs were taken aback by my behaviour and upbraided me for my rudeness. I explained that I had merely treated him in the manner that he had treated me. The chiefs were unconvinced, and clearly thought I was a hotheaded young man who would get himself into trouble. These were men I was trying to persuade to reject Bantu Authorities, and it was apparent that I had not made a very good impression. The incident reminded me that I had returned to my homeland a different man from the one who had left thirteen years before.

The police were unsophisticated in the Transkei, and from the moment I left the boarding-house, they followed me everywhere I went. After I talked to anyone, the police would confront the person and say, 'If you talk with Mandela, we will come and arrest you.'

I met briefly with a local ANC leader and was dismayed to learn of the organization's lack of funds, but at that moment I was thinking less about the organization than my next stop: Qunu, the village where I was brought up and where my mother still lived.

I roused my mother, who at first looked as though she was seeing a ghost. But she was overjoyed. I had brought some food – fruit, meat, sugar, salt and a chicken – and my mother lit the stove to make tea. We did not hug or kiss; that was not our custom. Although I was happy to be back, I felt a sense of guilt at the sight of her living all alone in such poor circumstances. I tried to persuade her to come to live with me in Johannesburg, but she swore that she would not leave the countryside she loved. I wondered – not for the first time – whether one was ever justified in neglecting the welfare of one's own family in order to fight for the welfare of others. Can there be anything more important than looking after one's ageing mother? Is politics merely a pretext for shirking one's responsibilities, an excuse for not being able to provide in the way one wanted?

After an hour or so with my mother, I left to spend the night at Mqhekezweni. It was night when I arrived, and in my enthusiasm I started to blow the horn of my car. I had not considered how this noise might be interpreted, and people emerged fearfully from their huts, thinking it might be the police. But when I was recognized, I was met with surprise and joy by a number of villagers.

But instead of sleeping like a child in my old bed, I tossed and turned that night, again wondering whether or not I had taken the right path. I did not doubt that I had chosen correctly. I do not mean to suggest that the freedom struggle is of a higher moral order than taking care of one's family. It is not; they are merely different.

Returning to Qunu the next morning, I spent the day reminiscing with people, and walking in the fields around the village. I also visited my sister Mabel, the most practical and easygoing of my sisters and of whom I was very fond. Mabel was married, but her union involved an interesting tale. My sister Baliwe, who was older than Mabel, had been engaged to be married, and *lobola* had already been paid. But two weeks before the wedding, Baliwa, who was a spirited girl, ran away. We could not return the cattle as they had already been accepted, so the family decided that Mabel would take Baliwe's place, and she did so.

I left late that afternoon to drive to Mqhekezweni. Again I arrived at night and announced my presence with loud hooting, only this time people emerged from their homes with the idea that Justice, their chief, had returned. Justice had been deposed from his chieftaincy by the government and was then living in Durban. Though the government had appointed someone in his stead, a chief is a chief by virtue of his birth and wields authority because of his blood. They were happy to see me, but they would have been happier still to welcome Justice home.

My second mother, No-England, the widow of the regent, had been fast asleep when I arrived, but when she appeared in her nightdress and saw me, she became so excited that she insisted I drive her immediately to a nearby relative to celebrate. She hopped into my car and we set off on a wild ride through the untamed veld to get to the remote rondavel of her relative. There we woke up another family, and I finally went to sleep, tired and happy, just before dawn.

Over the next fortnight I moved back and forth between Qunu and Mqhekezweni, staying by turns with my mother and No-England, visiting and receiving friends and relatives. I ate the same foods I had eaten as a boy, I walked the same fields and gazed at the same sky during the day, the same stars at night. It is important for a freedom fighter to remain in touch with his own roots, and the hurly-burly of city life has a way of erasing the past. The visit restored me and revived my feelings for the place in which I grew up. I was once again my mother's son in her house; I was once again the regent's charge in the Great Place.

The visit was also a way of measuring the distance I

had come. I saw how my own people had remained in one place, while I had moved on and seen new worlds and gained new ideas. If I had not realized it before, I knew that I was right not to have returned to the Transkei after Fort Hare. If I had returned, my political evolution would have been stunted.

When the Special Committee considering the introduction of the Bantu Authorities had adjourned, Daliwonga and I went to visit Sabata in hospital in Umtata. I had hoped to talk with Sabata about the Bantu Authorities, but his health made it impossible. I wanted Sabata and his brother, Daliwonga, to begin talks on this issue as soon as Sabata was well enough, and made this clear. I felt proud to be organizing a meeting between the descendants of Ngubengcuka, and mused for a moment on the irony that I was finally fulfilling the role of counsellor to Sabata for which I'd been groomed so many years before.

From Umtata, Daliwonga and I drove to Qamata, where we met his younger brother George, who was then a practising attorney. His two articled clerks were well known to me and I was pleased to see them both: A.P. Mda and Tsepo Letlaka. Both were still firm supporters of the organization who had given up teaching and decided to become lawyers. In Qamata, we all sat down to examine the issue of the proposed Bantu Authorities.

My mission was to persuade Daliwonga – a man destined to play a leading role in the politics of the Transkei – to oppose the imposition of the Bantu Authorities. I did not want our meeting to be a show-down, or even a debate; I did not want any grand-standing or fault-finding, but a serious discussion among men who all had the best interests of their people and their nation at heart.

In many ways, Daliwonga still regarded me as his junior, both in terms of my rank in the Thembu hierarchy and in my own political development. While I was his junior in the former realm, I believed I had advanced beyond my one-time mentor in my political views. Whereas his concerns focused on his own tribe, I had become involved with those who thought in terms of the entire nation. I did not want to complicate the discussion by introducing grand political theories; I would rely on common sense and the facts of our history. Before we began, Daliwonga invited Mda, Letlaka and his brother George, to participate, but they demurred, preferring to listen to the two of us. 'Let the nephew and the uncle conduct the debate,' Mda said as a sign of respect. Etiquette dictated that I would make my case first and Daliwonga would not interrupt; then he would answer while I listened.

In the first place, I said, the Bantu Authorities were impractical because more and more Africans were moving out of the rural homelands to the cities. The government's policy was to try to put Africans into ethnic enclaves because they feared the power of African unity. The people, I said, wanted democracy, and political leadership based on merit not birth. The Bantu Authorities was a retreat from democracy.

Daliwonga's response was that he was trying to re-store the status of his royal house that had been crushed by the British. He stressed the importance and vitality of the tribal system and traditional leader-ship, and did not want to reject a system that enshrined those things. He, too, wanted a free South Africa but he thought that goal could be achieved faster and more peacefully through the government's policy of separate development. The ANC, he said, would bring about bloodshed and bitterness. He ended by saying that he was startled and disturbed to learn that in spite of my own position in the Thembu royal house I did not support the principle of traditional leadership.

When Daliwonga finished, I replied that while I understood his personal position as a chief quite well, I believed that his own interests were in conflict with those of the community. I said that if I were in a similar position to his, I would try to subordinate my own interests to those of the people. I immediately regretted that last point because I have discovered that in discussions it never helps to take a morally superior tone to one's opponent. I noticed that Daliwonga stiffened when I made this remark and I quickly shifted the discussion to more general issues.

We talked the whole night, but came no closer to each other's position. As the sun was rising, we parted. We had embarked on different roads that put us in conflict with one another. This grieved me, because few men had inspired me as Daliwonga had, and nothing would have given me greater joy than to fight beside him. But it was not to be. On family issues, we remained friends; politically, we were in opposite and antagonistic camps.

I returned to Qunu that morning and spent another few days there. I tramped across the veld to visit friends and relatives, but the magic world of my childhood had fled. One evening I bade my mother and sister farewell. I visited Sabata in hospital to wish him a speedy recovery, and by 3 a.m. I was on my way to Cape Town.

The bright moonlight and crisp breeze kept me fresh all the way across the Kei River. The road winds up the rugged mountains and as the sun rose my mood lifted. I had last been on that road eighteen years before, when Jongintaba had driven me to Healdtown.

I was driving slowly when I noticed a limping man at the side of the road raising his hand to me. I instinctively pulled over and offered him a ride. He was about my own age, of small stature and rather unkempt; he had not bathed in quite a while. He told me that his car had broken down on the other side of Umtata and he had been walking for several days towards Port Elizabeth. I noticed a number of inconsistencies in his story, and I asked him the make of his car. A Buick, he replied. And the registration? I said. He told me a number. A few minutes later, I said, 'What did you say that registration number was?' He told me a slightly different figure. I suspected he was a policeman, and decided to say very little.

My reserve went unnoticed by my companion as he talked the entire way to Port Elizabeth. He pointed out various curiosities and was well versed in the history of the region. He never asked who I was and I did not tell him. But he was entertaining, and I found his conversation useful and interesting.

I made a stop in East London and spoke to a few ANC people. Before leaving I had a conversation with some other people, in the township, one of whom struck me as a possible undercover policeman. My companion had learned my identity, and a few minutes after we were back in the car, he said to me, 'You know, Mandela, I suspected that one chap at the end was a policeman.' This raised my own suspicions, and I said to my companion, 'Look here, how do I know you're not a policeman yourself? You must tell me who you are – otherwise I will dump you back on the road again.'

He protested and said, 'No, I will introduce myself properly.' He confessed that he was a smuggler and had been carrying *dagga* (marijuana) from the Pondoland coast when he ran into a police roadblock. When he saw it, he jumped out of the car and tried to make a run for it. The police fired, wounding him in the leg. That explained his limp and his lack of transportation. He waved me down because he assumed the police were hunting him.

I asked him why he had chosen such a dangerous livelihood. He had originally wanted to be a teacher, he told me, but his parents were too poor to send him to college. After school he had worked in a factory, but the wages were too meagre for him to live on his own. He started to supplement them by smuggling *dagga*, and soon found it so profitable that he left the factory altogether. He said that in any other country in the world he would have found an opportunity for his talents. 'I saw white men who were my inferiors in ability and brains earning fifty times what I was.' After a long pause, he announced in a solemn tone, 'I am also a member of the ANC.' He told me that he had defied during the 1952 Defiance Campaign and had served on various local committees in Port Elizabeth. I quizzed him on various personalities, all of whom he seemed to know, and later in Port Elizabeth I confirmed that he had told me the truth. In fact, he had been one of the most reliable of those who went to jail during the Defiance Campaign. The doors of the liberation struggle are open to all who choose to walk through them.

As an attorney with a fairly large criminal practice, I was conversant with such tales. Over and over again, I saw men as bright and talented as my companion resort to crime in order to make ends meet. While I do think certain individuals are disposed to crime because of their genetic inheritance or an abusive upbringing, I am convinced that apartheid turned many otherwise law-abiding citizens into criminals. It stands to reason that an immoral and unjust legal system would breed contempt for its laws and regulations.

We reached Port Elizabeth at sunset, and Joe Matthews, Z.K. Matthews's son, arranged accommodation. The next morning I met Raymond Mhlaba, Frances Baard, and Govan Mbeki, whom I was encountering for the first time. I knew his work, for as a student I had read his booklet *The Transkei in the Making*. He had been running a cooperative store in the Transkei which he was soon to give up to become an editor of the weekly *New Age*. Govan was serious, thoughtful and soft-spoken, equally at home in the world of scholarship and the world of political activism. He had been deeply involved in the planning of the Congress of the People and was destined for the highest levels of leadership in the organization.

I departed in the late morning for Cape Town, with only my radio for company. I had never before driven on roads between Port Elizabeth and Cape Town, and I was looking forward to many miles of entrancing scenery. It was hot, and the road was bordered by dense vegetation on either side. I had hardly left the city when I ran over a large snake slithering across the road. I am not superstitious and do not believe in omens, but the death of the snake did not please me. I do not like killing any living thing, even those creatures that fill some people with dread.

Once I had passed Humansdorp, the forests became denser and for the first time in my life I saw wild elephants and baboons. A large baboon crossed the road in front of me, and I stopped the car. He stood and stared at me as intently as if he were a Special Branch detective. It was ironic that I, an African, was seeing the Africa of storybooks and legend for the first time. Such a beautiful land, I thought, and all of it out of reach, owned by whites and untouchable for a black man. I could no more choose to live in such beauty than run for Parliament.

Seditious thoughts accompany a freedom fighter wherever he goes. At the town of Knysna, more than a hundred miles west of Port Elizabeth, I stopped to survey the surroundings. The road above the town affords a panoramic view as far as the eye can see. In every direction, I saw sprawling, dense forests and I dwelt not on the greenery but the fact that there were many places a guerrilla army could live and train undetected.

I arrived in Cape Town at midnight for what turned out to be a two-week stay. I stayed at the home of the Reverend Walter Teka, a leader in the Methodist Church, but I spent most of my days with Johnson Ngwevela and Greenwood Ngotyana. Ngwevela was chairman of the western Cape region of the ANC and Ngotyana a member of its executive. Both were communists as well as leading members of the Wesleyan Church. I travelled every day to meet ANC officials in places like Worcester, Paarl, Stellenbosch, Simonstown and Hermanus. I planned to work each day of my stay, and when I asked what had been arranged for Sunday – a working day for me in the Transvaal – they informed me that the sabbath was reserved for churchgoing. I protested, but to no avail. Communism and Christianity, at least in Africa, were not mutually exclusive.

While I was walking in the city one day, I noticed a white woman in the gutter gnawing on some fish bones. She was poor and apparently homeless, but she was young and not unattractive. I knew of course that there were poor whites, whites who were every bit as poor as Africans, but one rarely saw them. I was used to seeing black beggars on the street, and it startled me to see a white one. While I normally did not give to African beggars, I felt the urge to give this woman money. In that moment I realized the tricks that apartheid plays on one, for the everyday travails that afflict Africans are accepted as a matter of course, while my heart immediately went out to this bedraggled white woman. In South Africa, to be poor and black was normal, to be poor and white was a tragedy.

As I was preparing to leave Cape Town, I went to the offices of *New Age* to see some old friends and discuss their editorial policy. *New Age*, the successor to earlier banned left-wing publications, was a friend of the ANC. It was early in the morning of 27 September, and as I walked up the steps I could hear angry voices inside the office and furniture being moved. I recognized the voice of Fred Carneson, the manager of the newspaper and its guiding spirit. I also heard the gruff voices of the security police, who were in the process of searching the offices. I quietly left, and later discovered that this had not been an isolated incident but part of the largest nationwide raid undertaken in South African history. Armed with warrants authorizing the seizure of anything regarded as evidence of high treason, sedition or violations of the Suppression of Communism Act, the police searched more than five hundred people in their homes and offices around the country. My office in Johannesburg was searched, as well as the homes of Dr Moroka, Father Huddleston and Professor Matthews.

The raid cast a shadow over my last day in Cape Town, for it signalled the first move in the state's new and even more repressive strategy. At the very least, a new round of bannings would take place, and I was certain to be among them. That evening, Reverend Teka and his wife asked a number of people over to bid me farewell, and led by him, we knelt in prayer for the well-being of those whose homes had been raided. I left the house at my favoured departure time of 3 a.m., and within half an hour I was on the road to Kimberley, the rough-and-ready mining town where the South African diamond business had begun in the last century.

I was to stay at the home of Dr Arthur Letele for one night. Later to become the treasurer-general of the ANC, Arthur was a scrupulous medical practitioner. I had a cold, and when he greeted me on my arrival, he confined me to bed. He was a brave and dedicated man, and had led a small group of defiers to jail during the Defiance Campaign. This was a risky action for a doctor in a town where political action by blacks was rare. In Johannesburg, one has the support of hundreds and even thousands of others who are engaging in the same dangerous activities, but in a conservative place like Kimberley, with no liberal press or judiciary to oversee the police, such an action requires true valour. It was in Kimberley during the Defiance Campaign that one of the ANC's leading members was sentenced to lashes by the local magistrate.

Despite my cold, Arthur allowed me to address an ANC meeting in his house the following evening. I was preparing to leave the next morning at three, but Arthur and his wife insisted I remain for breakfast, which I did. I made good time on the way back to Johannesburg and arrived home just before supper, where I was met with excited cries from my children, who well knew that I was a father bearing gifts. One by one, I handed out the presents I had purchased in Cape Town and patiently answered the questions my children had for me about the trip. Though not a true holiday, it had the same effect: I felt rejuvenated and ready to take up the fight once more.

22

Immediately upon my return I reported on my trip to the Working Committee of the ANC. Their principal concern was whether or not the Congress Alliance was strong enough to halt the government's plans. I did not give them good news. I said the Transkei was not a well-organized ANC area and the power of the security police would soon immobilize what little influence the ANC had.

I put forth an alternative that I knew would be unpopular. Why shouldn't the ANC participate in the new Bantu Authority structures as a means of remaining in touch with the masses of the people? In time, such participation would become a platform for our own ideas and policies.

Any suggestion of participating in apartheid structures in any way was automatically met with angry opposition. In my early days, I, too, would have strenuously objected. But my sense of the country was that relatively few people were ready to make sacrifices to join the struggle. We should meet the people on their own terms, even if that meant appearing to collaborate. My idea was that our movement should be a great tent that included as many people as possible.

At the time, however, my report was given short shrift because of another related report with greater ramifications. The publication of the report of the Tomlinson Commission for the Socio-Economic Development of the Bantu Areas had set off a nationwide debate. The government-created commission proposed a plan for the development of the so-called Bantu Areas or Bantustans. The result was in fact a blueprint for 'separate development' or Grand Apartheid.

The Bantustan system had been conceived by Dr H.F. Verwoerd, the minister of native affairs, as a way of muting international criticism of South African racial policies but at the same time institutionalizing apartheid. The Bantustans, or reserves as they were also known, would be separate ethnic enclaves or homelands for all African citizens. Africans, Verwoerd said, 'should stand with both feet in the reserves' where they were to 'develop along their own lines'. The idea was to preserve the *status quo* where three million whites owned 87 per cent of the land, and relegate the eight million Africans to the remaining 13 per cent.

The central theme of the report was the rejection of the idea of integration between the races in favour of a policy of separate development of black and white. To that end, the report recommended the industrialization of the African areas, noting that any programme of development that did not aim to provide opportunities for Africans in their own regions was doomed to failure. The commission pointed out that the present geographical configuration of the African areas was too fragmentary, and recommended instead a consolidation of African areas into what it termed seven 'historical-logical' homelands of the principal ethnic groups.

But the creation of individual, self-contained Bantustans, as proposed by the commission, was farcical.

Transkei, the showpiece of the proposed homeland system, would be broken into three geographically separate blocks. The Swazi Bantustan, Lebowa and Venda were composed of three pieces each; Gazankule, four; the Ciskei, seventeen; Bophuthatswana, nineteen; and KwaZulu, twenty-nine. The Nationalists were creating a cruel jigsaw puzzle out of people's lives.

The government's intention in creating the homeland system was to keep the Transkei – and other African areas – as reservoirs of cheap labour for white industry. At the same time, the covert goal of the government was to create an African middle class to blunt the appeal of the ANC and the liberation struggle.

The ANC denounced the report of the Tomlinson Commission, despite some of its more liberal recommendations. As I told Daliwonga, separate development was a spurious solution to a problem that whites had no idea how to control. In the end, the government approved the report, but rejected a number of its recommendations as being too progressive.

Despite the encroaching darkness and my pessimism about the government's policies, I was thinking about the future. In February 1956 I returned to the Transkei to purchase a plot of land in Umtata. I have always thought a man should own a house near the place he was born, where he might find a restfulness that eludes him elsewhere.

With Walter, I journeyed down to the Transkei. He and I met various ANC people in both Umtata and Durban, where we went first. Once again, we were clumsily shadowed by Special Branch police. In Durban, we paid a call on our colleagues at the Natal Indian Congress in an effort to boost activism in the area.

In Umtata, with Walter's help, I made a down payment to C.K. Sakwe for a plot of land he owned in town. Sakwe was a member of the Bungha and had served on the Natives' Representative Council. While we were there he told us of an incident that had occurred the previous Saturday at Bumbhane, the Great Place of Sabata, at a meeting of government officials and chiefs about the introduction of the Bantustans. A number of the chiefs objected to the government's policy and verbally attacked the magistrate. The meeting broke up in anger; this gave us some sense of the grassroots objections to the Bantu Authorities Act.

In March 1956, after several months of relative freedom, I received my third ban, which restricted me to Johannesburg for five years and prohibited me from attending meetings for that same period. For the next sixty months I would be quarantined in the same district, seeing the same streets, the same mine dumps on the horizon, the same sky. I would have to depend on newspapers and other people for reports on what was occurring outside Johannesburg, another prospect I did not relish.

But this time my attitude towards my bans had changed radically. When I was first banned, I abided by the rules and regulations of my persecutors. I had now developed contempt for these restrictions. I was not going to let my involvement in the struggle and the scope of my political activities be determined by the enemy I was fighting against. To allow my activities to be circumscribed by my opponent was a form of defeat, and I resolved not to become my own jailer.

I soon became involved in mediating a bitter political dispute right in Johannesburg. It pitted two sides against each other, both of which were seeking my support. Each side within this particular organization had legitimate grievances and each was implacably opposed to the other. The altercation threatened to descend into an acrimonious civil war, and I did my best to prevent a rupture. I am speaking, of course, of the struggle at the boxing and weight-lifting club at the Donaldson Orlando Community Centre where I trained almost every evening.

I had joined the club in 1950, and on almost every free night I worked out at the Community Centre. For the previous few years I had taken my son Thembi with me, and by 1956, when he was ten years old, he was a keen if spindly paperweight boxer. The club was managed by Johannes (Skipper Adonis) Molotsi, and its membership consisted of both professional and amateur boxers, as well as a variety of dedicated weight-lifters. Our star boxer, Jerry (Uyinja) Moloi, later became the Transvaal lightweight champion and number one contender for the national title.

The gym was poorly equipped. We could not afford a ring and trained on a cement floor, which was particularly dangerous when a boxer was knocked down. We boasted a single punch-bag and a few pairs of boxing gloves. We had no medicine or speed balls, no proper boxing trunks or shoes, and no mouth guards. Almost no one owned head guards. Despite the lack of equipment, the gym produced such champions as Eric (Black Material) Ntsele, bantamweight champion of South Africa, and Freddie (Tomahawk)

Ngidi, the Transvaal flyweight champion, who spent his days working for me as an assistant at Mandela and Tambo. Altogether, we had perhaps twenty or thirty members.

Although I had boxed a bit at Fort Hare, it was not until I lived in Johannesburg that I took up the sport in earnest. I was never an outstanding boxer. I was in the heavyweight division, and I had neither enough power to compensate for my lack of speed nor enough speed to make up for my lack of power. I did not enjoy the violence of boxing so much as the science of it. I was intrigued by how one moved one's body to protect oneself, how one used a strategy both to attack and retreat, how one paced oneself over a match. Boxing is egalitarian. In the ring, rank, age, colour and wealth are irrelevant. When you are circling your opponent, probing his strengths and weaknesses, you are not thinking about his colour or social status. I never did any real fighting after I entered politics. My main interest was in training; I found the rigorous exercise to be an excellent outlet for tension and stress. After a strenuous workout, I felt both mentally and physically lighter. It was a way of losing myself in something that was not the struggle. After an evening's workout I would wake up the next morning feeling strong and refreshed, ready to take up the fight again.

I attended the gym for one and a half hours each evening from Monday to Thursday. I would go home directly after work, pick up Thembi, then drive to the Community Centre. We did an hour of exercise, some combination of roadwork, skipping rope, calisthenics or shadow boxing, followed by fifteen minutes of body-work, some weight-lifting and then sparring. If we were training for a fight or a tournament, we would extend the training time to two and a half hours.

We each took turns leading the training sessions in order to develop leadership, initiative and self-confidence. Thembi particularly enjoyed leading these sessions. Things would get a bit rough for me on the nights that my son was in charge, for he would single me out for criticism. He was quick to chastise me whenever I got lazy. Everybody in the gym called me 'Chief', an honorific he avoided, calling me 'Mr Mandela', and occasionally, when he felt sympathy for his old man, 'My bra', township slang meaning 'My brother'. When he saw me loafing, he would say in a stern voice, 'Mr Mandela, you are wasting our time this evening. If you cannot keep up, why not go home and sit with the old women?' Everyone enjoyed these jibes immensely, and it gave me pleasure to see my son so happy and confident.

The camaraderie of the club was shattered that year because of a spat between Skipper Molotsi and Jerry Moloi. Jerry and the other boxers felt that Skipper was not paying enough attention to the club. Skipper was a skilful coach, but was rarely present to impart his knowledge. He was a historian of boxing lore and could narrate all twenty-six rounds of Jack Johnson's famous bout in Havana in 1915 when the first black heavyweight champion of the world lost his title. But Skipper tended to appear only before a match or a tournament to collect the small fee that was his due. I myself was sympathetic to Jerry's point of view but did my best to patch up the quarrel in the interests of keeping harmony. In the end, even my son agreed with Jerry's criticism of Skipper and there was nothing I could do to prevent a rupture.

The boxers, under Jerry's leadership, threatened to secede from the club and start their own. I called a meeting for all the members and it was a lively session – conducted in Sesotho, Zulu, Xhosa and English. Shakespeare was even cited by Skipper in his attack against the rebellious boxers, accusing Jerry of double-crossing him as Brutus had betrayed Caesar. 'Who are Caesar and Brutus?' my son asked. Before I could answer, someone said, 'Aren't they dead?' To which Skipper replied, 'Yes, but the truth about the betrayal is very much alive!'

The meeting resolved nothing and the boxers left for another venue while the weight-lifters remained at the Community Centre. I joined the boxers and for the first few weeks of the separation we trained at an uncomfortable place for a freedom fighter, the police gymnasium. Thereafter, the Anglican Church gave us premises at a reasonable rental in Orlando East, and we trained under Simon (Mshengu) Tshabalala, who later became one of the ANC's leading underground freedom fighters.

Our new facilities were no better than the old, and the club was never reconstituted. African boxers, like all black athletes and artists, were shackled by the twin handicaps of poverty and racism. What money an African boxer earned was typically used on food, rent, clothing, and whatever was left went to boxing equipment and training. He was denied the opportunity of belonging to the white boxing clubs that had the equipment and trainers necessary to produce a first-rate, world-class boxer. Unlike white professional boxers, African professional boxers had full-time day jobs. Sparring partners were few and poorly paid; without proper drilling and practice, the performance greatly suffered. Yet a number of African fighters were able to triumph over these difficulties, and achieve great success. Boxers like Elijah (Maestro) Mokone, Enoch (Schoolboy) Nhlapo, Kangeroo Maoto, one of the greatest stylists of the ring, Levi (Golden Boy) Madi, Nkosana Mgxaji, Mackeed Mofokeng and Norman Sekgapane all won great victories, while Jake Tuli, our greatest hero, won the British and Empire flyweight title. He was the most eloquent example of what African boxers could achieve if given the opportunity.

PART FIVE

Treason

23

Just after dawn on the morning of 5 December 1956, I was woken by a loud knocking on my door. No neighbour or friend ever knocks in such a peremptory way, and I knew immediately that it was the security police. I dressed quickly and found Head Constable Rousseau, a security officer who was a familiar figure in our area, and two policemen. He produced a search warrant, at which point the three of them immediately began to comb through the entire house looking for incriminating papers or documents. By this time the children were awake, and with a stern look I bade them to be calm. The children looked to me for reassurance. The police searched drawers and cabinets and cupboards, any place where contraband might have been hidden. After forty-five minutes, Rousseau matter-of-factly said, 'Mandela, we have a warrant for your arrest. Come with me.' I looked at the warrant, and the words leapt out at me: 'HOOGVERRAAD – HIGH TREASON'.

I walked with them to the car. It is not pleasant to be arrested in front of one's children, even though one knows that what one is doing is right. But children do not comprehend the complexity of the situation; they simply see their father being taken away by the white authorities without an explanation.

Rousseau drove and I sat next to him, without handcuffs, in the front seat. He had a search warrant for my office in town, where we were now headed after dropping off the two other policemen in a nearby area. To get to downtown Johannesburg, one had to travel along a desolate highway that cut through an unpopulated area. While we were motoring along this stretch, I remarked to Rousseau that he must be very confident to drive with me alone and unhandcuffed. He was silent.

'What would happen if I seized you and overpowered you?' I said.

Rousseau shifted uncomfortably. 'You are playing with fire, Mandela,' he said.

'Playing with fire is my game,' I replied.

'If you continue speaking like this I will have to handcuff you,' Rousseau said threateningly.

'And if I refuse?'

We continued this tense debate for a few more minutes, but as we passed into a populated area near the Langlaagte police station, Rousseau said to me: 'Mandela, I have treated you well and I expect you to do the same to me. I don't like your jokes at all.'

After a brief stop at the police station, we were joined by another officer and went to my office, which they searched for another forty-five minutes. From there, I was taken to Marshall Square, the rambling red-brick Johannesburg prison where I had spent a few nights in 1952 during the Defiance Campaign. A number of my colleagues were already there, having been arrested and booked earlier that morning. Over the next few hours, more friends and comrades began to trickle in. This was the swoop the government had long been planning. Someone smuggled in a copy of the afternoon edition of *The Star*, and we learned from its banner headlines that the raid had been countrywide and that the premier leaders of the Congress Alliance were all being arrested on charges of high treason and an alleged conspiracy to overthrow the state. Those who had been arrested in different parts of the country – Chief Luthuli, Monty Naicker, Reggie September, Lilian Ngoyi, Piet Beyleveld – were flown by military planes to Johannesburg, where they were to be arraigned. One hundred and forty-four people had been arrested. The next day we appeared in court and were formally charged. A week later, Walter Sisulu and eleven others were arrested, bringing the total to one hundred and fifty-six. All told, there were one hundred and five Africans, twenty-one Indians, twenty-three whites and seven Coloureds. Almost the entire executive leadership of the ANC, both banned and unbanned, had been arrested. The government, at long last, had made its move.

We were soon moved to the Johannesburg Prison, popularly known as the Fort, a bleak, castle-like structure located on a hill in the heart of the city. Upon admission, we were taken to an outdoor quadrangle and ordered to strip completely and line up against the wall. We were forced to stand there for more than an hour, shivering in the breeze and feeling awkward – priests, professors, doctors, lawyers, businessmen, men of middle or old age, who were normally treated with deference and respect. Despite my anger, I could not suppress a laugh as I scrutinized the men around me. For the first time, the truth of the aphorism 'clothes make the man' came home to me. If fine bodies and impressive physiques were essential to being a leader, I saw that few among us would have qualified.

A white doctor finally appeared and asked whether any of us was ill. No one complained of any ailment. We were ordered to dress, and then escorted to two large cells with cement floors and no furniture. The cells had recently been painted and reeked of paint fumes. We were each given three thin blankets plus a sisal mat. Each cell had only one floor-level latrine, which was completely exposed. It is said that no one truly knows a nation until one has been inside its jails. A nation should not be judged by how it treats its highest citizens, but its lowest ones – and South Africa treated its imprisoned African citizens like animals.

We stayed in the Fort for two weeks, and despite the hardships, our spirits remained extremely high. We were permitted newspapers and read with gratification of the waves of indignation aroused by our arrests. Protest meetings and demonstrations were being held throughout South Africa; people carried signs declaring 'We Stand by Our Leaders'. We read of protests around the world over our incarceration.

Our communal cell became a kind of convention for far-flung freedom fighters. Many of us had been living under severe restrictions, making it illegal for us to meet and talk. Now, our enemy had gathered us all under one roof for what became the largest and longest unbanned meeting of the Congress Alliance in years. Younger leaders met older leaders they had only read about. Men from Natal mingled with leaders from the Transvaal. We revelled in the opportunity to exchange ideas and experiences for two weeks while we awaited trial.

Each day, we put together a programme of activities.

Patrick Molaoa and Peter Nthite, both prominent
Youth Leaguers, organized physical training. Talks
on a variety of subjects were scheduled, and we heard
Professor Matthews discourse on both the history of the
ANC and the American Negro. Debi Singh lectured on
the history of the SAIC, Arthur Letele discussed the
African medicine man, while the Reverend James
Calata spoke on African music – and sang in his
beautiful tenor voice. Every day Vuyisile Mini, who
years later was hanged by the government for political
crimes, led the group in singing freedom songs. One of
the most popular was: *'Nans' indod' emnyama Strijdom,
Bhasobha nans' indod' emnyama Strijdom'* ('Here's the
black man, Strijdom, beware the black man, Strijdom').
We sang at the top of our lungs, and it kept our spirits
high.

One time, Masabalala Yengwa (better known as M.B.
Yengwa), the son of a Zulu labourer and the provincial
secretary of the Natal ANC, contributed to a lecture on
music by reciting a praise song in honour of Shaka, the
legendary Zulu warrior and king. Yengwa draped himself with a blanket, rolled up a newspaper to imitate a
sword, and began to stride back and forth reciting the
lines from the praise song. All of us, even those who did
not understand Zulu, were entranced. Then he paused
dramatically and called out the lines *'Inyon' edl' ezinye!
Yath' Badl' ezinye, yadl' ezinye!'* The lines liken Shaka to a
great bird of prey that relentlessly slays its enemies. At
the conclusion of these words, pandemonium broke
out. Chief Luthuli, who until then had remained quiet,
sprang to his feet, and bellowed *'Ngu Shaka lowo!'*
('That is Shaka!'), and then began to dance and chant.
His movements electrified us, and we all took to our

feet. Accomplished ballroom dancers, sluggards who knew neither traditional nor Western dancing, all joined in the *indlamu*, the traditional Zulu war dance. Some moved gracefully, others resembled frozen mountaineers trying to shake off the cold, but all danced with enthusiasm and emotion. Suddenly there were no Xhosas or Zulus, no Indians or Africans, no rightists or leftists, no religious or political leaders; we were all nationalists and patriots bound together by a love of our common history, our culture, our country and our people. In that moment, something stirred deep inside all of us, something strong and intimate, that bound us to one another. In that moment we felt the hand of the great past that made us what we were and the power of the great cause that linked us all together.

After the two weeks, we appeared for our preparatory examination on 19 December at the Drill Hall in Johannesburg, a military structure not normally used as a court of justice. It was a great bare barn of a building with a corrugated iron roof, and considered the only public building large enough to support a trial of so many accused.

We were taken in sealed police vans escorted by half a dozen troop carriers filled with armed soldiers. One would have thought a full-scale civil war was under way from the precautions the state was taking with us. A massive crowd of our supporters was blocking traffic in Twist Street; we could hear them cheering and singing, and they could hear us answering from inside the van. The trip became like a triumphal procession as the slow-moving van was rocked by the crowd. The entire perimeter of the hall was surrounded by gun-toting policemen and soldiers. The vans were brought to an area behind the hall and parked so that we alighted straight from the van into the courtroom.

Inside, we were met by another crowd of supporters, so that the hall seemed more like a raucous protest meeting than a staid court of law. We walked in with our thumbs raised in the ANC salute and nodded to our supporters sitting in the Non-Whites Only section. The mood inside was more celebratory than punitive, as the accused mingled with reporters and friends.

The government was charging all 156 of us with high treason and a countrywide conspiracy to use violence to overthrow the present government and replace it with a communist state. The period covered by the indictment was 1 October 1952 to 13 December 1956: it included the Defiance Campaign, the Sophiatown removal and the Congress of the People. The South African law of high treason was based not on English law but on Roman Dutch antecedents, and defined high treason as a hostile intention to disturb, impair or endanger the independence or safety of the state. The punishment was death.

The purpose of a preparatory examination was to determine whether the government's charges were sufficient to put us on trial in the Supreme Court. There were two stages of giving evidence. The first stage was in a magistrates' court. If the magistrate determined that there was sufficient evidence against the accused, the case would move to the Supreme Court and be tried before a judge. If the magistrate decided there was insufficient evidence, the defendants were discharged.

The magistrate was Mr F.C.A. Wessel, the chief magistrate from Bloemfontein. That first day, when Wessel began to speak in his quiet voice, it was impossible to hear him. The state had neglected to provide microphones and loudspeakers, and the court was adjourned for two hours while amplification was sought. We assembled in a courtyard and had what was very much like a picnic, with food sent in from outside. The atmosphere was almost festive. Two hours later, court was recessed for the day because proper loudspeakers had not been found. To the cheers of the crowd, we were once again escorted back to the Fort.

The next day, the crowds outside were even larger; the police more tense. Five hundred armed police surrounded the Drill Hall. When we arrived, we discovered that the state had erected an enormous wire cage for us to sit in. It was made of diamond-mesh wire, attached to poles and scaffolding with a grille at the front and top. We were led inside and sat on benches, surrounded by sixteen armed guards.

In addition to its symbolic effect, the cage cut us off from communication with our lawyers, who were not permitted to enter. One of my colleagues scribbled on a piece of paper, which he then posted on the side of the cage: 'Dangerous. Please Do Not Feed'.

Our supporters and organization had assembled a formidable defence team, including Bram Fischer, Norman Rosenberg, Israel Maisels, Maurice Franks and Vernon Berrangé. None of them had ever seen such a structure in court before. Franks lodged a powerful protest in open court against the state's humiliating his clients in such a 'fantastic' fashion and treating them, he said, 'like wild beasts'. Unless the cage was removed forthwith, he announced, the entire defence team would walk out of court. After a brief adjournment, the magistrate decided that the cage would be pulled down; in the meantime, the front of it was removed.

Only then did the state begin its case. The chief prosecutor, Mr van Niekerk, began reading part of an 18,000-word address outlining the Crown case against us. Even with amplification he was barely audible against the shouting and singing outside, and at one point a group of policemen rushed out. We heard a revolver shot, followed by shouts and more gunfire. The court was adjourned while the magistrate held a meeting with counsel. Twenty people had been injured.

The reading of the charges continued for the next two days. Van Niekerk said that he would prove to the court that the accused, with help from other countries, were plotting to overthrow the existing government by violence and impose a communist government on South Africa. This was the charge of high treason. The state cited the Freedom Charter as both proof of our communist intentions and evidence of our plot to overthrow the existing authorities. By the third day, much of the cage had been dismantled. Finally, on the fourth day, we were released on bail. Bail was another example of the sliding scale of apartheid: £250 for whites, £100 for Indians and £25 for Africans and Coloureds. Even treason was not colour-blind. Well-wishers from diverse walks of life came forward to guarantee bail for each of the accused, gestures of support that later became the foundation for the Treason Trial Defence Fund started by Bishop Reeves,

Alan Paton and Alex Hepple. The fund was ably administered during the trial by Mary Benson and then Freda Levson. We were released provided we reported once a week to the police, and were forbidden to attend public gatherings. Court was to resume in early January.

The following day I was at my office bright and early. Oliver and I had both been in prison, and our case-load had mounted in the meantime. While trying to work that morning, I was visited by an old friend named Jabavu, a professional interpreter whom I had not seen for several months. Before the arrests I had deliberately cut down my weight, in anticipation of prison, where one should be lean and able to survive on little. In jail, I had continued my exercises and was pleased to be so trim. But Jabavu eyed me suspiciously. 'Madiba,' he said, 'why must you look so thin?' In African cultures, portliness is often associated with wealth and well-being. He burst out: 'Man, you were scared of jail, that is all. You have disgraced us, we Xhosas!'

24

Even before the trial, my marriage to Evelyn had begun to unravel. In 1953, Evelyn had become set on upgrading her four-year certificate in general nursing. She enrolled in a midwifery course at King Edward VII Hospital in Durban that would keep her away from home for several months. This was possible because my mother and sister were staying with us and could look after the children. During her stay in Durban, I visited her on at least one occasion.

Evelyn returned, having passed her examinations. She was pregnant again, and later that year gave birth to Makaziwe, named after the daughter we had lost six years before. In our culture, to give a new child the name of a deceased child is considered a way of honouring the earlier child's memory and retaining a mystical attachment to the child who left too soon.

Over the course of the next year Evelyn became involved with the Watch Tower organization, part of the church of Jehovah's Witnesses. Whether this was due to some dissatisfaction with her life at the time, I do not know. The Jehovah's Witnesses took the Bible as the sole rule of faith and believed in a coming Armageddon between good and evil. Evelyn zealously began distributing their publication *The Watchtower*, and began to work on me as well, urging me to convert my commitment to the struggle to a commitment to God. Although I found some aspects of the Watch Tower's system to be interesting and worthwhile, I could not and did not share her devotion. There was an obsessional element to it that put me off. From what I could discern, her faith taught passivity and submissiveness in the face of oppression, something I could not accept.

My devotion to the ANC and the struggle was unremitting. This disturbed Evelyn. She had always assumed that politics was a youthful diversion, that I would someday return to the Transkei and practise there as a lawyer. Even as that possibility became remote, she never resigned herself to the fact that Johannesburg would be our home, or let go of the idea that we might move back to Umtata. She believed that once I was back in the Transkei, in the bosom of my family, acting as counsellor to Sabata, I would no longer miss politics. She encouraged Daliwonga's efforts to persuade me to come back to Umtata. We had many arguments about this, and I patiently explained to her that politics was not a distraction but my lifework, that it was an essential and fundamental part of my being. She could not accept this. A man and a woman who hold such different views of their respective roles in life cannot remain close.

I tried to persuade her of the necessity of the struggle, while she attempted to persuade me of the value of religious faith. When I would tell her that I was serving the nation, she would reply that serving God was above serving the nation. We were finding no common ground, and I was becoming convinced that the marriage was no longer tenable.

We also waged a battle for the minds and hearts of the children. She wanted them to be religious, and I thought they should be political. She would take them to church at every opportunity and read them Watch Tower literature. She even gave the boys *Watchtower* pamphlets to distribute in the township. I used to talk politics to the boys. Thembi was a member of the Pioneers, the juvenile section of the ANC, so he was already politically cognizant. I would explain to Makgatho in the simplest terms how the black man was persecuted by the white man.

Hanging on the walls of the house I had pictures of Roosevelt, Churchill, Stalin, Gandhi and the storming of the Winter Palace in St Petersburg in 1917. I explained to the boys who each of the men was, and what he stood for. They knew that the white leaders of South Africa stood for something very different. One day, Makgatho came running into the house, and said, 'Daddy, Daddy, there is Malan on the hill!' Malan had been the first Nationalist prime minister and the boy had confused him with a Bantu Education official, Willie Maree, who had announced that he would that day address a public meeting in the township. I went outside to see what Makgatho was talking about, for the ANC had organized a demonstration to ensure that the meeting did not succeed. As I went out, I saw a couple of police vans escorting Maree to the place he was meant to speak, but there was trouble from the start and Maree had fled without delivering his speech. I told Makgatho that it was not Malan but might as well have been.

My schedule in those days was relentless. I would leave the house very early in the morning and return late at night. After a day at the office, I would usually have meetings of one kind or another. Evelyn could not understand my meetings in the evening, and when

I returned home late suspected that I was seeing other women. Time after time, I would explain what meeting I was at, why I was there and what was discussed. But she was not convinced. In 1955, she gave me an ultimatum: I had to choose between her and the ANC.

Walter and Albertina Sisulu were very close to Evelyn, and their fondest wish was for us to stay together. Evelyn confided in Albertina. At one point, Walter intervened in the matter and I was very short with him, telling him it was none of his business. I regretted the tone I took, because Walter had always been a brother to me and his friendship and support had never faltered.

One day, Walter told me he wanted to bring someone over to the office for me to meet. He did not tell me that it was my brother-in-law, and I was surprised but not displeased to see him. I was pessimistic about the marriage and I thought it only fair to inform him of my feelings.

We were discussing this issue cordially among the three of us, when either Walter or I used a phrase like 'Men such as ourselves', or something of that sort. Evelyn's brother-in-law was a businessman, opposed to politics and politicians. He became very huffy and said, 'If you chaps think you are in the same position as myself, that is ridiculous. Do not compare yourselves to me.' When he left, Walter and I looked at each other and started laughing.

After we were arrested in December and kept in prison for two weeks, I had one visit from Evelyn. But when I left on bail, I found that she had moved out and taken the children. I returned to an empty, silent house. She had even removed the curtains, and for some reason I found this small detail shattering. She had moved in with her brother, who told me, 'Perhaps it is for the best; maybe when things will have cooled down you will come back together.' It was reasonable advice, but it was not to be.

Evelyn and I had irreconcilable differences. I could not give up my life in the struggle, and she could not live with my devotion to something other than herself and the family. She was a very good woman, charming, strong and faithful, and a fine mother. I never lost my respect and admiration for her, but in the end we could not make our marriage work.

The breakup of any marriage is traumatic, especially for the children. Our family was no exception, and all the children were wounded by our separation. Makgatho took to sleeping in my bed. He was a gentle child, a natural peacemaker, and he tried to bring about some sort of reconciliation between me and his mother. Makaziwe was still very small, and I remember one day, when I was not in prison or in court, I visited her crèche unannounced. She had always been a very affectionate child, but that day when she saw me, she froze. She did not know whether to run to me or retreat, to smile or frown. She had some conflict in her small heart, which she did not know how to resolve. It was very painful.

Thembi, who was ten at the time, was the most deeply affected. He stopped studying and became withdrawn. He had once been keen on English and Shakespeare, but after the separation he seemed to become apathetic about learning. The principal of his school spoke to me on one occasion, but there was little that I was able to do. I would take him to the gym

whenever I could, and occasionally he would brighten
a bit. There were many times when I could not be there
and later, when I was underground, Walter would take
Thembi with him along with his own son. Once he took
him to an event, and afterwards Walter said to me,
'Man, that chap is quiet.' Following the breakup,
Thembi would frequently wear my clothes, even
though they were far too large for him; they gave
him some kind of attachment to his too often distant
father.

25

On 9 January 1957 we once again assembled in the Drill Hall. It was the defence's turn to refute the state's charges. After summarizing the Crown's case against us, Vernon Berrangé, our lead counsel, announced our argument. 'The defence,' he said, 'will strenuously repudiate that the terms of the Freedom Charter are treasonable or criminal. On the contrary, the defence will contend that the ideas and beliefs which are expressed in this charter, although repugnant to the policy of the present government, are such as are shared by the overwhelming majority of mankind of all races and colours, and also by the overwhelming majority of the citizens of this country.' In consultation with our attorneys, we had decided that we were not merely going to prove that we were innocent of treason, but that this was a political trial in which the government was persecuting us for taking actions that were morally justified.

But the drama of the opening arguments was succeeded by the tedium of court logistics. The first month of the trial was taken up by the state's submission of evidence. One by one, every paper, pamphlet, document, book, notebook, letter, magazine and clipping that the police had accumulated in the last three years of searches was produced and numbered; 12,000 in all. The submissions ranged from the United Nations Declaration of Human Rights to a Russian cookery book. They even submitted the two signs from the Congress of the People: 'SOUP WITH MEAT', and 'SOUP WITHOUT MEAT'.

During the preparatory examination, which was to last for months, we listened day after day as African and Afrikaner detectives read out their notes of ANC meetings, or transcripts of speeches. These accounts were always garbled, and often either nonsensical or downright false. Berrangé later revealed in his deft cross-examination that many of the African detectives were unable to understand or write English, the language in which the speeches were made.

To support the state's extraordinary allegation that we intended to replace the existing government with a Soviet-style state, the Crown relied on the evidence of Professor Andrew Murray, head of the Department of Political Science at the University of Cape Town. Murray labelled many of the documents seized from us, including the Freedom Charter itself, as communistic.

Professor Murray seemed, at the outset, relatively knowledgeable, but that was until Berrangé began his cross-examination. Berrangé said that he wanted to read Murray a number of passages from various documents and then ask Murray to label them as communistic or not. Berrangé read him the first passage, which concerned the need for ordinary workers to cooperate with each other and not exploit one another. Communistic, Murray said. Berrangé then noted that the statement had been made by the former premier of South Africa, Dr Malan. Berrangé proceeded to read him two other statements, both of which Professor Murray described as communistic.

These passages had in fact been uttered by the American presidents Abraham Lincoln and Woodrow Wilson. The highlight came when Berrangé read Murray a passage that the professor unhesitatingly described as 'communism straight from the shoulder'. Berrangé then revealed that it was a statement that Professor Murray himself had written in the 1930s.

In the seventh month of the trial, the state said it would produce evidence of planned violence that occurred during the Defiance Campaign. The state called the first of their star witnesses, Solomon Ngubase, who offered sensational evidence that seemed to implicate the ANC. Ngubase was a soft-spoken fellow in his late thirties, with a shaky command of English, who was currently serving a sentence for fraud. In his opening testimony, Ngubase told the court he had obtained a BA degree from Fort Hare, and that he was a practising attorney. He said he became secretary of the Port Elizabeth branch of the ANC as well as a member of the National Executive. He claimed to have been present at a meeting of the National Executive when a decision was made to send Walter Sisulu and David Bopape to the Soviet Union to procure arms for a violent revolution in South Africa. He said he was present at a meeting that planned the 1952 Port Elizabeth riot and that he had witnessed an ANC decision to murder all whites in the Transkei in the same manner as the Mau Mau in Kenya. Ngubase's dramatic testimony caused a stir in and out of court. Here at long last was evidence of a conspiracy.

But when Ngubase was cross-examined by Vernon Berrangé, it was revealed that he was equal parts madman and liar. Berrangé, whose cross-examining skills earned him the nickname of 'Isangoma' (a diviner or healer who exorcises an illness) among the accused, quickly established that Ngubase was neither a university graduate nor a member of the ANC, much less a member of the National Executive. Berrangé produced evidence that Ngubase had forged certificates for a university degree, had practised law illegally for several years and had a further case of fraud pending against him. At the time of the meeting he claimed to have attended to plan the Port Elizabeth riot, he was serving a sentence for fraud in a Durban jail. Almost none of Ngubase's testimony bore even a remote resemblance to the truth. At the end of his cross-examination, Berrangé asked the witness, 'Do you know what a rogue is?' Ngubase said he did not. 'You, sir, are a rogue!' Berrangé exclaimed.

Joe Slovo, one of the accused and a superb advocate, conducted his own defence. He was an irritant to the state because of his sharp questions and attempts to show that the state was the violator of laws, not the Congress. Slovo's cross-examination was often as devastating as Berrangé's. Detective Jeremiah Mollson, one of the few African members of the Special Branch, claimed to recall lines verbatim from ANC speeches that he had heard. But what he reported was usually gibberish or outright fabrication.

Slovo: 'Do you understand English?'

Mollson: 'Not so well.'

Slovo: 'Do you mean to say that you reported these speeches in English but you don't understand English well?'

Mollson: 'Yes, Your Worship.'

Slovo: 'Do you agree that your notes are a lot of rubbish?'

Mollson: 'I don't know.'

This last response caused an outbreak of laughter from the defendants. The magistrate scolded us for laughing, and said, 'The proceedings are not as funny as they may seem.'

At one point, Wessel told Slovo that he was impugning the integrity of the court and fined him for contempt. This provoked the fury of most of the accused, and it was only Chief Luthuli's restraining hand that kept a number of the defendants from being cited for contempt as well.

As the testimony continued, much of it tedious legal manoeuvring, we began to occupy ourselves with other matters. I often brought a book to read or a legal brief to work on. Others read newspapers, did crossword puzzles or played chess or Scrabble. Occasionally the bench would reprimand us for not paying attention, and the books and puzzles would disappear. But, slowly, as the testimony resumed its snail's pace, the games and reading material re-emerged.

As the preparatory examination continued the state became increasingly desperate. It became more and more apparent that the state was gathering – often fabricating – evidence as it went along, to help in what seemed to be a lost cause.

Finally, on 11 September, ten months after we had first assembled in the Drill Hall, the prosecutor announced that the state's case in the preparatory examination was completed. The magistrate gave the defence four months to sift through the 8,000 pages of typed evidence and 12,000 documents to prepare its case.

The preparatory examination had lasted for the whole of 1957. Court adjourned in September, and the defence began reviewing the evidence. Three months later, without warning and without explanation, the Crown announced that charges against sixty-one of the accused were to be dropped. Most of these defendants were relatively minor figures in the ANC, but also among them were Chief Luthuli and Oliver Tambo. The Crown's release of Luthuli and Tambo pleased but bewildered us.

In January, when the government was scheduled to sum up its charges, the Crown brought in a new prosecutor, the formidable Oswald Pirow, QC. Pirow was a former minister of justice and of defence and a pillar of National Party politics. He was a longtime Afrikaner nationalist, and an outspoken supporter of the Nazi cause; he once described Hitler as the 'greatest man of his age'. He was a virulent anti-communist. The appointment of Pirow was new evidence that the state was worried about the outcome and attached tremendous importance to a victory.

Before Pirow's summing-up, Berrangé announced that he would apply for our discharge on the ground that the state had not offered sufficient evidence against us. Pirow opposed this application for dismissal, and quoted from several inflammatory speeches by the accused, informing the court that the police had unearthed more evidence of a highly dangerous conspiracy. The country, he said portentously, was sitting on top of a volcano. It was an effective and highly dramatic performance. Pirow changed the atmosphere of the trial. We had become over-confident, and were reminded that we were facing a serious charge. Don't fool yourselves, counsel told us, you people might go to jail. Their warnings sobered us.

After thirteen months of the preparatory examination, the magistrate ruled that he had found 'sufficient reason' for putting us on trial in the Transvaal Supreme Court for high treason. Court adjourned in January with ninety-five remaining defendants committed to stand trial. When the actual trial would begin, we did not know.

26

One afternoon, during a recess in the preparatory examination, I drove a friend from Orlando to the medical school at the University of the Witwatersrand and went past Baragwanath Hospital, the leading black hospital in Johannesburg. As I passed a nearby bus stop, I noticed out of the corner of my eye a lovely young woman waiting for the bus. I was struck by her beauty, and I turned my head to get a better look at her, but my car had gone by too fast. This woman's face stayed with me – I even considered turning round to drive by her in the other direction – but I went on.

Some weeks thereafter, a curious coincidence occurred. I was at the office, and when I popped in to see Oliver, there was this same young woman with her brother, sitting in front of Oliver's desk. I was taken aback, and did my best not to show my surprise – or my delight – at this. Oliver introduced me to them and explained that they were visiting him on a legal matter.

Her name was Nomzamo Winifred Madikizela, but she was known as Winnie. She had recently completed her studies at the Jan Hofmeyr School of Social Work in Johannesburg and was working as the first black female social worker at Baragwanath Hospital. At the time I paid little attention to her background or legal problem, for something in me was deeply stirred by her presence. I was thinking more of how I could ask her out than how our firm would handle her case. I cannot

At the age of nineteen, in Umtata, Transkei. *(P. K. A. Gaeshwe/Black Star)*

Oliver and I opened the doors to our office on Fox Street in 1952; it was the first black law practice in Johannesburg. *(Jurgen Schadeberg/Bailey's African History Archives)*

Opposite: Under the Suppression of Communism Act, bans became a routine part of the life of a freedom fighter. *(Bailey's African History Archives)*

Outside the courtroom with Dr James Moroka and Yusuf Dadoo during the Defiance Campaign. *(Jurgen Schadeberg/ Bailey's African History Archives)*

With Patrick Moloa and Robert Resha at the Transvaal Supreme Court after receiving a nine-month suspended sentence. *(Jurgen Schadeberg/ Bailey's African History Archives)*

Yusuf Dadoo, ex-president, SAIC.

Nelson Mandela, ex-president, Tvl. ANC.

James Phillips, ex-chairman, Tvl. CPAC.

Duma Nokwe, secretary, ANC Y.L.

Walter Sisulu, secretary, ANC.

Albert Luthuli, president, ANC.

Yusuf Cachalia, secretary, SAIC.

John B. Marks, ex-president, Tvl. ANC.

Stephen Sello, ex-acting secretary.

David Bopape, ex-secretary, Tvl. ANC.

Moses Kotane, ex-leader, ANC.

Dr. Z. Njongwe, ex-chairman, ANC.

The Effects of New Laws: 2

BANNED MEN

DURING the last few months, nearly all the non-White leaders in South Africa have been restricted in their movements and activities. Most of them have been called upon to resign their positions in the African National Congress or the South African Indian Congress. Many of them have been forbidden to attend any gatherings, or to enter certain magisterial districts in the Union.

Albert Luthuli, for instance, president of the African National Congress, is forbidden to move away from his own district at Groutville, Natal. He cannot visit the shops in Durban, thirty miles away, or attend the cathedral there.

Most of the bans are in force for two years, after which time they may be renewed: some have already been removed.

The bans take effect under the Suppression of Communism Act of 1950. This allows the Minister of Justice to prohibit from gatherings or organisations anyone suspected of furthering the aims of Communism. 'Communism' is defined under the act as aiming to bring about social, economic or political changes in the country.

Many of those convicted or 'banned' under the Suppression of Communism Act are not 'Communists' in the usual sense of the term, but 'Statutory Communists' who come within the definition of the act.

Kassim Amra, ex-leader, Indian C.

Dr. Silas M. Molema, ex-treasurer, ANC.

Diliza Mji, ex-secretary, ANC.

Maulvi Cachalia, co-secretary, Tvl. I.C.

Nevum, ex-Transvaal ANC leader.

Nana Sitha, ex-president, Transvaal I.C.

Dan Tihoome, ex-leader, ANC.

Flag Boshielo, ex-leader, Transvaal ANC.

N. Thandray, ex-Tvl. secretary, I.C.

Hoola Seperepera, ex-leader, ANC.

nk Marquard, ex-president, Cape F.W.U.

Joseph Matthews, ex-president, ANC Y.L.

Robert Matji, ex-secretary, Cape ANC.

MacDon. Maseko, ex-leader, ANC.

Ismail Bhoola, ex-sec., Tvl. Indian YC.

Harrison Motlana, ex-secretary, Tvl.

Dr Moroka, after handing over the presidency of the ANC to Chief Albert Luthuli. *(G. R. Naidoo/ Bailey's African History Archives)*

Chief Luthuli giving the 'Afrika' salute to ANC delegates at the forty-first annual congress in Queenstown. *(Bob Gosani/ Bailey's African History Archives)*

With youth leader Peter Nthite in 1955. *(Peter Magubane/Bailey's African History Archives)*

Under the Group Areas Act, the vital township of Sophiatown was declared a 'black spot'; removals to Meadowlands were scheduled to begin in 1955. *(Jurgen Schadeberg/Bailey's African History Archives)*

One of the lessons I took away from the failed Western Areas anti-removal campaign was that it is the oppressor who defines the nature of the struggle; in the end, we would have no alternative but to resort to an armed resistance. *(Jurgen Schadeberg/Bailey's African History Archives)*

Speaking to a group of women during their march to Pretoria Union Buildings to protest the pass laws. *(Peter Magubane/Bailey's African History Archives)*

Tense times, 1956.
*(Ian Berry/
Magnum)*

The Treason Trial,
1956. The accused
were bussed
every day from
Johannesburg to
Pretoria. *(Peter
Magubane/Bailey's
African History
Archives)*

We were
forbidden from
attending political
gatherings of any
kind, but so many
leaders had been
brought together
for the Treason
Trial that our
afternoon breaks
often felt like
meetings of
the National
Executive
Committee. *(Ian
Berry/Magnum)*

Our supporters
joined us in song
outside the court
in Pretoria, 1958.
*(Peter Magubane/
Bailey's African
History Archives)*

Sparring with Jerry
Moloi. *(Bob Gosani/
Bailey's African
History Archives)*

With Ruth First outside the court. *(Peter Magubane/ Bailey's African History Archives)*

A triumphant moment with Moses Kotane outside the court; we had just learned that the Crown was withdrawing its indictment. But the victory was to be short-lived: three months later, in 1959, twenty-nine of us found ourselves on trial once again. *(Peter Magubane/ Bailey's African History Archives)*

After the second
trial I went
underground,
becoming known
for a time as "the
black pimpernel".
*(photographer
unknown)*

In hiding after
my return from
abroad, 1962.
*(Eli Weinberg/
Camera Press Ltd.)*

Oliver Tambo and
Robert Resha at
the Dar es Salaam
airport after the
banning of the
ANC, 1962.
(Associated Press)

say for certain if there is such a thing as love at first sight, but I do know that the moment I first glimpsed Winnie Nomzamo, I knew that I wanted to have her as my wife.

Winnie was the sixth of eleven children of C.K. Madikizela, a school principal turned businessman. Her given name was Nomzamo, which means one who strives or undergoes trials, a name as prophetic as my own. She came from Bizana in Pondoland, an area adjacent to the part of the Transkei where I grew up. She is from the Phondo clan of amaNgutyana, and her great-grandfather was Madikizela, a powerful chief in nineteenth-century Natal who had settled in the Transkei at the time of the iMfecane.

I telephoned Winnie the next day at the hospital and asked her for help in raising money for the Treason Trial Defence Fund from the Jan Hofmeyr School. It was merely a pretext to invite her to lunch, which I did. I picked her up where she was staying in town, and took her to an Indian restaurant near my office, one of the few places that served Africans and where I frequently ate. Winnie was dazzling, and even the fact that she had never before tasted curry and drank glass after glass of water to cool her palate only added to her charm.

After lunch I took her for a drive to an area between Johannesburg and Evaton, an open veld just past Eldorado Park. We walked on the long grass, grass so similar to that of the Transkei where we had both been raised. I told her of my hopes and of the difficulties of the Treason Trial. I knew at once that I wanted to marry her – and I told her so. Her spirit, her passion, her youth, her courage, her wilfulness – I felt all of these things the moment I first saw her.

Over the next weeks and months we saw each other whenever we could. She visited me at the Drill Hall and at my office. She came to see me work out in the gym; she met Thembi, Makgatho and Makaziwe. She came to meetings and political discussions; I was both courting her and politicizing her. As a student, Winnie had been attracted to the Non-European Unity Movement, for she had a brother who was involved with that party. In later years, I would tease her about this early allegiance, telling her that had she not met me, she would have married a leader of the NEUM.

Shortly after I filed for divorce from Evelyn, I told Winnie she should visit Ray Harmel, the wife of Michael Harmel, for a fitting for a wedding dress. In addition to being an activist, Ray was an excellent dressmaker. I asked Winnie how many bridesmaids she intended to have, and suggested she go to Bizana to inform her parents that we were to be married. Winnie has laughingly told people that I never proposed to her, but I always told her that I asked her on our very first date and that I simply took it for granted from that day forward.

The Treason Trial was in its second year and it put a suffocating weight on our law practice. The Mandela and Tambo firm was falling apart as we could not be there, and both Oliver and I were experiencing grave financial difficulties. Since the charges against Oliver had been dropped, he was able to do some remedial work, but the damage had already been done. We had gone from a bustling practice that turned people away to one that was practically begging for clients. I could not even afford to pay the balance of £50 still owing on the plot of land that I had purchased in Umtata, and had to give it up.

I explained all this to Winnie. I told her it was more than likely that we would have to live on her small salary as a social worker. Winnie understood, and said she was prepared to take the risk and throw in her lot with me. I never promised her gold and diamonds, and I was never able to give them to her.

The wedding took place on 14 June 1958. I applied for a relaxation of my banning orders and was given six days' leave of absence from Johannesburg. I also arranged for *lobola*, the traditional brideprice, to be paid to Winnie's father.

The wedding party left Johannesburg very early on the morning of 12 June, and we arrived in Bizana late that afternoon. My first stop, as always when one was banned, was the police station to report that I had arrived. At dusk, we then went to the bride's place, Mbongweni, as was customary. We were met by a great chorus of local women ululating with happiness, and Winnie and I were separated; she went to the bride's house, while I went with the groom's party to the house of one of Winnie's relations.

The ceremony itself was at a local church, after which we celebrated at the home of Winnie's eldest brother, which was the ancestral home of the Madikizela clan. The bridal car was swathed in ANC colours. There was dancing and singing, and Winnie's exuberant grandmother did a special dance for all of us. The entire executive of the ANC had been invited, but bans limited their attendance. Among those who came were Duma Nokwe, Lilian Ngoyi, Dr James Njongwe, Dr Wilson Conco and Victor Tyamzashe.

The final reception was at the Bizana Town Hall. The speech I recall best was given by Winnie's father. He took note, as did everyone, that among the uninvited guests at the wedding were a number of security Police. He spoke of his love for his daughter, my commitment to the country and my dangerous career as a politician. When Winnie had first told him of the marriage, he had exclaimed, 'But you are marrying a jailbird!' At the wedding, he said he was not optimistic about the future, and that such a marriage, in such difficult times, would be unremittingly tested. He told Winnie she was marrying a man who was already married to the struggle. He bade his daughter good luck, and ended his speech by saying, 'If your man is a wizard, you must become a witch!' It was a way of saying that you must follow your man on whatever path he takes. Then, Constance Mbekeni, my sister, spoke on my behalf at the ceremony.

After the ceremony, a piece of the wedding cake was wrapped up for the bride to bring to the groom's ancestral home for the second part of the wedding. But it was never to be, for my leave of absence was up and we had to return to Johannesburg. Winnie carefully stored the cake in anticipation of that day. At our house, No. 8115 Orlando West, a large party of friends and family were there to welcome us back. A sheep had been slaughtered and there was a feast in our honour.

There was no time or money for a honeymoon, and life quickly settled into a routine dominated by the trial. We woke very early in the morning, usually at about four. Winnie prepared breakfast before I left. I would then take the bus to the trial or make an early morning visit to my office. As much as possible, afternoons and evenings were spent at my office attempting to keep our practice going and to earn some money. Evenings were often taken up with political work and meetings. The wife of a freedom fighter is often like a widow, even when her husband is not in prison. Though I was on trial for treason, Winnie gave me cause for hope. I felt as though I had a new and second chance at life. My love for her gave me added strength for the struggles that lay ahead.

27

The major event facing the country in 1958 was the general election – 'general' only in the sense that three million whites could participate, but none of the thirteen million Africans. We debated whether or not to stage a protest. The central issue was: did an election in which only whites could participate make any difference to Africans? The answer, as far as the ANC was concerned, was that we could not remain indifferent even when we were shut out of the process. We were excluded, but not unaffected: the defeat of the Nationalist Party would be in our interest and that of all Africans.

The ANC joined with the other congresses and SACTU, the South African Congress of Trade Unions, to call a three-day strike during the elections in April. Leaflets were distributed in factories and shops, at railway stations and bus stops, in beer halls and hospitals, and from house to house. 'THE NATS MUST GO!' was the main slogan of this campaign. Our preparations worried the government; four days before the election, the state ruled that a gathering of more than ten Africans in any urban area was illegal.

The night before a planned protest, boycott or stay-away, the leaders of the event would go underground in order to foil the police swoop that inevitably took place. The police were not yet monitoring us around the clock and it was easy to disappear for a day or two.

The night before the strike, Walter, Oliver, Moses Kotane, J.B. Marks, Dan Tloome, Duma Nokwe and I stayed in the house of my physician, Dr Nthato Motlana, in Orlando. Very early the next morning, we moved to another house in the same neighbourhood where we were able to keep in touch by telephone with other leaders around the city. Communications were not very efficient in those days, particularly in the townships where few people owned telephones, and it was a frustrating task to oversee a strike. Early the next morning, we dispatched men to strategic places around the townships to watch the trains, buses and taxis in order to determine whether people were going to work. They returned with bad news: the buses and trains were filled; people were ignoring the strike. Only then did we notice that the gentleman in whose house we were staying was nowhere to be found – he had slipped out and gone to work. The strike was shaping up as a failure.

We resolved to call off the strike. A three-day strike that is cancelled on the first day is only a one-day failure; a strike that fails three days running is a fiasco. It was humiliating to have to retreat, but we felt that it would have been more humiliating not to. Less than an hour after we had released a statement calling off the strike, the government-run South African Broadcasting Corporation read our announcement in full. Normally, the SABC ignored the ANC altogether; only in defeat did we make their broadcasts. This time, they even complimented us on our decision. This greatly annoyed Moses Kotane. 'To be praised by the SABC, that is too much,' he said, shaking his head. Kotane questioned whether we had acted too hastily and played into the state's hands. It was a legitimate concern, but decisions should not be taken out of pride or embarrassment, but out of pure strategy – and strategy here suggested we call off the strike. The fact that the enemy had exploited our surrender didn't mean we were wrong to surrender.

But some areas did not hear that the strike was called off, while others spurned our call. In Port Elizabeth, an ANC stronghold, the response was better on the second and third days than the first. In general, however, we could not hide the fact that the strike was a failure. As if that were not enough, the Nationalists increased their popular vote in the election by more than 10 per cent.

We had heated discussions about whether we ought to have relied on coercive measures. Should we have used pickets, which generally prevent people from entering their place of work? The hard-liners suggested that if we had deployed pickets, the strike would have been a success. But I have always resisted such methods. It is best to rely on the freely given support of the people; otherwise that support is weak and fleeting. The organization should be a haven, not a prison. However, if the majority of the organization or the people support a decision, coercion can be used in certain cases against the dissident minority in the interests of the majority. A minority, however vocal it might be, should not be able to frustrate the will of the majority.

In my own house, I attempted to use a different sort of coercion, but without success. Ida Mthimkhulu, a Sotho-speaking woman of my own age, was then our house assistant. Ida was more a member of the family than an employee, and I called her Kgaitsedi, which means 'Sister' and is a term of endearment. Ida ran the house with military efficiency, and Winnie and I took our orders willingly; I often ran out to do errands at her command.

The day before the strike, I was driving Ida and her twelve-year-old son home, and I mentioned that I needed her to wash and press some shirts for me the following day. A long and uncharacteristic silence followed. Ida then turned to me and said with barely concealed disdain, 'You know very well that I can't do that.'

'Why not?' I replied, surprised by the vehemence of her reaction.

'Have you forgotten that I, too, am a worker?' she said with some satisfaction. 'I will be on strike tomorrow with my people and fellow workers!'

Her son saw my embarrassment and in his boyish way tried to ease the tension by saying that 'Uncle Nelson' had always treated her as a sister, not a worker. In irritation, she turned on her well-meaning son and said, 'Boy, where were you when I was struggling for my rights in that house? If I had not fought hard against your "Uncle Nelson" I would not today be treated like a sister!' Ida did not come to work the next day, and my shirts went unpressed.

28

Few issues touched a nerve as much as that of passes for women. The state had not weakened in its resolve to impose passes on women, and women had not weakened in their resolve to resist. Although the government now called passes 'reference books', women weren't fooled: they could still be fined £10 or imprisoned for a month for failing to produce their 'reference book'.

In 1957, spurred by the efforts of the ANC Women's League, women all across the country, in rural areas and in cities, reacted with fury to the state's insistence that they carry passes. The women were courageous, persistent, enthusiastic, indefatigable, and their protest against passes set a standard for anti-government protest that was never equalled. As Chief Luthuli said, 'When the women begin to take an active part in the struggle, no power on earth can stop us from achieving freedom in our lifetime.'

All across the southeastern Transvaal, in Standerton, Heidelberg, Balfour and other dorps, thousands of women protested. On recess from the Treason Trial, Frances Baard and Florence Matomela organized women to refuse passes in Port Elizabeth, their home town. In Johannesburg in October a large group of women gathered at the central pass office, and chased away women who had come to collect passes and clerks who worked in the office, bringing the office to a standstill. Police arrested hundreds of the women.

Not long after these arrests, Winnie and I were relaxing after supper when she quietly informed me that she intended to join the group of Orlando women who would be protesting the following day at the pass office. I was a bit taken aback, and while I was pleased at her sense of commitment and admired her courage, I was also wary. Winnie had become increasingly politicized since our marriage, and had joined the Orlando West branch of the ANC's Women's League, all of which I encouraged.

I told her I welcomed her decision, but that I had to warn her about the seriousness of her action. It would, I said, in a single act, radically change her life. By African standards, Winnie was from a well-to-do family and had been shielded from some of the more unpleasant realities of life in South Africa. At the very least, she had never had to worry about where her next meal was coming from. Before our marriage, she had moved in circles of relative wealth and comfort, a life very different from the often hand-to-mouth existence of the freedom fighter.

I told her that if she was arrested she would be certain to be sacked by her employer, the provincial administration – we both knew it was her small income that was supporting the household – and that she could probably never work again as a social worker, since the stigma of imprisonment would make public agencies reluctant to hire her. Finally, she was pregnant, and I warned her of the physical hardship and humiliations of jail. My response may sound harsh, but I felt responsibility, both as a husband and as a leader of the struggle, to be as clear as possible about the ramifications of her action. I myself had mixed emotions, for the concerns of a husband and a leader do not always coincide.

But Winnie is a determined person, and I suspect my pessimistic reaction only strengthened her resolve. She listened to all I said and informed me that her mind was made up. The next morning I rose early to make her breakfast, and we drove over to the Sisulus' house to meet Walter's wife, Albertina, one of the leaders of the protest. We then drove to the Phefeni station in Orlando, where the women would get the train into town. I embraced her before she boarded the train. Winnie was nervous yet resolute as she waved to me from the window, and I felt as though she were setting out on a long and perilous journey, the end of which neither of us could know.

Hundreds of women converged on the Central Pass Office in downtown Johannesburg. They were old and young; some carried babies on their backs, some wore tribal blankets while others dressed in smart suits. They sang, marched and chanted. Within minutes they were surrounded by dozens of armed police, who arrested all of them, packed them into vans and drove them to Marshall Square police station. The women were cheerful throughout; as they were being driven away, some called out to reporters, 'Tell our madams we won't be at work tomorrow!' All told, more than a thousand women were arrested.

I knew this not because I was the husband of one of the detainees but because Mandela and Tambo were called on to represent most of the women who had been arrested. I quickly made my way to Marshall Square to visit the prisoners and arrange bail. I managed to see Winnie, who beamed when she saw me and seemed as happy as one could be in a bare police cell. It was as though she had given me a great gift that she knew would please me. I told her I was proud of her, but I could not stay and talk as I had quite a lot of legal work to do.

By the end of the second day, the number of arrests had increased and nearly two thousand women were incarcerated, many of them remanded to the Fort to await trial. This created formidable problems not only for Oliver and me, but for the police and the prison authorities. There was simply not enough space to hold them all. There were too few blankets, too few mats and toilets, and too little food. Conditions at the Fort were cramped and dirty. While many in the ANC, including myself, were eager to bail out the women, Lilian Ngoyi, the national president of the Women's League, and Helen Joseph, secretary of the South African Women's Federation, believed that for the protest to be genuine and effective, the women should serve whatever time the magistrate ordered. I remonstrated with them but was told in no uncertain terms that the matter was the women's affair and that the ANC – as well as anxious husbands – should not meddle. I did tell Lilian that I thought she should discuss the issue with the women themselves before making a decision, and escorted her down to the cells where she could take a poll of the prisoners. Many were desperate to be bailed out and had not been adequately prepared for what would await them in prison. As a compromise, I suggested to Lilian that the women spend a fortnight in prison, after which we would bail them out. Lilian accepted.

Over the next two weeks I spent many hours in court

arranging bail for the women. A few were frustrated and took their anger out on me. 'Mandela, I am tired of this case of yours,' one woman said to me. 'If this does not end today I will not ever reappear in court.' With the help of relatives and fund-raising organizations, we managed to bail them all out within two weeks.

Winnie did not seem the worse for wear from her prison experience. If she had suffered, she would not have told me anyway. While she was in prison she became friendly with two teenage Afrikaner wardresses. They were sympathetic and curious, and after Winnie was released on bail, we invited them to visit us. They accepted and travelled by train to Orlando. We gave them lunch at the house and afterwards Winnie took them for a tour of the township. Winnie and the two wardresses were about the same age and got on well. They laughed together as though they were all sisters. The two girls had an enjoyable day and thanked Winnie, saying that they would like to return. As it turned out, this was not to be, for in travelling to Orlando they had, of necessity, sat in a Non-European carriage. (There were no white trains to Orlando for the simple reason that no whites went to Orlando.) As a result, they attracted a great deal of attention and it was soon widely known that two Afrikaner wardresses from the Fort had visited Winnie and me. This was not a problem for us, but it proved to be one for them, because the prison authorities dismissed them. We never saw or heard from them again.

29

For six months – ever since the end of the preparatory hearings in January – we had been awaiting and preparing for our formal trial, which was to start in August 1958. The government set up a special high court – Mr Justice F.L. Rumpff, president of the three-man court, Mr Justice Kennedy and Mr Justice Ludorf. The panel was not promising: it consisted of three white men, all with ties to the ruling party. While Judge Rumpff was an able man and better informed than the average white South African, he was rumoured to be a member of the Broederbond, a secret Afrikaner organization whose aim was to solidify Afrikaner power. Judge Ludorf was a well-known member of the National Party, as was Judge Kennedy. Kennedy had a reputation as a hanging judge, having sent a group of twenty-three Africans to the gallows for the murder of two white policemen.

Shortly before the case resumed, the state played another unpleasant trick on us. They announced that the venue of the trial was to be shifted from Johannesburg to Pretoria, thirty-six miles away. The trial would be conducted in an ornate former synagogue that had been converted into a court of law. All of the accused as well as our defence team resided in Johannesburg, so we would be forced to travel each day to Pretoria. The trial would now take up even more of our time and money – neither of which we had in abundance. Those who had managed to keep their jobs had been able to do so because the court had been near their work. Changing the venue was also an attempt to crush our spirits by separating us from our natural supporters. Pretoria was the home of the National Party, and the ANC barely had a presence there.

Nearly all the ninety-two accused commuted to Pretoria in a lumbering, uncomfortable bus, with stiff wooden slats for seats, which left every day at six in the morning and took two hours to reach the Old Synagogue. The round-trip took us nearly five hours – time far better spent earning money to pay for food, rent and clothes for the children.

Once more we were privileged to have a brilliant and aggressive defence team, ably led by advocate Israel Maisels, and assisted by Bram Fischer, Rex Welsh, Vernon Berrangé, Sydney Kentridge, Tony O'Dowd and G. Nicholas. On the opening day of the trial, they displayed their combativeness with a risky legal manoeuvre that a number of us had decided on in consultation with the lawyers. Issy Maisels rose dramatically and applied for the recusal of Judges Ludorf and Rumpff on the grounds that both had conflicts of interest that prevented them from being fair arbiters of our case. There was an audible murmur in the courtroom. The defence contended that Rumpff, as the judge at the 1952 Defiance Trial, had already adjudicated on certain aspects of the present indictment and therefore it was not in the interest of justice that he try this case. We argued that Ludorf was prejudiced, because he had represented the government in 1954 as a lawyer for the police when Harold Wolpe had sought a court interdict to eject the police from a meeting of the Congress of the People.

This was a dangerous strategy, for we could easily win this legal battle but lose the war. Although we regarded both Ludorf and Rumpff as strong supporters of the National Party, there were far worse judges in the country who could replace them. In fact, while we were keen to have Ludorf step down, we secretly hoped that Rumpff, whom we respected as an honest broker, would decide not to recuse himself. Rumpff always stood for law, no matter what his own political opinions might be, and we were convinced that when it came to law, we could only be found innocent.

That Monday, the atmosphere was expectant when the three red-robed judges marched into the court-room. Judge Ludorf announced that he would with-draw, adding that he had completely forgotten about the previous case. But Rumpff refused to recuse him-self and instead offered the assurance that his judg-ment in the Defiance case would have no influence on him in this one. We were happy with his decision. To replace Ludorf, the state appointed Mr Justice Bekker, a man we liked right from the start and who was not linked to the National Party.

After the success of this first manoeuvre, we tried a second, nearly as risky. We began a long and detailed argument contesting the indictment itself. We claimed, among other things, that the indictment was vague and lacked particularity. We also argued that the planning of violence was necessary to prove high treason, and the prosecution needed to provide examples of its claim that we intended to act violently. It became apparent by the end of our argument that the three judges agreed. In August, the court quashed one of the two charges under the Suppression of Communism

Act. On 13 October, after two more months of legal wrangling, the Crown suddenly announced the withdrawal of the indictment altogether. This was extraordinary, but we were too well versed in the devious ways of the state to celebrate. A month later the prosecution issued a new, more carefully worded, indictment and announced that the trial would proceed against only thirty of the accused; the others would be tried later. I was among the first thirty, all of whom were members of the ANC.

Under the new indictment, the prosecution was now required to prove the intention to act violently. As Pirow put it, the accused knew that the achievement of the goals of the Freedom Charter would 'necessarily involve the overthrow of the State by violence'. The legal sparring continued until the middle of 1959, when the court dismissed the Crown's indictment against the remaining sixty-one accused. For months on end, the activity in the courtroom consisted of the driest legal manoeuvring imaginable. Despite the defence's successes in showing the shoddiness of the government's case, the state was obdurately persistent. As the minister of justice said, 'This trial will be proceeded with, no matter how many millions of pounds it costs. What does it matter how long it takes?'

Just after midnight on 4 February 1958, I returned home after a meeting to find Winnie alone and in pain, about to go into labour. I rushed her to Baragwanath Hospital, but was told that it would be many hours before her time. I stayed until I had to leave for the trial in Pretoria. Immediately after the session ended, I sped back with Duma Nokwe to find mother and daughter doing extremely well. I held my newborn daughter in my arms and pronounced her a true Mandela. My relative, Chief Mdingi, suggested the name Zenani, which means 'What have you brought to the world?' – a poetic name that embodies a challenge, suggesting that one must contribute something to society. It is a name one does not simply possess, but has to live up to.

My mother came from the Transkei to help Winnie, and planned to give Zenani a Xhosa baptism by calling in an *inyanga*, a tribal healer, to give the baby a traditional herbal bath. But Winnie was adamantly opposed, thinking it unhealthy and outdated, and instead smeared Zenani with olive oil, plastered her little body with Johnson's Baby Powder, and filled her stomach with shark oil.

As soon as Winnie was up and about, I undertook the task of teaching the new mother of the household how to drive. Driving, in those days, was a man's business; very few women, especially African women, were to be seen in the driver's seat. But Winnie was independent-minded and intent on learning, and it would be useful because I was away so much of the time and could not act as her chauffeur. Perhaps I am an impatient teacher or perhaps I had a headstrong pupil, but when I attempted to give Winnie lessons along a relatively flat and quiet Orlando road, we could not seem to shift gears without quarrelling. Finally, after she had ignored one too many of my suggestions, I stormed out of the car and walked home. Winnie seemed to do better without my tutelage than with it, for she proceeded to drive around the township on her own for the next hour. By that time we were ready to make up, and it is a story we subsequently laughed about.

Married life and motherhood was an adjustment for Winnie. She was then a young woman of twenty-five who had yet to form her own character completely. I was already formed and rather stubborn. I knew that others often saw her as 'Mandela's wife'. It was undoubtedly difficult for her to form her own identity in my shadow. I did my best to let her bloom in her own right, and she soon did so without any help from me.

30

On 6 April 1959, the anniversary of Jan van Riebeeck's landing at the Cape, a new organization was born that sought to rival the ANC as the country's premier African political organization and repudiate the white domination that began three centuries before. With a few hundred delegates from around the country at the Orlando Communal Hall, the Pan-Africanist Congress launched itself as an Africanist organization that expressly rejected the multiracialism of the ANC. Like those of us who had formed the Youth League fifteen years before, the founders of the new organization thought the ANC was insufficiently militant, out of touch with the masses and dominated by non-Africans.

Robert Sobukwe was elected president and Potlako Leballo became national secretary, both of them former ANC Youth Leaguers. The PAC presented a manifesto and a constitution, along with Sobukwe's opening address, in which he called for a 'government of the Africans by the Africans and for the Africans'. The PAC declared that it intended to overthrow white supremacy and establish a government Africanist in origin, socialist in content and democratic in form. They disavowed communism in all its forms and considered whites and Indians 'foreign minority groups' or 'aliens' who had no natural place in South Africa. South Africa was for Africans, and no one else.

The birth of the PAC did not come as a surprise to

us. The Africanists within the ANC had been loudly voicing their grievances for more than three years. In 1957 the Africanists had called for a vote of no confidence in the Transvaal Executive at the national conference, but had been defeated. They had opposed the election-day stay-at-home of 1958, and their leader, Potlako Leballo, had been expelled from the ANC. At the November 1958 ANC conference, a group of Africanists had declared their opposition to the Freedom Charter, claiming it violated the principles of African nationalism.

The PAC claimed that it drew its inspiration from the principles surrounding the ANC's founding in 1912, but its views derived principally from the emotional African nationalism put forth by Anton Lembede and A.P. Mda during the founding of the Youth League in 1944. The PAC echoed the axioms and slogans of that time: Africa for the Africans and a United States of Africa. But the immediate cause for the breakaway was its objection to the Freedom Charter and the presence of whites and Indians in the Congress Alliance leadership. It was opposed to interracial cooperation, in large part because it believed that white communists and Indians had come to dominate the ANC.

The founders of the PAC were all well known to me. Robert Sobukwe was an old friend. He was the proverbial gentleman and scholar (his colleagues called him 'Prof'). His consistent willingness to pay the penalty for his principles earned my enduring respect. Potlako Leballo, Peter Raboroko and Zephania Mothopeng were all friends and colleagues. I was astonished and indeed somewhat dismayed to learn that my political mentor Gaur Radebe had joined the PAC. I found it curious that a former member of the Communist Party's Central Committee had decided to align himself with an organization that then explicitly rejected Marxism.

Many of those who cast their lot with the PAC did so out of personal grudges or disappointments, and were thinking not of the advancement of the struggle, but of their own feelings of jealousy or revenge. I have always believed that to be a freedom fighter one must suppress many of the personal feelings that make one feel like a separate individual rather than part of a mass movement. One is fighting for the liberation of millions of people, not the glory of one individual. I am not suggesting that a man become a robot and rid himself of all personal feelings and motivations. But in the same way that a freedom fighter subordinates his own family to the family of the people, he must subordinate his own individual feelings to the movement.

I found the views and the behaviour of the PAC immature. A philosopher once noted that something is odd if a person is not liberal when he is young and conservative when he is old. I am not a conservative, but one matures and regards some of the views of one's youth as undeveloped and callow. While I sympathized with the views of the Africanists and once shared many of them, I believed that the freedom struggle required one to make compromises and accept the kind of discipline that one resisted as a younger, more impulsive man.

The PAC put forward a dramatic and over-ambitious programme that promised quick solutions. Its most dramatic – and naive – promise was that liberation would be achieved by the end of 1963, and it urged

Africans to ready themselves for that historic hour. 'In 1960 we take our first step,' it promised, 'in 1963, our last towards freedom and independence.' Although this prediction inspired hope and enthusiasm among people who were tired of waiting, it is always dangerous for an organization to make promises it cannot keep.

Because of the PAC's anti-communism, it became the darling of the Western press and the American State Department, which hailed its birth as a dagger in the heart of the African left. Even the National Party saw a potential ally in the PAC: they viewed the PAC as mirroring their anti-communism and supporting their views on separate development. The Nationalists also rejected interracial cooperation, and both the National Party and the American State Department saw fit to exaggerate the size and importance of the new organization for their own ends.

While we welcomed anyone brought into the struggle by the PAC, the role of the organization was almost always that of a spoiler. They divided the people at a critical moment, and that was hard to forget. They would ask the people to go to work when we called a general strike, and make misleading statements to counter any pronouncement we would make. Yet the PAC aroused in me the hope that even though the founders were breakaway ANC men, unity between our two groups was possible. I thought that once the heated polemics had cooled, the essential commonality of the struggle would bring us together. Animated by this belief, I paid particular attention to their policy statement and activities, with the idea of finding affinities rather than differences.

The day after the PAC's inaugural conference I

approached Sobukwe for a copy of his presidential address, as well as the constitution and other policy material. Sobukwe, I thought, seemed pleased by my interest, and said he would make sure I received the requested material. I saw him again not long afterwards and reminded him of my request and he said the material was on its way. I subsequently met Potlako Leballo and said, 'Man, you chaps keep promising me your material, but no one has given it to me.' He said, 'Nelson, we have decided not to give it to you because we know you only want to use it to attack us.' I disabused him of this notion, and he relented, giving me all that I had sought.

31

In 1959, Parliament passed the Promotion of Bantu Self Government Act, which created eight separate ethnic Bantustans. This was the foundation of what the state called *groot* or grand apartheid. At roughly the same time, the government introduced the deceptively named Extension of University Education Act, another leg of grand apartheid, which barred non-whites from racially 'open' universities. In introducing the Bantu Self Government Act, de Wet Nel, the minister of Bantu administration and development, said that the welfare of every individual and population group could best be developed within its own national community. Africans, he said, could never be integrated into the white community.

The immorality of the Bantustan policy, whereby 70 per cent of the people would be apportioned only 13 per cent of the land, was obvious. Under the new policy, even though two-thirds of Africans lived in so-called white areas, they could have citizenship only in their own 'tribal homelands'. The scheme gave us neither freedom in white areas nor independence in what they deemed 'our' areas. Verwoerd said the creation of the Bantustans would engender so much goodwill that they would never become the breeding grounds for rebellion.

In reality, it was quite the opposite. The rural areas were in turmoil. Few areas fought so stubbornly as

Zeerust, where Chief Abram Moilaw (with the able assistance of advocate George Bizos), led his people to resist the so-called Bantu Authorities. Such areas are usually invisible to the press, and the government uses their inaccessibility to veil the cruelty of the state's actions. Scores of innocent people were arrested, prosecuted, jailed, banished, beaten, tortured and murdered. The people of Sekhukhuneland also revolted, and the paramount chief, Moroamotshe Sekhukhune, Godfrey Sekhukhune, and other counsellors were arrested and banished. A Sekhukhune chief, Kolane Kgoloko, who was perceived as a government lackey was assassinated. By 1960, resistance in Sekhukhuneland had reached open defiance and people were refusing to pay taxes.

In Zeerust and Sekhukhuneland, ANC branches played a prominent part in the protests. In spite of the severe repression, a number of new ANC branches sprang up in the Zeerust area, one of them having recruited about two thousand members. Sekhukhuneland and Zeerust were the first areas in South Africa where the ANC was banned by the government, evidence of our power in these remote areas.

Protest erupted in eastern Pondoland, where government henchmen were assaulted and killed. Thembuland and Zululand fiercely resisted, and were among the last areas to yield. People were beaten, arrested, deported and imprisoned. In Thembuland, resistance had been going on since 1955, with Sabata part of the forces of protest.

It was especially painful to me that in the Transkei, the wrath of the people was directed against my nephew and one-time mentor K.D. Matanzima. There was no doubt that Daliwonga was collaborating with the government. All the appeals I had made to him over the years had come to naught. There were reports that *impis* (traditional warriors) from Matanzima's headquarters had burned down villages that opposed him. There were several assassination attempts against him. Equally painful was the fact that Winnie's father was serving on Matanzima's council and was an unwavering supporter. This was terribly difficult for Winnie: her father and her husband were on opposite sides of the same issue. She loved her father, but she rejected his politics.

On a number of occasions, tribesmen and kinsmen from the Transkei visited me in Orlando to complain about chiefs collaborating with the government. Sabata was opposed to the Bantu Authorities and would not capitulate, but my visitors were afraid that Matanzima would depose him, which is eventually what happened. At one time, Daliwonga himself came to visit during the Treason Trial and I brought him with me to Pretoria. In the courtroom, Issy Maisels introduced him to the judges and they accorded him a seat of honour. But outside – among the accused – he was not treated so deferentially. He began aggressively to ask the various defendants, who regarded him as a turncoat, why they objected to separate development. Lilian Ngoyi remarked: '*Tyhini, uyadelela lo mntu*' ('Gracious, this man is provocative').

32

It is said that the mills of God grind exceedingly slowly, but even the Lord's machinations cannot compete with those of the South African judicial system. On 3 August 1959, two years and eight months after our arrests, and after a full year of legal manoeuvring, the actual trial commenced at the Old Synagogue in Pretoria. We were finally formally arraigned and all thirty of us pleaded not guilty.

Our defence team was once again led by Issy Maisels, and he was assisted by Sydney Kentridge, Bram Fischer and Vernon Berrangé. This time, at long last, the trial was in earnest. During the first two months of the case, the Crown entered some two thousand documents into the record and called 210 witnesses, 200 of whom were members of the Special Branch. These detectives admitted to hiding in wardrobes and under beds, posing as ANC members, perpetrating virtually any deception that would enable them to get information about our organization. Yet many of the documents the state submitted and the speeches they transcribed were public documents, public speeches, information available to all. As before, much of the Crown's evidence consisted of books, papers and documents seized from the accused during numerous raids that took place between 1952 and 1956, as well as notes taken by the police at Congress meetings during this same period. As before, the reports of our speeches by the Special

Branch officers were generally muddled. We used to joke that between the poor acoustics of the hall and the confused and inaccurate reports of the Special Branch detectives, we could be fined for what we did not say, imprisoned for what we could not hear and hanged for what we did not do.

At lunchtime we were permitted to sit outside in the spacious garden of a neighbouring vicarage where we were supplied with a meal cooked by the redoubtable Mrs Thayanagee Pillay and her friends. They prepared a spicy Indian lunch for us almost every day, and also tea, coffee and sandwiches during the morning and afternoon breaks. These respites were like tiny vacations from court, and were a chance for us to discuss politics with each other. Those moments under the shade of the jacaranda trees on the vicarage lawn were the most pleasant of the trial, for in many ways the case was more a test of our endurance than a trial of justice.

On the morning of 11 October, as we were preparing to go to court, we heard an announcement on the radio that the prosecutor, Oswald Pirow, had died suddenly from a stroke. His death was a severe setback to the government, and the effectiveness and aggressiveness of the Crown team diminished from that point on. In court that day, Judge Rumpff paid an emotional eulogy to Pirow, and praised his legal acumen and thoroughness. Although we would benefit from his absence, we did not rejoice at his death. We had developed a certain affection for our opponent, for despite Pirow's noxious political views, he was a humane man without the virulent personal racism of the government he was acting for. His habitual polite reference to us as 'Africans' (even one of our own

attorneys occasionally slipped and referred to us as
'natives') contrasted with his supremacist political lean-
ings. In a curious way, our small world inside the Old
Synagogue seemed balanced when, each morning, we
observed Pirow reading the right-wing *Nuwe Order* at his
table and Bram Fischer reading the left-wing *New Age* at
ours. His donation to us of the more than a hundred
volumes of the preparatory examination free of charge
was a generous gesture that saved the defence a great
deal of money. Advocate de Vos became the new leader
of the Crown's team, but could not match the eloquence or acuity of his predecessor.

Shortly after Pirow's death, the prosecution concluded its submission of evidence. It was then that
the prosecution began its examination of expert witnesses commencing with the long-suffering Professor
Murray, its supposed expert in communism who had
proved so inept in his subject during the preparatory
examination. In a relentless cross-examination by Maisels, Murray admitted that the charter was in fact a
humanitarian document that might well represent the
natural reaction and aspirations of non-whites to the
harsh conditions in South Africa.

Murray was not the only Crown witness who did little
to advance the state's case. Despite the voluminous
amount of Crown evidence and the pages and pages of
testimony from their expert witnesses, the prosecution
had not managed to produce any valid evidence that
the ANC plotted violence, and they knew it. Then, in
March, the prosecution displayed a new burst of confidence. They were about to release their most damn-
ing evidence. With great fanfare and a long drumroll in
the press, the state played for the court a secretly

recorded speech of Robert Resha's. This had been given in his capacity as Transvaal Volunteer-in-Chief to a roomful of Freedom Volunteers in 1956, a few weeks before we were all to be arrested. The courtroom was very quiet, and despite the static of the recording and the background din, one could make out Robert's words very clearly.

> When you are disciplined and you are told by the organization not to be violent, you must not be violent . . . but if you are a true volunteer and you are called upon to be violent, you must be absolutely violent, you must murder! Murder! That is all.

The prosecution believed it had sealed its case. Newspapers prominently featured Resha's words and echoed the sensibilities of the state. To the Crown, the speech revealed the ANC's true and secret intent, unmasking the ANC's public pretence of non-violence. But in fact, Resha's words were an anomaly. Robert was an excellent if rather excitable platform speaker, and his choice of analogy was unfortunate. But as the defence would show, he was merely emphasizing the importance of discipline and that the volunteer must do whatever he is ordered, however unsavoury. Over and over, our witnesses would show that Resha's speech was not only taken out of context but did not represent ANC policy.

The prosecution concluded its case on 10 March 1960 and we were to call our first witness for the defence four days later. We had been in the doldrums for months, but as we started to prepare ourselves for our testimony, we were eager to go on the offensive. We had been parrying the enemy's attacks for too long.

There had been much speculation in the press that our first witness would be Chief Luthuli. The Crown apparently believed that as well, for there was great consternation among the prosecution when, on 14 March, our first witness was not Luthuli but Dr Wilson Conco.

Conco was the son of a Zulu cattle farmer from the beautiful Ixopo district of Natal. In addition to being a practising physician, he had been one of the founders of the Youth League, an active participant in the Defiance Campaign and the treasurer of the ANC. As a preparation for his testimony, he was asked about his brilliant academic record at the University of the Witwatersrand, where he graduated top of his medical school class, ahead of all the sons and daughters of white privilege. As Conco's credentials were cited, I got the distinct impression that Justice Kennedy, who was also from Natal, seemed proud. Natalians are noted for their loyalty to their region, and these peculiar bonds of attachment can sometimes even transcend colour. Indeed, many Natalians thought of themselves as white Zulus. Justice Kennedy had always seemed to be a fair-minded man and I sensed that, through Wilson Conco's example, he began to see us not as heedless rabble-rousers but men of worthy ambitions who could help their country if their country would only help them. At the end of Conco's testimony, when Conco was quoted for some medical achievement, Kennedy said in Zulu, a language in which he was fluent, '*Sinjalo thina maZulu*', which means, 'We Zulus are like that.' Dr Conco proved a calm and articulate witness who reaffirmed the ANC's commitment to non-violence.

Chief Luthuli was next. With his dignity and sincerity, he made a deep impression on the court. He was suffering from high blood pressure, and the court agreed to sit only in the mornings while he gave evidence. His evidence-in-chief lasted several days and he was cross-examined for nearly three weeks. He carefully outlined the evolution of the ANC's policy, putting things simply and clearly, and his former positions as teacher and chief imparted an added gravity and authority to his words. As a devout Christian, he was the perfect person to discuss how the ANC had sincerely strived for racial harmony.

The chief testified to his belief in the innate goodness of man and how moral persuasion plus economic pressure could well lead to a change of heart on the part of white South Africans. In discussing the ANC's policy of non-violence, he emphasized that there was a difference between non-violence and pacifism. Pacifists refused to defend themselves even when violently attacked, but that was not necessarily the case with those who espoused non-violence. Sometimes men and nations, even when non-violent, had to defend themselves when they were attacked.

As I listened to Conco and Luthuli, I thought that here, probably for the first time in their lives, the judges were listening not to their domestic servants who said only what they knew their masters would like to hear, but to independent and articulate Africans spelling out their political beliefs and how they hoped to realize them.

The chief was cross-examined by Advocate Tren-

grove, who doggedly attempted to get him to say the
ANC was dominated by communists and had a dual
policy of non-violence intended for the public and a
secret plan of waging violent revolution. The chief
steadfastly refuted the implications of what Trengrove
was suggesting. He himself was the soul of moderation,
particularly as Trengrove seemed to lose control. At
one point, Trengrove accused the chief of hypocrisy.
The chief ignored Trengrove's aspersion and calmly
remarked to the bench, 'My Lord, I think the Crown is
running wild.'

But on 21 March the chief's testimony was interrupted by a shattering event outside the courtroom.
On that day, the country was rocked by an occurrence
of such magnitude that when Chief Luthuli returned to
testify a month later, the courtroom – and all of South
Africa – was a different place.

33

The December 1959 ANC annual conference was held in Durban during that city's dynamic anti-pass demonstrations. The conference unanimously voted to initiate a massive countrywide anti-pass campaign beginning on 31 March and climaxing on 26 June with a great bonfire of passes.

The planning began immediately. On 31 March, deputations were sent to local authorities. ANC officials toured the country, talking to the branches about the campaign. ANC field-workers spread the word in townships and factories. Leaflets, stickers and posters were printed and circulated and posted in trains and buses.

The mood of the country was grim. The state was threatening to ban the organization, with cabinet ministers warning the ANC that it would soon be battered with 'an ungloved fist'. Elsewhere in Africa the freedom struggle was marching on: the emergence of the independent republic of Ghana in 1957 and its pan-Africanist, anti-apartheid leader, Kwame Nkrumah, had alarmed the Nationalists and made them even more intent on clamping down on dissent at home. In 1960 seventeen former colonies in Africa were scheduled to become independent states. In February, the British prime minister Harold Macmillan visited South Africa and gave a speech before Parliament in which he talked of 'winds of change' sweeping Africa.

The PAC at the time appeared lost; they were a

leadership in search of followers, and they had yet to initiate any action that put them on the political map. They knew of the ANC's anti-pass campaign and had been invited to join, but instead of linking arms with the Congress movement, they sought to sabotage us. The PAC announced that it was launching its own anti-pass campaign on 21 March, ten days before ours was to begin. No conference had been held by them to discuss the date, no organizational work of any significance had been undertaken. It was a blatant case of opportunism. Their actions were motivated more by a desire to eclipse the ANC than to defeat the enemy.

Four days before the scheduled demonstration, Sobukwe invited us to join with the PAC. Sobukwe's offer was not a gesture of unity but a tactical move to prevent the PAC from being criticized for not including us. He made the offer at the eleventh hour, and we declined to participate. On the morning of 21 March Sobukwe and his executive walked to the Orlando police station to turn themselves in for arrest. The tens of thousands of people going to work ignored the PAC men. In the magistrate's court, Sobukwe announced that the PAC would not attempt to defend itself, in accordance with its slogan: 'No bail, no defence, no fine'. They believed the defiers would receive sentences of a few weeks. But Sobukwe was sentenced not to three weeks but three years' imprisonment without the option of a fine.

The response to the PAC's call in Johannesburg was minimal. No demonstrations at all took place in Durban, Port Elizabeth or East London. But in Evaton Z.B. Molete, ably assisted by Joe Molefi, and Vusumuzi Make, mustered the support of the entire township as several hundred men presented themselves for arrest without passes. Cape Town saw one of the biggest anti-pass demonstrations in the history of the city. In Langa township, outside Cape Town, some thirty thousand people, led by the young student, Philip Kgosana, gathered and were spurred to rioting by a police baton-charge. Two people were killed. But the last of the areas where demonstrations took place was the most calamitous and the one whose name still echoes with tragedy: Sharpeville.

Sharpeville was a small township about thirty-five miles south of Johannesburg in the grim industrial complex around Vereeniging. PAC activists had done an excellent job of organizing the area. In the early afternoon, a crowd of several thousand surrounded the police station. The demonstrators were controlled and unarmed. The police force of seventy-five was greatly outnumbered and panicky. No one heard warning shots or an order to shoot, but suddenly the police opened fire on the crowd and continued to shoot as the demonstrators turned and ran in fear. When the area had cleared, sixty-nine Africans lay dead, most of them shot in the back as they were fleeing. All told, more than seven hundred shots had been fired into the crowd, wounding more than four hundred people, including dozens of women and children. It was a massacre, and the next day press photos displayed the savagery on front pages around the world.

The shootings at Sharpeville provoked national turmoil and a government crisis. Outraged protests came in from across the globe, including one from the American State Department. For the first time, the UN Security Council intervened in South African affairs, blaming the government for the shootings and urging it to initiate measures to bring about racial equality. The Johannesburg stock exchange plunged, and capital started to flow out of the country. South African whites began making plans to emigrate. Liberals urged Verwoerd to offer concessions to Africans. The government insisted that Sharpeville was the result of a communist conspiracy.

The massacre at Sharpeville created a new situation in the country. In spite of the amateurishness and opportunism of their leaders, the PAC rank and file displayed great courage and fortitude in their demonstrations at Sharpeville and Langa. In just one day, they had moved to the front lines of the struggle, and Robert Sobukwe was being hailed inside and outside the country as the saviour of the liberation movement. We in the ANC had to make rapid adjustments to this new situation, and we did so.

A small group of us – Walter, Duma Nokwe, Joe Slovo and I – held an all-night meeting in Johannesburg to plan a response. We knew we had to acknowledge the events in some way and give the people an outlet for their anger and grief. We conveyed our plans to Chief Luthuli, and he readily accepted them. On 26 March, in Pretoria, the chief publicly burned his pass, calling on others to do the same. He announced a nationwide stay-at-home for 28 March, a national Day of Mourning and protest for the atrocities at Sharpeville. In Orlando, Duma Nokwe and I then burned our passes before hundreds of people and dozens of press photographers.

Two days later, on the 28th, the country responded magnificently as several hundred thousand Africans observed the chief's call. Only a truly mass organization could coordinate such activities, and the ANC did so. In Cape Town a crowd of fifty thousand met in Langa township to protest against the shootings. Rioting broke out in many areas. The government declared a State of Emergency, suspending habeas corpus and assuming sweeping powers to act against all forms of subversion. South Africa was now under martial law.

34

At 1.30 in the morning on 30 March I was awakened by sharp, unfriendly knocks at my door, the unmistakable signature of the police. 'The time has come,' I said to myself as I opened the door to find half-a-dozen armed security policemen. They turned the house upside down, taking virtually every piece of paper they could find, including the transcripts I had recently been making of my mother's recollections of family history and tribal fables. I was never to see them again. I was then arrested without a warrant, and given no opportunity to call my lawyer. They refused to inform my wife as to where I was to be taken. I simply nodded at Winnie; it was no time for words of comfort.

Thirty minutes later we arrived at Newlands police station, which was familiar to me from the many occasions when I had visited clients there. The station was located in Sophiatown, or rather what was left of it, for the once bustling township was now a ruin of bulldozed buildings and vacant plots. Inside I found a number of my colleagues who had been similarly roused out of bed, and over the course of the night, more arrived; by morning we totalled forty in all. We were put in a cramped yard with only the sky as a roof and a dim bulb for light, a space so small and dank that we remained standing all night.

At 7.15 we were taken into a tiny cell with a single drainage hole in the floor which could be flushed only from the outside. We were given no blankets, no food, no mats and no toilet paper. The hole regularly became blocked and the stench in the room was insufferable. We issued numerous protests, among them the demand to be fed. These were met with surly rejoinders, and we resolved that the next time the door opened, we would surge out into the adjacent courtyard and refuse to return to the cell until we had been fed. The young policeman on duty took fright and left as we stampeded through the door. A few minutes later, a burly no-nonsense sergeant entered the courtyard and ordered us to return to the cell. 'Go inside!' he yelled. 'If you don't, I'll bring in fifty men with batons and we'll break your skulls!' After the horrors of Sharpeville, the threat did not seem empty.

The station commander approached the gate of the courtyard to observe us, and then came over and berated me for standing with my hands in my pockets. 'Is that the way you act around an officer?' he yelled. 'Take your bloody hands out of your pockets!' I kept my hands firmly rooted in my pockets as though I were taking a walk on a chilly day. I told him that I might condescend to remove my hands if we were fed.

At 3 p.m., more than twelve hours after most of us had arrived, we were delivered a container of thin mealie pap and no utensils. Normally I would have considered this unfit for consumption, but we reached in with our unwashed hands and ate as though we had been provided with the most delicious delicacies under the sun. After our meal, we elected a committee to represent us, which included Duma Nokwe and Z.B. Molete, the publicity secretary of the Pan-Africanist Congress, and me. I was elected spokesman. We immediately drew up a petition protesting at the unfit conditions and demanding our immediate release on the ground that our detention was illegal.

At 6 p.m. we received sleeping-mats and blankets. I do not think words can do justice to a description of the foulness and filthiness of this bedding. The blankets were encrusted with dried blood and vomit, ridden with lice, vermin and cockroaches, and reeked with a stench that actually competed with the stink of the drain.

Near midnight, we were told we were to be called out, but for what we did not know. Some of the men smiled at the expectation of release. Others knew better. I was the first to be called, and I was ushered over to the front gate of the prison where I was briefly released in front of a group of police officers. But before I could move, an officer shouted: 'Name!'

'Mandela,' I said.

'Nelson Mandela,' the officer said, 'I arrest you under the powers vested in me by the Emergency Regulations.' We were not to be released at all, but rearrested under the terms of what we only then discovered was a State of Emergency. Each of us in turn was released for mere seconds and then re-arrested. We had been arrested illegally before the State of Emergency; now we were being properly arrested under the State of Emergency that had come into force at midnight. We drafted a memorandum to the commander asking to know our rights.

The next morning I was called to the commander's office, where I found my colleague Robert Resha, who had been arrested and was being interrogated by the station commander. When I walked into the room,

Resha asked the commander why he had erupted at me the previous night. His answer was that of the typical white *baas*: 'Mandela was cheeky.' I responded, 'I'm not bound to take my hands out of my pockets for the likes of you, then or now.' The commander jumped out of his chair, but was restrained by other officers. At this moment, Special Branch Detective Sergeant Helberg entered the office and said, 'Hello, Nelson!' in a pleasant way. To which I shot back, 'I am not Nelson to you, I am Mr Mandela.' The room was on the brink of becoming a full-scale battle when we were informed that we had to leave to attend the Treason Trial in Pretoria. I did not know whether to laugh or despair, but in the midst of this thirty-six hours of mistreatment and the declaration of a State of Emergency, the government still saw fit to take us back to Pretoria to continue their desperate and now seemingly outdated case against us. We were taken straight to Pretoria Local Prison and detained.

35

In the meantime, court resumed in our absence, on 31 March, but the witness box was conspicuously empty. Those who did attend, were the accused whom the police had failed to pick up under the State of Emergency. Chief Luthuli had been in the middle of his evidence, and Judge Rumpff asked for an explanation for his absence. He was informed that the chief had been taken into custody the night before. Judge Rumpff expressed irritation with the explanation and said he did not see why the State of Emergency should stand in the way of his trial. He demanded that the police bring the chief to court so that he could resume his testimony, and court was adjourned.

Later we discovered that after the chief's arrest, he had been assaulted. He had been walking up some stairs when he was jostled by a warder, causing his hat to fall to the floor. As he bent to pick it up, he was smacked across the head and face. This was hard for us to take. A man of immense dignity and achievement, a lifelong devout Christian and a man with a dangerous heart condition was treated like a barnyard animal by men who were not fit to tie his shoes.

When we were called back into session that morning, Judge Rumpff was informed that the police refused to bring the chief to court. The judge then adjourned court for the day, and we expected to go home. But as they were leaving the court grounds to find transport, we were all once again arrested.

But the police, with their usual disorganized over-zealousness, made a comical mistake. Wilton Mkwayi, one of the accused and a longtime union leader and ANC man, had travelled to Pretoria for the trial from Port Elizabeth. Somehow he had become separated from his colleagues, and when he approached the gate and saw the commotion of his fellow accused being rearrested, he asked a policeman what was going on. The policeman ordered him to leave. Wilton stood there. The policeman again ordered him to leave, whereupon Wilton informed the officer he was one of the accused. The officer called him a liar, and threatened to arrest him for obstruction of justice. The officer then angrily ordered him to leave the area. Wilton shrugged his shoulders and walked out of the gate; that was the last anyone saw of him in court. He went underground for the next two months, success-fully evading arrest, and then was smuggled out of the country, soon emerging as a foreign representative for the Congress of Trade Unions and later going for military training in China.

That night, we were joined by detainees from other parts of the Transvaal. The countrywide police raid had led to the detention without trial of more than two thousand people. These men and women belonged to all races and all anti-apartheid parties. A call-up of soldiers had been announced, and units of the army had been mobilized and stationed in strategic areas around the country. On 8 April both the ANC and the PAC were declared illegal organizations under the Suppression of Communism Act. Overnight, being a member of the ANC had become a felony punishable by a term in jail and a fine. The penalty for furthering the aims of the ANC was imprisonment for up to ten years. Now even non-violent law-abiding protests under the auspices of the ANC were illegal. The struggle had entered a new phase. We were now, all of us, outlaws.

For the duration of the State of Emergency we stayed at Pretoria Local, where the conditions were as bad as those at Newlands. Groups of five prisoners were pressed into cells measuring nine by seven feet; the cells were filthy, with poor lighting and worse ventilation. We had a single sanitary pail with a loose lid, and vermin-infested blankets. We were allowed outside for an hour a day.

On our second day in Pretoria, we sent a deputation to complain about the conditions to the prison's commanding officer, Colonel Snyman. The colonel's response was rude and abrupt. He demanded that we produce evidence, calling our complaints lies. 'You have brought the vermin into my prison from your filthy homes,' he sneered.

I said we also required a room that was quiet and well lit so that we could prepare our case. The colonel was again contemptuous: 'Government regulations do not require prisoners to read books, if you can read at all.' Despite the colonel's disdainful attitude, the cells were soon painted and fumigated and we were supplied with fresh blankets and sanitary pails. We were permitted to stay out in the yard for much of the day, while those of us involved in the Treason Trial were provided with a large cell for consultations, in which we were also permitted to keep legal books.

Pretoria Local would be our home for the foreseeable future. We would leave for the trial in the morning and return to the prison in the afternoon. The prison, according to apartheid dictates, separated detainees by colour. We were of course already separated from our white colleagues, but the separation from our Indian and Coloured comrades within the same non-white facility seemed like madness. We demanded to be accommodated together, and were given all sorts of absurd explanations why this was impossible. When the proverbial inflexibility of red tape is combined with the petty small-mindedness of racism, the result can be mind-boggling. But the authorities eventually yielded, allowing the Treason Trialists to be kept together.

Although we were kept together, our diet was fixed according to race. For breakfast, Africans, Indians and Coloureds received the same quantities, except that Indians and Coloureds received a half-teaspoonful of sugar, which we did not. For supper, the diets were the same, except that Indians and Coloureds received four ounces of bread while we received none. This latter distinction was made on the curious premise that Africans did not naturally like bread, which was a more sophisticated or 'Western' taste. The diet for white detainees was far superior to that for Africans. So colour-conscious were the authorities that even the type of sugar and bread supplied to blacks and whites differed: white prisoners received white sugar and white bread, while Coloured and Indian prisoners were given brown sugar and brown bread.

We complained vociferously about the inferior quality of the food and, as a result, our advocate Sydney Kentridge made a formal complaint in court. I stated that the food was unfit for human consumption. Judge

Rumpff agreed to sample the food himself that day. Samp and beans was the best meal that the prison prepared, and in this case the authorities put in more beans and gravy than usual. Judge Rumpff ate a few spoonfuls and pronounced the food well cooked and tasty. He did allow that it should be served warm. We laughed among ourselves at the idea of 'warm' jail food; it was a contradiction in terms. Eventually the authorities supplied the detainees with what they called an Improved Diet: Africans received bread, while Indians and Coloureds received the same food as that provided for white prisoners.

I enjoyed one extraordinary privilege during our detention: weekend trips to Johannesburg. These were not a vacation from prison but a busman's holiday. Shortly before the State of Emergency, Oliver left South Africa on the instructions of the ANC. We had long suspected a clamp-down was coming, and Congress decided that certain members needed to leave the country to strengthen the organization abroad in anticipation of the time when it would be banned entirely.

Oliver's departure was one of the best-planned and most fortunate actions ever taken by the movement. At the time we hardly suspected how absolutely vital the external wing would become. With his wisdom and calmness, his patience and organizational skills, his ability to lead and inspire without stepping on toes, Oliver was the perfect choice for this assignment.

Before leaving, Oliver had retained a mutual friend of ours, Hymie Davidoff, a local attorney, to close our office and wind up our practice. Davidoff made a special request to Colonel Prinsloo to permit me to come to Johannesburg at weekends to help him put things in order. In a fit of generosity, the colonel agreed, allowing me to be driven to Johannesburg on Friday afternoons to work in the office all weekend and then be driven back to the trial on Monday morning. Sergeant Kruger and I would leave after court adjourned at one o'clock on Friday, and after arriving at my office I would work with Davidoff and our accountant Nathan Marcus. I would spend the nights in Marshall Square prison and the days at the office.

Sergeant Kruger was a tall and imposing fellow who treated us with fairness. On the way from Pretoria to Johannesburg he would often stop the car and leave me inside while he went into a shop to buy biltong, oranges and chocolate for both of us. I thought about jumping out of the car, especially on Fridays, when the pavements and streets were busy and one could get lost in a crowd.

While at the office, I could walk downstairs to the ground-floor café to buy incidentals, and he turned his head aside on one or two occasions when Winnie came to visit me. We had a kind of gentleman's code between us: I would not escape and thereby get him into trouble, while he permitted me a degree of freedom.

36

On 25 April, the day before the trial was to resume, Issy Maisels called us together to discuss the grave effect the State of Emergency was having on the conduct of the trial. Because of the Emergency Regulations, consultations between the accused and our lawyers had become virtually impossible. Our lawyers, who were based in Johannesburg, had trouble seeing us in prison and were unable to prepare our case. They would often drive up and be informed that we were not available. Even when we were able to see them, consultations were harassed and cut short. More important, Maisels explained that under the Emergency Regulations, those already in detention would be exposing themselves to further detention merely by testifying, for they would inevitably make statements regarded as 'subversive', thereby subjecting themselves to greater penalties. Defence witnesses who were not imprisoned now risked detainment if they testified.

The defence team proposed that they withdraw from the case in protest. Maisels explained the serious implications of such a withdrawal and the consequences of our conducting our own defence in a capital case. Under the hostile atmosphere at the time, he said, the judges might see fit to give us longer terms of imprisonment. We discussed the proposal among ourselves, and each of the twenty-nine accused – we were now minus Wilton Mkwayi – was able to express his opinion.

The resolution was unanimously endorsed, and it was agreed that Duma Nokwe and I would help in preparing the case in the absence of our lawyers. I was in favour of this dramatic gesture, for it highlighted the iniquities of the State of Emergency.

On 26 April Duma Nokwe, the first African advocate in the Transvaal, rose in court and made the sensational announcement that the accused were instructing defence counsel to withdraw from the case. Maisels then said simply, 'We have no further mandate and we will consequently not trouble Your Lordships any further,' after which the defence team silently filed out of the synagogue. This shocked the three-judge panel, who warned us in direst terms about the dangers of conducting our own defence. But we were angry and eager to take on the state. For the next five months, until the virtual end of the Emergency, we conducted our own defence.

Our strategy was simple and defensive in nature: to drag out the case until the State of Emergency was lifted and our lawyers could return. The case had gone on so long already that it did not seem to matter if we stretched it out even further. In practice, this strategy became rather comical. Under the law, each one of us was now entitled to conduct his own defence and was able to call as a witness each of the other accused; and each of the accused was entitled to cross-examine each witness. We were arranged in alphabetical order according to the docket and accused No. 1 was Farid Adams, of the Transvaal Indian Youth Congress. Farid would open his case by calling accused No. 2, Helen Joseph, as his first witness. After being examined by Farid, Helen would then be cross-examined by the

other twenty-seven co-accused. She would then be
cross-examined by the Crown and re-examined by
accused No. 1. Adams would then proceed to call
accused No. 3 and so on, and the whole procedure
would duplicate itself until every accused was called in
this fashion. At that rate, we would be at trial until the
millennium.

It is never easy to prepare a case from prison, and in
this instance we were hampered by the customary
apartheid barriers. All of the accused needed to be
able to meet together, but prison regulations prohibited meetings between male and female prisoners, and
between black and white, so we were not permitted to
consult with Helen Joseph, Leon Levy, Lilian Ngoyi
and Bertha Mashaba.

Helen, as the first witness to be called, needed to
prepare her evidence in the presence of Duma, myself
and Farid Adams, who would be examining her. After
protracted negotiations with the prison authorities, we
were permitted to have consultations under very strict
conditions. Helen Joseph, Lilian, Leon, and Bertha
were to be brought from their various prisons and
sections (separated by race and gender) to the African
men's prison. The first stipulation was that there could
be no physical contact between white and black prisoners, and between male and female prisoners. The
authorities erected an iron grille to separate Helen
and Leon (as whites) from us and a second partition to
separate them from Lilian and Bertha (as African
women), who were also participating in the preparations. Helen needed to be separated from Lilian because of colour, and from us because of sex and colour.

Even a master architect would have had trouble designing such a structure. In prison we were separated from each other by this elaborate metal contraption, while in court we all mingled freely.

We first needed to coach Farid in the art of courtroom etiquette, and rehearse Helen's testimony. To help Helen, I was playing the role that Farid would play in court. I assumed the proper courtroom manner and began the examination.

'Name?' I said.

'Helen Joseph,' she replied.

'Age?'

Silence. I repeated, 'Age?'

Helen pursed her lips and waited. Then, after some moments, she scowled at me and said sharply, 'What has my age to do with this case, Nelson?'

Helen was as charming as she was courageous, but she also had an imperious side. She was a woman of a certain age, and sensitive about it. I explained that it was customary to note down the witness's particulars, such as name, age, address and place of birth. A witness's age helps the court to weigh her testimony and influences the sentencing.

I continued: 'Age?'

Helen stiffened. 'Nelson,' she said, 'I will cross that bridge when I come to it in court, but not until then. Let us move on.'

I then asked her a series of questions that she might expect from the Crown in a manner perhaps too realistic for her, because at one point Helen turned to me and said, 'Are you Mandela or are you the prosecutor?'

There were other light moments, some of which were quite encouraging. I was permitted to visit Helen

Joseph at weekends and bring her records of the proceedings. On these occasions I met other women detainees and consulted with them as possible witnesses. I was always very cordial with the white wardresses, and I noticed that my visits caused considerable interest. The wardresses had never known there *was* such a species as an African lawyer or doctor, and regarded me as an exotic creature. But as I became more familiar they became more friendly and at ease, and I joked with them that I would handle any of their legal problems. Seeing prominent and educated white women discussing serious matters with a black man on the basis of perfect equality could only lead to the weakening of the wardresses' apartheid assumptions.

Once during a long interview with Helen, I turned to the wardress who was required to sit in on our conversation and said, 'I'm sorry to bore you with this endless consultation.' 'No,' she said, 'you are not boring me at all, I am enjoying it.' I could see she was following our conversation, and once or twice she even offered small suggestions. I saw this as one of the side benefits of the trial. Most of these wardresses had no idea why we were in prison, and gradually began to discover what we were fighting for and why we were willing to risk jail in the first place.

This is precisely why the National Party was violently opposed to all forms of integration. Only a white electorate indoctrinated with the idea of the black threat, ignorant of African ideas and policies, could support the monstrous racist philosophy of the National Party. Familiarity, in this case, would breed not contempt but understanding, and even, eventually, harmony.

The light moments in prison could not make up for the low ones. Winnie was allowed to visit on a number of occasions while I was in Pretoria, and each time she brought Zenani, who was then beginning to walk and talk. I would hold her and kiss her if the guards permitted, and towards the end of the interview, hand her back to Winnie. As Winnie was saying good-bye, and the guards were ushering them out, Zeni would often motion for me to come with them, and I could see from her small puzzled face that she did not understand why I could not.

In court, Farid Adams deftly led Helen through her evidence-in-chief. He argued frequently and fairly competently with the judges and sometimes outpointed them. We were now energized: no longer was anyone doing crossword puzzles to pass the time. As the accused took turns cross-examining the witnesses, the Crown and the prosecution began to get a sense for the first time of the true calibre of the men and women on trial.

According to South African law, since we were in the Supreme Court, Duma, as an advocate, was the only one permitted to address the judges direct. I, as an attorney, could instruct him, but I was not technically permitted to address the court, and neither were any of the other defendants. We dismissed our advocates under the correct assumption that an accused, in the absence of representation, would be permitted to address the court. I addressed the court and Justice Rumpff trying to frustrate us, interrupted me. 'You appreciate the fact, Mr Mandela,' he said, 'that Mr Nokwe, as an advocate, is the only lawyer who is permitted to address the court.' To which I replied,

'Very well, My Lord, I believe we are all prepared to abide by that as long as you are prepared to pay Mr Nokwe his fees.' From then on no one objected to any of the accused addressing the court.

While Farid was questioning Helen and the subsequent witnesses, Duma and I sat on either side of him, supplying him with questions, helping him to deal with legal issues as they arose. In general, he did not need much prompting. But one day, when we were under constant pressure, we were whispering suggestions to him every few seconds. Farid seemed weary, and Duma and I were running out of material. Then, without consulting us, Farid suddenly asked the judges for a postponement, saying he was fatigued. The judges refused his application, saying it was not sufficient reason for a postponement and reiterating the warning they gave us the day our lawyers withdrew.

That afternoon there was no singing as we returned to prison, and everyone sat with sullen faces. A crisis was brewing among the accused. Upon our arrival in prison, a handful of them demanded a meeting. I called all the men together, and J. Nkampeni, a businessman from Port Elizabeth who had helped out the families of defiers during the Defiance Campaign, led what turned out to be an attack.

'Madiba,' he said, using my clan name as a sign of respect, 'I want you to tell us why you drove away our lawyers.' I reminded him that the lawyers were not released by any one individual; their withdrawal had been approved by all, including himself. 'But what did we know about court procedure, Madiba?' he said. 'We relied on you lawyers.'

A substantial number of men shared Nkampeni's

misgivings. I warned them against the dangers of being disheartened and insisted that we were doing quite well. I said that today was a minor setback, and that we would face worse difficulties. Our case was far more than a trial of legal issues between the Crown and a group of people charged with breaking the law. It was a trial of strength, a test of the power of a moral idea versus an immoral one, and I said we needed to worry about more than the legal technique of our advocates. The protest abated.

After Helen Joseph had been cross-examined and re-examined, accused No. 3, Ahmed Kathrada, opened his case. It was during the testimony of Kathy's second witness, accused No. 4, Stanley Lollan, a member of the executive of the Coloured People's Congress, that Prime Minister Verwoerd announced that the State of Emergency would soon be lifted. The Emergency had never been intended to be permanent, and the government believed that it had successfully stifled the liberation struggle. At this point our defence lawyers returned, to the general relief of all of us, though we remained in prison for another few weeks. We had been kept in detention and had functioned without our lawyers for more than five months.

My own testimony began on 3 August. I felt well prepared through my preparation of the others. After three years of silence, banning and internal exile, I looked forward to the chance to speak out before the people attempting to judge me. During my evidence-in-chief I preached moderation and reaffirmed the ANC's commitment to non-violent struggle. In answer to a question as to whether democracy could be achieved through gradual reforms, I suggested that it could.

> We demand universal adult franchise and we are prepared to exert economic pressure to attain our demands. We will launch defiance campaigns, stay-at-homes, either singly or together, until the Government should say, 'Gentlemen, we cannot have this state of affairs, laws being defied, and this whole situation created by stay-at-homes. Let's talk.' In my own view I would say, 'Yes, let us talk,' and the Government would say, 'We think that the Europeans at present are not ready for a type of government where they might be dominated by non-Europeans. We think we should give you 60 seats. The African population to elect 60 Africans to represent them in Parliament. We will leave the matter over for five years and we will review it at the end of five years.' In my view, that would be a victory, My Lords; we would have taken a significant step towards the attainment of universal adult suffrage for Africans, and we would then for the five years say that we will suspend civil disobedience.

The state was determined to prove that I was a dangerous, violence-spouting communist. While I was not a communist or a member of the party, I did not want to be seen as distancing myself from my communist allies. Although I could have been sent back to jail for voicing such views, I did not hesitate to reaffirm the tremendous support the communists had given us. At one point, the bench posed the question as to whether or not I thought a one-party state was a viable option for South Africa.

> NM: My Lord, it is not a question of form, it is a question of democracy. If democracy would be best expressed by a one-party system then I would examine the proposition very carefully. But if a democracy could best be expressed by a multiparty system, then I would examine that carefully. In this country, for example, we have a multiparty system at present, but so far as the non-Europeans are concerned, this is the most vicious despotism that you could think of.

I became testy with Judge Rumpff when he fell into the mistake made by so many white South Africans about the idea of a universal franchise. Their notion was that to exercise this responsibility, voters must be 'educated'. To a narrow-thinking person, it is hard to explain that to be 'educated' does not only mean being literate and having a BA, and that an illiterate man can be a far more 'educated' voter than someone with an advanced degree.

> JUSTICE RUMPFF: What is the value of participation in the Government of a state of people who know nothing?
> NM: My Lord, what happens when illiterate whites vote . . .
> JUSTICE RUMPFF: Are they not subject as much to the influence of election leaders as children would be?
> NM: No, My Lord, this is what happens in practice.

A man stands up to contest a seat in a particular area; he draws up a manifesto, and he says, 'These are the ideas for which I stand'; it is a rural area and he says, 'I am against stock limitation'; then, listening to the policy of this person, you decide whether this man will advance your interests if you return him to Parliament, and on that basis you vote for a candidate. It has nothing to do with education.

JUSTICE RUMPFF: He only looks to his own interests?

NM: No, a man looks at a man who will be able to best present his point of view and votes for that man.

I told the court that we believed we could achieve our demands without violence, through our numerical superiority.

We had in mind that in the foreseeable future it will be possible for us to achieve these demands, and we worked on the basis that Europeans themselves, in spite of the wall of prejudice and hostility which we encountered, that they can never remain indifferent indefinitely to our demands, because we are hitting them in the stomach with our policy of economic pressure. The Europeans dare not look at it with indifference. They would have to respond to it and indeed, My Lord, they are responding to it.

The Emergency was lifted on the last day of August. We would be going home for the first time in five months.

When people in Johannesburg heard about the end of the Emergency, they drove up on the chance that we might be released; when we were let go, we were met with a jubilant reception from friends and family. Winnie had got a ride to Pretoria and our reunion was joyous. I had not held my wife in five months or seen her smile with joy. For the first time in five months, I slept in my own bed that night.

After one has been in prison, it is the small things that one appreciates: being able to take a walk whenever one wants, going into a shop and buying a newspaper, speaking or choosing to remain silent. The simple act of being able to control one's person.

Even after the end of the Emergency, the trial continued for another nine months until 29 March 1961. In many ways, these were the glory days for the accused, for our own people were on the stand fearlessly enunciating ANC policy. Robert Resha forcefully disputed the government's absurd contention that the ANC wanted to induce the government to use violence so that we could use violence in return. Gert Sibande eloquently told the court of the miseries of African farmworkers. The venerable Isaac Behndy of Ladysmith, eighty-one years old, a lay preacher of the African Native Mission Church, explained why we opted for stay-at-homes instead of strikes.

In October the redoubtable Professor Matthews was called as our final witness. He was imperturbable on the witness stand and treated the prosecutors as though they were errant students who needed stern admonishment. Often he would reply to the arrogant prosecutor with some version of the following: 'What you really want me to say is that the speech which you allege is violent represents the policy of my organization. First, your contention is incorrect and second, I am not going to say that.'

He explained in beautiful language that the African people knew that a non-violent struggle would entail suffering but had chosen it because they prized freedom above all else. People, he said, will willingly undergo the severest suffering in order to free themselves from oppression. With Professor Matthews in the dock, the defence ended on a high note. After he finished testifying, Justice Kennedy shook his hand and expressed the hope that they would meet again under better circumstances.

37

After the lifting of the Emergency, the National Executive met secretly in September to discuss the future. We had had discussions in jail during the trial, but this was our first formal session. The state was arming itself not for an external threat but an internal one. We would not disband but carry on from underground. We would have to depart from the democratic procedures outlined in the ANC's constitution of holding conferences, branch meetings and public gatherings. New structures had to be created for communication with unbanned Congress organizations. But all of these new structures were illegal and would subject the participants to arrest and imprisonment. The Executive Committee and its subordinate structures would have to be severely streamlined to adapt to illegal conditions. Of necessity, we dissolved the ANC Youth League and Women's League. Some fiercely resisted these changes; but the fact was that we were now an illegal organization. For those who would continue to participate, politics went from being a risky occupation to a truly perilous one.

Though Mandela and Tambo had closed its doors and settled its remaining accounts, I continued to do whatever legal work I could. Numerous colleagues readily made their offices, staff and phone facilities available to me, but most of the time I preferred to work from Ahmed Kathrada's flat, No. 13 Kholvad

House. Although my practice had dissolved, my reputation as a lawyer was undimmed. Soon, the lounge of No. 13 and the passage outside were crammed with clients. Kathy would return home and discover that the only room in which he could be alone was his kitchen.

During this period, I hardly had time for meals and saw very little of my family. I would stay late in Pretoria preparing for our case, or rush back to handle another case. When I could actually sit down to supper with my family, the telephone would ring and I would be called away. Winnie was pregnant again and infinitely patient. She was hoping her husband might actually be at the hospital when she gave birth. But it was not to be.

During the Christmas adjournment in 1960, I learned that Makgatho was ill in the Transkei where he was at school, and I violated my banning orders and went down to see him. I drove the entire night, stopping only for petrol. Makgatho required surgery, and I decided to bring him back with me to Johannesburg. I again drove all night, and took him to his mother's place while I went to arrange for his surgery. When I returned, I learned that Winnie had already gone into labour. I rushed to the non-European wing of Bridgman Memorial Hospital to find that mother and daughter were already in residence. The newborn girl was fine, but Winnie was very weak.

We named our new daughter Zindziswa, after the daughter of the poet laureate of the Xhosa people, Samuel Mqhayi, who had inspired me so many years before at Healdtown. The poet returned home after a very long trip to find that his wife had given birth to a daughter. He had not known that she was pregnant and assumed that the child had been fathered by another man. In our culture, when a woman gives birth, for ten days the husband does not enter the house where she is confined. In this case, the poet was too enraged to observe this custom, and he stormed into the house with an assegai, ready to stab both mother and daughter. But when he looked at the baby girl and saw that she was the image of himself, he stepped back, and said, '*u Zindzile*,' which means, 'You are well established.' He named her Zindziswa, the feminine version of what he had said.

38

The Crown took over a month to do its summing up, which was often interrupted by interjections from the bench pointing out lapses in the argument. In March it was our turn. Issy Maisels categorically refuted the charges of violence. 'We admit that there is a question of non-cooperation and passive resistance,' he said. 'We shall say quite frankly that if non-cooperation and passive resistance constitute high treason, then we are guilty. But these are plainly not encompassed in the law of treason.'

Maisels's argument was continued by Bram Fischer, but on 23 March the bench cut short Bram's concluding argument. We still had weeks of argument ahead, but the judges asked for a week's adjournment. This was irregular, but we regarded it as a hopeful sign, for it suggested that they had already formed their opinion. We were to return to court six days later for what we presumed would be the verdict. In the meantime, I had work to do.

My bans were due to expire two days after the adjournment. I was almost certain that the police would not be aware of this, as they rarely kept track of when bans ended. It would be the first time in nearly five years that I would be free to leave Johannesburg, free to attend a meeting. That weekend was the long-planned All-in Conference in Pietermaritzburg. Its aim was to agitate for a national constitutional convention for all South Africans. I was secretly scheduled to be the main speaker at the conference. I would make the 300-mile drive down to Pietermaritzburg the night before I was down to speak.

The day before I was to leave, the National Working Committee met secretly to discuss strategy. After many meetings in prison and outside, we had decided that we would work from underground, adopting a strategy along the lines of the M-Plan. The organization would survive clandestinely. It was decided that if we were not convicted, I would go underground to travel about the country organizing the proposed national convention. Only someone operating full-time from underground would be free from the paralysing restrictions imposed by the enemy. It was decided that I would surface at certain events, hoping for a maximum of publicity, to show that the ANC was still fighting. It was not a proposal that came as a surprise to me, nor was it one I particularly relished, but it was something I knew I had to do. This would be a hazardous life, and I would be apart from my family, but when a man is denied the right to live the life he believes in, he has no choice but to become an outlaw.

When I returned home from the meeting it was as though Winnie could read my thoughts. Seeing my face, she knew that I was about to embark on a life that neither of us wanted. I explained what had transpired and that I would be leaving the next day. She took this stoically, as though she had expected it all along. She understood what I had to do, but that did not make it any easier for her. I asked her to pack a small suitcase for me. I told her that friends and relatives would look after her while I was gone. I did not tell her how long I would be away, and she did not ask. It was just as well, because I did not know the answer. I would return to Pretoria for what would probably be the verdict on Monday. No matter what the result, I would not be returning home: if we were convicted, I would go directly to prison; if we were discharged, I would immediately go underground.

My eldest son Thembi was in school in the Transkei, so I could not say good-bye to him, but that afternoon I fetched Makgatho and my daughter Makaziwe from their mother in Orlando East. We spent some hours together, walking on the veld outside town, talking and playing. I said good-bye to them, not knowing when I would see them again. The children of a freedom fighter also learn not to ask their father too many questions, and I could see in their eyes that they understood that something serious was occurring.

At home, I kissed the two girls good-bye and they waved as I got in the car with Wilson Conco and began the long drive to Natal.

Fourteen hundred delegates from all over the country representing 150 different religious, social, cultural and political bodies converged on Pietermaritzburg for the All-in Conference. When I walked out on stage on Saturday evening, 25 March, in front of this loyal and enthusiastic audience, it had been nearly five years since I had been free to give a speech on a public platform. I was met with a joyous reaction. I had almost forgotten the intensity of the experience of addressing a crowd.

In my speech I called for a national convention in which all South Africans, black and white, Indian and Coloured, would sit down in brotherhood and create a constitution that mirrored the aspirations of the country as a whole. I called for unity, and said we would be invincible if we spoke with one voice.

The All-in Conference called for a national convention of elected representatives of all adult men and women on an equal basis to determine a new non-racial democratic constitution for South Africa. A National Action Council was elected, with myself as honorary secretary, to communicate this demand to the government. If the government failed to call such a convention, we would call a countrywide three-day stay-away beginning on 29 May to coincide with the declaration of South Africa as a republic. I had no illusions that the state would agree to our proposal.

In October 1960 the government had held an all-white referendum on whether South Africa should become a republic. This was one of the long-cherished dreams of Afrikaner nationalism, to cast off ties with the country they had fought against in the Anglo-Boer war. The pro-republic sentiment won with 52 per cent of the vote, and the proclamation of the republic was set for 31 May 1961. We set our stay-at-home on the date of the proclamation to indicate that, for us, such a change was merely cosmetic.

Directly after the conference I sent Prime Minister Verwoerd a letter in which I formally enjoined him to call a national constitutional convention. I warned him that if he failed to call it we would stage the country's most massive three-day strike ever, beginning on 29 May. 'We have no illusions about the counter-measures your government might take,' I wrote. 'During the last twelve months we have gone through a period of grim dictatorship.' I also issued press statements affirming that the strike was a peaceful and non-violent stay-at-home. Verwoerd did not reply, except to describe my letter in Parliament as 'arrogant'. The government instead began to mount one of the most intimidating displays of force ever assembled in the country's history.

39

Even before the doors of the Old Synagogue opened on the morning of 29 March 1961, the day of the long-anticipated verdict in the Treason Trial, a crowd of supporters and press people jostled to get inside. Hundreds were turned away. When the judges brought the court to order, the visitors' gallery and the press bench were packed. Moments after Justice Rumpff pounded his gavel, the Crown made an extraordinary application to change the indictment. This was the fifty-ninth minute of the eleventh hour, and it was two years too late. The court rebuffed the prosecution and the gallery murmured its approval.

'Silence in court!' the orderly yelled, and Judge Rumpff announced that the three-judge panel had reached a verdict. Silence now reigned. In his deep, even voice, Judge Rumpff reviewed the court's conclusions. Yes, the African National Congress had been working to replace the government with a 'radically and fundamentally different form of state'; yes, the African National Congress had used illegal means of protest during the Defiance Campaign; yes, certain ANC leaders had made speeches advocating violence; and yes, there was a strong left-wing tendency in the ANC that was revealed in its anti-imperialist, anti-West, pro-Soviet attitudes, but:

> On all the evidence presented to this court and on our finding of fact it is impossible for this court to

come to the conclusion that the African National Congress had acquired or adopted a policy to overthrow the state by violence, that is, in the sense that the masses had to be prepared or conditioned to commit direct acts of violence against the state.

The court said the prosecution had failed to prove that the ANC was a communist organization or that the Freedom Charter envisioned a communist state. After speaking for forty minutes, Justice Rumpff said, 'The accused are accordingly found not guilty and are discharged.'

The spectators' gallery erupted in cheers. We stood and hugged one another, and waved to the happy courtroom. All of us then paraded into the courtyard, smiling, laughing, crying. The crowd yelled and chanted as we emerged. A number of us hoisted our defence counsels on our shoulders, which was no easy task in the case of Issy Maisels, for he was such a large man. Flash-bulbs were popping all around us. We looked around for friends, wives, relatives. Winnie had come up, and I hugged her in joy, though I knew that while I might be free for this moment, I would not be able to savour that freedom. When we were all outside together, the Treason Trialists and the crowd all began to sing '*Nkosi Sikelel' iAfrika*'.

After more than four years in court and dozens of prosecutors, thousands of documents and tens of thousands of pages of testimony, the state had failed in its mission. The verdict was an embarrassment to the government, both at home and abroad. Yet the result only made the state more bitter towards us. The lesson they took away was not that we had legitimate grievances but that they needed to be far more ruthless.

I did not regard the verdict as a vindication of the legal system or evidence that a black man could get a fair trial in a white man's court. It was the right verdict and a just one, but it was largely as a result of a superior defence team and the fair-mindedness of the panel of these particular judges.

The court system, however, was perhaps the only place in South Africa where an African could possibly receive a fair hearing and where the rule of law might still apply. This was particularly true in courts presided over by enlightened judges who had been appointed by the United Party. Many of these men still stood by the rule of law.

As a student, I had been taught that South Africa was a place where the rule of law was paramount and applied to all persons, regardless of their social status or official position. I sincerely believed this and planned my life based on that assumption. But my career as a lawyer and activist removed the scales from my eyes. I saw that there was a wide difference between what I had been taught in the lecture room and what I learned in the courtroom. I went from having an idealistic view of the law as a sword of justice to a perception of the law as a tool used by the ruling class to shape society in a way favourable to itself. I never expected justice in court, however much I fought for it, and though I sometimes received it.

In the case of the Treason Trial, the three judges rose above their prejudices, their education and their background. There is a streak of goodness in men that can be buried or hidden and then emerge unexpectedly. Justice Rumpff, with his aloof manner, gave the impression throughout the proceedings that he shared the point of view of the ruling white minority. Yet, in the end, an essential fairness dominated his judgment. Kennedy was less conservative than his colleagues and seemed attracted by the idea of equality. Once, for example, he and Duma Nokwe flew on the same plane from Durban to Johannesburg, and when the airline bus to town refused to take Duma, Kennedy also refused to ride in it. Judge Bekker always struck me as open-minded and seemed aware that the accused before him had suffered a great deal at the hands of the state. I commended these three men as individuals, not as representatives of the court or of the state or even of their race, but as exemplars of human decency under adversity.

Judge Bekker's wife was a person sensitive to the needs of others. During the State of Emergency, she collected goods which she brought to the accused.

But the consequence of the government's humiliating defeat was that the state decided never to let it happen again. From that day forth they were not going to rely on judges whom they had not themselves appointed. They were not going to observe what they considered the legal niceties that protected terrorists or permitted convicted prisoners certain rights in jail. During the Treason Trial, there were no examples of individuals being isolated, beaten and tortured in order to elicit information. All of those things became commonplace shortly thereafter.

PART SIX

The Black Pimpernel

40

I did not return home after the verdict. Although others were in a festive mood and eager to celebrate, I knew the authorities could strike at any moment, and I did not want to give them the opportunity. I was anxious to be off before I was banned or arrested, and I spent the night in a safe house in Johannesburg. It was a restless night in a strange bed, and I started at the sound of every car, thinking it might be the police.

Walter and Duma saw me off on the first leg of my journey, which was to take me to Port Elizabeth. There I met Govan Mbeki and Raymond Mhlaba to discuss the new underground structures of the organization. We met at the house of Dr Masla Pather, who would later be sentenced to two years in prison for allowing us to meet at his home. At safe houses arranged by the organization, I met the editor of the liberal *Port Elizabeth Morning Post* to discuss the campaign for a national convention, a goal several newspapers subsequently endorsed. I later visited Patrick Duncan, the editor and publisher of the liberal weekly *Contact*, a founding member of the Liberal Party, and one of the first white defiers during the Defiance Campaign. His newspaper had repeatedly been decrying ANC policy as being dictated by communists but, when he saw me, the first thing he said was that a close reading of the Treason Trial record had disabused him of that notion and he would correct it in his paper.

That night I addressed a meeting of African township ministers in Cape Town. I mention this because the opening prayer of one of the ministers has stayed with me over these many years and was a source of strength at a difficult time. He thanked the Lord for His bounty and goodnesss, for His mercy and His concern for all men. But then he took the liberty of reminding the Lord that some of His subjects were more downtrodden than others, and that it sometimes seemed as though He was not paying attention. The minister then said that if the Lord did not show a little more initiative in leading the black man to salvation, the black man would have to take matters into his own two hands. Amen.

On my last morning in Cape Town, I was leaving my hotel in the company of George Peake, a founding member of the South African Coloured People's Organization, and stopped to thank the Coloured manager of the hotel for looking after me so well. He was grateful, but also curious. He had discovered my identity and told me that the Coloured community feared that under an African government they would be just as oppressed as under the present white government. He was a middle-class businessman who probably had little contact with Africans, and feared them in the same way as whites did. This was a frequent anxiety on the part of the Coloured community, especially in the Cape, and though I was running late, I explained the Freedom Charter to this man and stressed our commitment to non-racialism. A freedom fighter must take every opportunity to make his case to the people.

The following day I joined a secret meeting of the ANC National Executive and the joint executives of the

Congress movement in Durban to discuss whether the
planned action should take the form of a stay-at-home
or a fully fledged strike with organized pickets and
demonstrations. Those who argued for the strike said
that the stay-at-home strategy we had used since 1950
had outlasted its usefulness, that at a time when the
PAC was appealing to the masses, more militant forms
of the struggle were necessary. The alternative view,
which I advocated, was that stay-at-homes allowed us to
strike at the enemy while preventing him from striking
back. I argued that the confidence of the people in our
campaigns had grown precisely because they realized
that we were not reckless with their lives. Sharpeville, I
said, for all the heroism of the demonstrators, had
allowed the enemy to shoot down our people. I argued
for stay-at-homes even though I was aware that our
people around the country were becoming impatient
with passive forms of struggle, but I did not think we
should depart from our proven tactics without com-
prehensive planning, and we had neither the time nor
the resources to do so. The decision was for a stay-at-
home.

Living underground requires a seismic psychological
shift. One has to plan every action, however small and
seemingly insignificant. Nothing is innocent. Everything is questioned. You cannot be yourself; you must
fully inhabit whatever role you have assumed. In some
ways, this was not much of an adaptation for a black
man in South Africa. Under apartheid, a black man
lived a shadowy life between legality and illegality,
between openness and concealment. To be a black
man in South Africa meant not to trust anything, which

was not unlike living underground for one's entire life.

I became a creature of the night. I would keep to my hideout during the day, and emerge to do my work when it became dark. I operated mainly from Johannesburg, but I would travel as necessary. I stayed in empty flats, in people's houses, wherever I could be alone and inconspicuous. Although I am a gregarious person, I love solitude even more. I welcomed the opportunity to be by myself, to plan, to think, to plot. But one can have too much solitude. I was terribly lonesome for my wife and family.

The key to being underground is to be invisible. Just as there is a way to walk into a room in order to make yourself stand out, there is a way of walking and behaving that makes you inconspicuous. As a leader, one often seeks prominence; as an outlaw, the opposite is true. When underground I did not walk as tall or stand as straight. I spoke more softly, with less clarity and distinction. I was more passive, more unobtrusive; I did not ask for things but let people tell me what to do. I did not shave or cut my hair. My most frequent disguise was as a chauffeur, chef or a 'garden boy'. I would wear the blue overalls of the field-worker and often wore round, rimless glasses known as Mazzawatee tea-glasses. I had a car and I wore a chauffeur's cap with my overalls. The pose of chauffeur was convenient because I could travel under the pretext of driving my master's car.

During those early months, when there was a warrant for my arrest and I was being pursued by the police, my outlaw existence caught the imagination of the press. Articles claiming that I had been here and there were on the front pages. Roadblocks were instituted all over the country, but the police repeatedly came up empty-handed. I was dubbed the Black Pimpernel, a somewhat derogatory adaptation of Baroness Orczy's fictional character the Scarlet Pimpernel, who daringly evaded capture during the French Revolution.

I travelled secretly about the country: I was with Muslims in the Cape, with sugar-workers in Natal, with factory workers in Port Elizabeth. I moved through townships in different parts of the country attending secret meetings at night. I would even feed the mythology of the Black Pimpernel by taking a pocketful of 'tickeys' (threepenny bits) and phoning individual newspaper reporters from telephone boxes and relaying stories of what we were planning or of the ineptitude of the police. I would pop up here and there to the annoyance of the police and to the delight of the people.

There were many wild and inaccurate stories about my experiences underground. People love to embellish tales of daring. I did have a number of narrow escapes, however, which no one knew about. On one occasion, I was driving in town and stopped at a traffic light. I looked to my left and in an adjacent car saw Colonel Spengler, the chief of the Witwatersrand Security Branch. It would have been a great plum for him to catch the Black Pimpernel. I was wearing a workman's cap, my blue overalls, and my glasses. He never looked my way, but even so the seconds I spent waiting for the light to change seemed like hours.

One afternoon, when I was in Johannesburg posing as a chauffeur and wearing my long dust-coat and cap, I was waiting on a corner to be picked up and I saw an African policeman striding deliberately towards me. I looked around to see if I had a place to run, but before I did, he smiled at me and surreptitiously gave me the thumbs-up ANC salute and was gone. Incidents like this happened many times, and I was reassured when I saw that we had the loyalty of many African policemen. There was a black sergeant who used to tip off Winnie as to what the police were doing. He would whisper to her, 'Make sure Madiba is not in Alexandra on Wednesday night because there is going to be a raid.' Black policemen have often been severely criticized during the struggle, but many have played covert roles that have been extremely valuable.

When I was underground, I remained as unkempt as possible. My overalls looked as though they had been through a lifetime of hard toil. The police had one picture of me with a beard, which they widely distributed, and my colleagues urged me to shave it off. But I had become attached to my beard, and I resisted all their efforts.

Not only was I not recognized, I was sometimes snubbed. Once, I was planning to attend a meeting in a distant area of Johannesburg and a well-known priest arranged with friends of his to put me up for the night. I arrived at the door, and before I could announce who I was, the elderly lady who answered exclaimed, 'No, we don't want such a man as you here!' and shut the door.

41

My time underground was mainly taken up in planning the 29 May stay-at-home. It was shaping up to be a virtual war between the state and the liberation movement. Late in May, the government staged countrywide raids on opposition leaders. Meetings were banned, printing presses were seized and legislation was rushed through Parliament permitting the police to detain charged prisoners for twelve days without bail.

Verwoerd declared that those supporting the strike, including sympathetic newspapers, were 'playing with fire', an ominous declaration, given the ruthlessness of the state. The government urged industries to provide sleeping accommodation for workers so that they would not have to return home during the strike. Two days before the stay-at-home, the government staged the greatest peacetime show of force in South African history. The military exercised its largest call-up since the war. Police holidays were cancelled. Military units were stationed at the entrances and exits of townships. While Saracen tanks rumbled through the dirt streets of the townships, helicopters hovered above, swooping down to break up any gathering. At night, the helicopters trained searchlights on houses.

The English-language press had widely publicized the campaign until a few days before it was to begin. But on the eve of the stay-at-home the entire English-language press crumbled and urged people to go to

work. The PAC played the role of saboteur and released thousands of leaflets telling people to oppose
the stay-at-home, and denouncing the ANC leaders as
cowards. The PAC's actions shocked us. It is one thing
to criticize, and that we can accept, but to attempt to
break a strike by calling upon the people to go to work
directly serves the interests of the enemy.

The night before the stay-at-home, I was scheduled to
meet the Johannesburg leadership of the ANC at a safe
house in Soweto. To avoid police roadblocks, I entered
Soweto through Kliptown, which was normally not
patrolled. But as I went around a blind corner I drove
straight into what I had been trying to avoid: a roadblock. A white policeman indicated I should stop. I was
dressed in my usual costume of overalls and chauffeur's
cap. He squinted through the window at me and then
stepped forward and searched the car on his own.
Normally, this was the duty of the African police. After
he had found nothing, he demanded my pass. I told
him that I had left it at home by mistake, and casually
recited a fictitious pass number. This seemed to satisfy
him and he motioned me through.

On Monday 29 May, the first day of the stay-at-home,
hundreds of thousands of people risked their jobs and
livelihoods by not going to work. In Durban, Indian
workers walked out of factories, while in the Cape
thousands of Coloured workers stayed home. In Johannesburg, more than half of all employees stayed at
home and in Port Elizabeth the rate was even higher. I
praised the response as 'magnificent' to the press,
lauding our people for 'defying unprecedented intimidation by the state'. The white celebration of Re-

public Day was drowned out by our protest.

Although reports on the first day of the stay-at-home suggested strong reactions in various parts of the country, the response as a whole appeared less than we had hoped. Communication was difficult, and bad news always seems to travel more efficiently than good. As more reports came in, I felt let down and disappointed by the reaction. That evening, feeling demoralized and rather angry, I had a conversation with Benjamin Pogrund of the *Rand Daily Mail* in which I suggested that the days of non-violent struggle were over.

On the second day of the stay-at-home, after consultations with my colleagues, I called it off. That morning in a safe flat in a white suburb I met various members of the local and foreign press, and I once again called the stay-at-home 'a tremendous success'. But I did not mask the fact that I believed a new day was dawning. I said, 'If the government reaction is to crush by naked force our non-violent struggle, we will have to reconsider our tactics. In my mind we are closing a chapter on this question of a non-violent policy.' It was a grave declaration, and I knew it. I was criticized by our Executive for making that remark before it was discussed by the organization, but sometimes one must go public with an idea to push a reluctant organization in the direction you want it to go.

The debate on the use of violence had been going on among us since early 1960. I had first discussed the armed struggle as far back as 1952 with Walter Sisulu. Now, I again conferred with him and we agreed that the organization had to set out on a new course. The Communist Party had secretly reconstituted itself underground and was now considering forming its own military wing. We decided that I should raise the issue of the armed struggle within the Working Committee, and I did so in a meeting in June of 1961.

I had barely commenced my proposal when Moses Kotane, the secretary of the Communist Party and one of the most powerful figures in the ANC Executive, staged a counter-assault, accusing me of not having thought out the proposal carefully enough. He said that I had been outmanoeuvred and paralysed by the government's actions, and now in desperation I was resorting to revolutionary language. 'There is still room,' he stressed, 'for the old methods if we are imaginative and determined enough. If we embark on the course Mandela is suggesting, we will be exposing innocent people to massacres by the enemy.'

Moses spoke persuasively and I could see that he had defeated my proposal. Even Walter did not speak on my behalf, and I backed down. Afterwards I spoke with Walter and voiced my frustration, chiding him for not coming to my aid. He laughed and said it would have been as foolish as attempting to fight a pride of angry lions. Walter is a diplomat and extremely resourceful. 'Let me arrange for Moses to come and see you privately,' he said, 'and you can make your case that way.' I was underground, but Walter managed to put the two of us together in a house in the township and we spent the whole day talking.

I was candid and explained why I believed we had no choice but to turn to violence. I used an old African expression: '*Sebatana ha se bokwe ka diatla*' ('The attacks of the wild beast cannot be averted with only bare hands'). Moses was a long-time communist, and I told him that his opposition was like the Communist Party in Cuba under Batista. The party had insisted that the appropriate conditions had not yet arrived, and waited because they were simply following the textbook definitions of Lenin and Stalin. Castro did not wait, he acted – and he triumphed. If you wait for textbook conditions, they will never occur. I told Moses point blank that his mind was stuck in the old mould of the ANC's being a legal organization. People were already forming military units on their own, and the only organization that had the muscle to lead them was the ANC. We had always maintained that the people were ahead of us, and now they were.

We talked the entire day, and at the end, Moses said to me, 'Nelson, I will not promise you anything, but raise the issue again in committee, and we will see what happens.' A meeting was scheduled in a week's time, and once again I raised the issue. This time, Moses was silent, and the general consensus of the meeting was that I should make the proposal to the National Executive in Durban. Walter simply smiled.

The Executive meeting in Durban, like all ANC meetings at the time, was held in secret and at night in order to avoid the police. I suspected I would encounter difficulties because Chief Luthuli was to be in attendance and I knew of his moral commitment to non-violence. I was also wary because of the timing: I was raising the issue of violence so soon after the Treason Trial, where we had contended that for the ANC non-violence was an inviolate principle, not a tactic to be changed as conditions warranted. I myself believed precisely the opposite; that non-violence was a tactic that should be abandoned when it no longer worked.

At the meeting I argued that the state had given us no alternative to violence. I said it was wrong and immoral to subject our people to armed attacks by the state without offering them some kind of alternative. I mentioned again that people on their own had taken up arms. Violence would begin whether we initiated it or not. Would it not be better to guide this violence ourselves, according to principles where we saved lives by attacking symbols of oppression, and not people? If we did not take the lead now, I said, we would soon be latecomers and followers to a movement we did not control.

The chief initially resisted my arguments. For him, non-violence was not simply a tactic. But we worked on him the whole night; and I think that in his heart he realized we were right. He ultimately agreed that a military campaign was inevitable. When someone later insinuated that perhaps the chief was not prepared for such a course, he retorted, 'If anyone thinks I'm a pacifist, let him try to take my chickens, and he will know how wrong he is!'

The National Executive formally endorsed the preliminary decision of the Working Committee. The chief and others suggested that we should treat this new resolution as if the ANC had not discussed it. He did not want to jeopardize the legality of our unbanned allies. His idea was that a military movement should be a separate and independent organ, linked to the ANC and under the overall control of the ANC, but fundamentally autonomous. There would be two separate streams of the struggle. We readily accepted the chief's suggestion. The chief and others warned against this new phase becoming an excuse for neglecting the essential tasks of organization and the traditional methods of struggle. That, too, would be self-defeating because the armed struggle, at least in the beginning, would not be the centrepiece of the movement.

The following night a meeting of the joint Executive was scheduled in Durban. This would include the Indian Congress, the Coloured People's Congress, the South African Congress of Trade Unions and the Congress of Democrats. Although these other groups customarily accepted ANC decisions, I knew that some of my Indian colleagues would strenuously oppose the move towards violence.

The meeting had an inauspicious beginning. Chief Luthuli, who was presiding, announced that even though the ANC had endorsed a decision on violence, 'it is a matter of such gravity, I would like my colleagues here tonight to consider the issue afresh.' It was apparent that the chief was not fully reconciled to our new course.

We began our session at 8 p.m., and it was tumultuous. I made the identical arguments that I had been making all along, but many people expressed reservations. Yusuf Cachalia and Dr Naicker pleaded with us not to embark on this course, arguing that the state would slaughter the whole liberation movement. J.N. Singh, an effective debater, uttered words that night which still echo in my head. 'Non-violence has not failed us,' he said, 'we have failed non-violence.' I countered by saying that in fact non-violence had failed us, for it had done nothing to stem the violence of the state or change the heart of our oppressors.

We argued the entire night, and in the early hours of

the morning I began to feel we were making progress. Many of the Indian leaders were now speaking in a sorrowful tone about the end of non-violence. But then suddenly M.D. Naidoo, a member of the South African Indian Congress, burst forth and said to his Indian colleagues, 'Ah, you are afraid of going to jail, that is all!' His comment caused pandemonium in the meeting. When you question a man's integrity, you can expect a fight. The entire debate went back to square one. But towards dawn, there was a resolution. The Congresses authorized me to go ahead and form a new military organization, separate from the ANC. The policy of the ANC would still be that of non-violence. I was authorized to join with whomever I wanted or needed to create this organization and would not be subject to the direct control of the mother organization.

This was a fateful step. For fifty years, the ANC had treated non-violence as a core principle, beyond question or debate. Henceforth, the ANC would be a different kind of organization. We were embarking on a new and more dangerous path, a path of organized violence, the results of which we did not and could not know.

42

I, who had never been a soldier, who had never fought in battle, who had never fired a gun at an enemy, had been given the task of starting an army. It would be a daunting task for a veteran general, much less a military novice. The name of this new organization was Umkhonto we Sizwe (The Spear of the Nation) – or MK for short. The symbol of the spear was chosen because with this simple weapon Africans had resisted the incursions of whites for centuries.

Although the Executive of the ANC did not allow white members, MK was not thus constrained. I immediately recruited Joe Slovo and along with Walter Sisulu we formed the High Command with myself as chairman. Through Joe, I enlisted the efforts of white Communist Party members who had resolved on a course of violence and had already executed acts of sabotage such as cutting government telephone and communication lines. We recruited Jack Hodgson, who had fought in the Second World War and was a member of the Springbok Legion, and Rusty Bernstein, both party members. Jack became our first demolition expert. Our mandate was to wage acts of violence against the state – precisely what form those acts would take was yet to be decided. Our intention was to begin with what was least violent to individuals but most damaging to the state.

I began in the only way I knew how, by reading and

talking to experts. What I wanted to find out were the fundamental principles for starting a revolution. I discovered that there was a great deal of writing on this very subject, and I made my way through the available literature on armed warfare and in particular guerrilla warfare. I wanted to know what circumstances were appropriate for a guerrilla war; how one created, trained and maintained a guerrilla force; how it should be armed; where it gets its supplies – all basic and fundamental questions.

Any and every source was of interest to me. I read the report of Blas Roca, the general secretary of the Communist Party of Cuba, about their years as an illegal organization during the Batista regime. In *Commando* by Deneys Reitz, I read of the unconventional guerrilla tactics of the Boer generals during the Anglo-Boer War. I read works by and about Che Guevara, Mao Tse-tung, Fidel Castro. In Edgar Snow's brilliant *Red Star Over China* I saw that it was Mao's determination and non-traditional thinking that had led him to victory. I read *The Revolt* by Menachem Begin and was encouraged by the fact that the Israeli leader had led a guerrilla force in a country with neither mountains nor forests, a situation similar to our own. I was eager to know more about the armed struggle of the people of Ethiopia against Mussolini, and of the guerrilla armies of Kenya, Algeria and the Cameroons.

I went into the South African past. I studied our history both before and after the white man. I probed the wars of African against African, of African against white, of white against white. I made a survey of the country's chief industrial areas, the nation's transportation system, its communication network. I accumulated detailed maps and systematically analysed the terrain of different regions of the country.

On 26 June 1961, our Freedom Day, I released a letter to South African newspapers from underground, which commended the people for their courage during the recent stay-at-home, once more calling for a national constitutional convention. I again proclaimed that a countrywide campaign of non-cooperation would be launched if the state failed to hold such a convention. My letter read in part:

> I am informed that a warrant for my arrest has been issued, and that the police are looking for me. The National Action Council has given full and serious consideration to this question . . . and has advised me not to surrender myself. I have accepted this advice, and will not give myself up to a Government I do not recognize. Any serious politician will realize that under present day conditions in the country, to seek for cheap martyrdom by handing myself to the police is naive and criminal . . .
>
> I have chosen this course which is more difficult and which entails more risk and hardship than sitting in gaol. I have had to separate myself from my dear wife and children, from my mother and sisters, to live as an outlaw in my own land. I have had to close my business, to abandon my profession and live in poverty, as many of my people are doing . . . I shall fight the Government side by side with you, inch by inch, and mile by mile, until victory is won. What are you going to do? Will you

come along with us, or are you going to co-operate with the Government in its efforts to suppress the claims and aspirations of your own people? Are you going to remain silent and neutral in a matter of life and death to my people, to our people? For my own part I have made my choice. I will not leave South Africa, nor will I surrender. Only through hardship, sacrifice and militant action can freedom be won. The struggle is my life. I will continue fighting for freedom until the end of my days.

43

During those first few months underground I lived for a few weeks with a family in Market Street, after which I shared a one-room ground-floor bachelor flat with Wolfie Kodesh in Berea, a quiet white suburb a short distance north of downtown. Wolfie was a member of the Congress of Democrats, a reporter for *New Age*, and had fought in North Africa and Italy during the Second World War. His knowledge of warfare and his firsthand battle experience were extremely helpful to me. At his suggestion I read the Prussian general Karl von Clausewitz's classic work *On War*. Clausewitz's central thesis, that war was a continuation of diplomacy by other means, dovetailed with my own instincts. I relied on Wolfie to procure reading material for me and I fear that I took over his life, infringing on both his work and pleasure. But he was such an amiable, modest fellow that he never complained.

I spent nearly two months in his flat, sleeping on a camp bed, staying inside during the day with the blinds drawn reading and planning, leaving only for meetings or organizing sessions at night. I annoyed Wolfie every morning, for I would wake up at five, change into my running clothes and run on the spot for more than an hour. Wolfie eventually surrendered to my regimen and began working out with me in the morning before he left for town.

MK was then practising setting off explosions. One night I accompanied Wolfie to an old brickworks on the outskirts of town for a demonstration. It was a security risk, but I wanted to attend MK's first test of an explosive device. Explosions were common at the brickworks, for companies would use dynamite to loosen the clay before the great machines scooped it up to make bricks. Jack Hodgson had brought along a paraffin tin filled with nitroglycerine; he had created a timing device that used the inside of a ball-point pen. It was dark and we had only a small light, and we stood to the side as Jack worked. When it was ready, we stood back and counted down to thirty seconds; there was a great roar and much displaced earth. The explosion had been a success, and we all quickly returned to our cars and went off in different directions.

I felt safe in Berea. I did not go outside, and because it was a white area, the police would probably not think to look for me there. While I was reading in the flat during the day, I would often place a pint of milk on the windowsill to allow it to ferment. I am very fond of this sour milk, which is known as *amasi* among the Xhosa people and is greatly prized as a healthy and nourishing food. It is very simple to make and merely involves letting the milk stand in the open air and curdle. It then becomes thick and sour, rather like yogurt. I even prevailed upon Wolfie to try it, but he grimaced when he tasted it.

One evening, after Wolfie had returned, we were chatting in the flat when I overheard a conversation going on near the window. I could hear two young black men speaking in Zulu, but I could not see them, as the curtains were drawn. I motioned Wolfie to be quiet.

'What is "our milk" doing on that window ledge?' one of the fellows said.

'What are you talking about?' replied the other fellow.

'The sour milk – *amasi* – on the window ledge,' he said. 'What is it doing there?' Then there was silence. The sharp-eyed fellow was suggesting that only a black man would place milk on the ledge like that and what was a black man doing living in a white area? I realized then that I needed to move on. I left for a different hideout the next night.

I stayed at a doctor's house in Johannesburg, sleeping in the servants' quarters at night, and working in the doctor's study during the day. Whenever anyone came to the house during the day, I would dash out to the backyard and pretend to be the gardener. I then spent about a fortnight on a sugar plantation in Natal, living with a group of African labourers and their families in a small community called Tongaat, just up the coast from Durban. I lived in a hostel and posed as an agricultural demonstrator who had come at the behest of the government to evaluate the land.

I had been equipped by the organization with a demonstrator's tools and I spent part of each day testing the soil and performing experiments. I little understood what I was doing and I do not think I fooled the people of Tongaat. But these men and women, who were mostly farmworkers, had a natural kind of discretion and did not question my identity, even when they began seeing people arriving at night in cars, some of them well-known local politicians. Often I was at meetings all night and would sleep all day – not the normal schedule of an agricultural demonstrator. But even though I was involved in other matters I felt a closeness with the community. I would attend services on Sunday, and I enjoyed the old-fashioned Bible-thumping style of these Zionist Christian ministers. Shortly before I was planning to leave, I thanked one elderly fellow for having looked after me. He said, 'You are of course welcome, but, Kwedeni [young man], please tell us, what does Chief Luthuli want?' I was taken aback but quickly responded, 'Well, it would be better to ask him yourself and I cannot speak for him, but as I understand it, he wants our land returned, he wants our kings to have their power back, and he wants us to be able to determine our own future and run our own lives as we see fit.'

'And how is he going to do that if he does not have an army?' the old man said.

I wanted very much to tell the old man that I was busy attempting to form that army, but I could not. While I was encouraged by the old man's sentiments, I was nervous that others had discovered my mission as well. Again I had stayed too long in one place, and the following night I left as quietly as I had arrived.

44

My next address was more of a sanctuary than a hideout: Liliesleaf Farm, located in Rivonia, a bucolic northern suburb of Johannesburg, and I moved there in October. In those days Rivonia consisted mainly of farms and smallholdings. The farmhouse and property had been purchased by the movement for the purpose of having a safe house for those underground. It was an old house that needed work and no one lived there.

I moved in under the pretext that I was the houseboy or caretaker who would look after the place until my master took possession. I had taken the alias David Motsamayi, the name of one of my former clients. At the farm, I wore the simple blue overalls that were the uniform of the black male servant. During the day, the place was busy with workers, builders and painters who were repairing the main house and extending the outbuildings. We wanted to have a number of small rooms added to the house so that more people could stay. The workers were all Africans from Alexandra township and they called me 'waiter' or 'boy' (they never bothered to ask my name). I prepared breakfast for them and made them tea in the late morning and afternoon. They also sent me on errands about the farm, or ordered me to sweep the floor or pick up rubbish.

One afternoon, I informed them that I had prepared

tea in the kitchen. They came in and I passed around a tray with cups, tea, milk and sugar. Each man took a cup, and helped himself. As I was carrying the tray, I came to one fellow who was in the middle of telling a story. He took a cup of tea, but he was concentrating more on his story than on me, and he simply held his teaspoon in the air while he was talking, using it to gesture and tell his tale rather than help himself to some sugar. I stood there for what seemed like several minutes and finally, in mild exasperation, I started to move away. At that point he noticed me, and said sharply, 'Waiter, come back here, I didn't say you could leave.'

Many people have painted an idealistic picture of the egalitarian nature of African society, and while in general I agree with this portrait, the fact is that Africans do not always treat each other as equals. Industrialization has played a large role in introducing the urban African to the perceptions of status common to white society. To those men, I was an inferior, a servant, a person without a trade, and therefore to be treated with disdain. I played the role so well that none of them suspected I was anything other than what I seemed.

Every day at sunset the workers would return to their homes and I would be alone until the next morning. I relished these hours of quiet, but on most evenings I would leave the property to attend meetings, returning in the middle of the night. I often felt uneasy coming back at such hours to a place I did not know well and where I was living illegally under an assumed name. I recall being frightened one night when I thought I saw someone lurking in the bushes; although I investigated, I found nothing. An underground freedom fighter sleeps very lightly.

After a number of weeks I was joined at the farm by Raymond Mhlaba, who had journeyed up from Port Elizabeth. Ray was a staunch trade unionist, a member of the Cape Executive and the Communist Party, and the first ANC leader to be arrested in the Defiance Campaign. He had been chosen by the ANC to be one of the first recruits for Umkhonto we Sizwe. He had come to prepare for his departure, with three others, for military training in the People's Republic of China; we had renewed the contacts that Walter had made back in 1952. Ray stayed with me for a fortnight and provided me with a clearer picture of the problems the ANC was having in the eastern Cape. I also enlisted his assistance in writing the MK constitution. We were joined by Joe Slovo as well as Rusty Bernstein, who both had hands in drafting it.

After Raymond left, I was joined for a brief time by Michael Harmel, a key figure in the underground Communist Party, a founding member of the Congress of Democrats, and an editor of the magazine *Liberation*. Michael, a brilliant theorist, was working on policy matters for the Communist Party and needed a quiet and safe place to work on this full time.

During the day, I kept my distance from Michael as it would have seemed exceedingly curious if a white professional man and an African houseboy were having regular conversations. But at night, after the workers left, we had long conversations about the relationship between the Communist Party and the ANC. One night I returned to the farm late after a meeting. When I was there alone, I made sure that all the gates were locked and the lights were out. I took quite a few precautions because a black man driving a car into a smallholding in Rivonia in the middle of the night would attract unwanted questions. But I saw that the house lights were on, and as I approached the house I heard a radio blaring. The front door was open and I walked in and found Michael in bed fast asleep. I was furious at this breach of security, and I woke him up and said, 'Man, how can you leave the lights on and the radio playing!' He was groggy but angry. 'Nel, must you disturb my sleep? Can't this wait until tomorrow?' I said it couldn't, it was a matter of security, and I reprimanded him for his lax conduct.

Soon after this Arthur Goldreich and his family moved into the main house as official tenants and I took over the newly built domestic worker's cottage. Arthur's presence provided a safe cover for our activities. He was an artist and designer by profession, a member of the Congress of Democrats and one of the first members of MK. His politics were unknown to the police and he had never been questioned or raided. In the 1940s, Arthur had fought with the Palmach, the military wing of the Jewish National Movement in Palestine. He was knowledgeable about guerrilla warfare and helped fill many gaps in my understanding. A flamboyant person, he gave the farm a buoyant atmosphere.

The final addition to the regular group at the farm was Mr Jelliman, an amiable white pensioner and old friend of the movement who became the farm foreman. Jelliman brought in several young workers from Sekhukhuneland, and the place soon appeared to be like any other smallholding in the country. He was not a member of the ANC, but he was loyal, discreet, and hard working. I used to prepare breakfast for him as well as supper, and he was unfailingly gracious. Much later, Jelliman risked his own life and livelihood in a courageous attempt to help me.

The loveliest times at the farm were when I was visited by my wife and family. Once the Goldreichs were in residence, Winnie would visit me at weekends. We were careful about her movements, and she would be picked up by one driver, dropped off at another place, and then picked up by a second driver before finally being delivered to the farm. Later, she would drive herself and the children, taking the most circuitous route possible. The police were not yet following her every move.

At these weekends time would sometimes seem to stop as we pretended that these stolen moments together were the rule not the exception of our lives. Ironically, we had more privacy at Liliesleaf than we ever had at home. The children could run about and play, and we were secure, however briefly, in this idyllic bubble.

Winnie brought me an old air rifle that I had in Orlando and Arthur and I would use it for target practice or hunting doves on the farm. One day, I was on the front lawn of the property and aimed the gun at a sparrow perched high in a tree. Hazel Goldreich, Arthur's wife, was watching me and jokingly remarked that I would never hit my target. But she had hardly finished the sentence when the sparrow fell to the ground. I turned to her and was about to boast, when the Goldreichs' son Paul, then about five years old, turned to me with tears in his eyes and said, 'David, why did you kill that bird? Its mother will be sad.' My mood immediately shifted from one of pride to shame; I felt that this small boy had far more humanity than I did. It was an odd sensation for a man who was the leader of a nascent guerrilla army.

45

In planning the direction and form that MK would take, we considered four types of violent activities: sabotage, guerrilla warfare, terrorism and open revolution. For a small and fledgling army, open revolution was inconceivable. Terrorism inevitably reflected poorly on those who used it, undermining any public support it might otherwise garner. Guerrilla warfare was a possibility, but since the ANC had been reluctant to embrace violence at all, it made sense to start with the form of violence that inflicted the least harm against individuals: sabotage.

Because it did not involve loss of life, it offered the best hope for reconciliation among the races afterwards. We did not want to start a blood-feud between white and black. Animosity between Afrikaner and Englishman was still sharp fifty years after the Anglo-Boer war; what would race relations be like between white and black if we provoked a civil war? Sabotage had the added virtue of requiring the least manpower.

Our strategy was to make selective forays against military installations, power plants, telephone lines and transportation links; targets that would not only hamper the military effectiveness of the state, but frighten National Party supporters, scare away foreign capital, and weaken the economy. This we hoped would bring the government to the bargaining table. Strict instructions were given to members of MK that we would countenance no loss of life. But if sabotage did not produce the results we wanted, we were prepared to move on to the next stage: guerrilla warfare and terrorism.

The structure of MK mirrored that of the parent organization. The National High Command was at the top; below it were Regional Commands in each of the provinces, and below that there were local commands and cells. Regional Commands were set up around the country, and an area like the eastern Cape had over fifty cells. The High Command determined tactics and general targets and was in charge of training and finance. Within the framework laid down by the High Command, the Regional Commands had authority to select local targets to be attacked. All MK members were forbidden to go armed into an operation and were not to endanger life in any way.

One problem we encountered early on was the question of divided loyalties between MK and the ANC. Most of our recruits were ANC members who were active in the local branches, but we found that once they were working for MK, they stopped doing the local work they had been performing before. The secretary of the local branch would find that certain men were no longer attending meetings. He might approach one and say, 'Man, why were you not at the meeting last night?' and the fellow would say, 'Ah, well, I was at another meeting.'

'What kind of meeting?' the secretary would say.

'Oh, I cannot say.'

'You cannot tell me, your own secretary?' But the secretary would soon discover the member's other loyalty. After some initial misunderstandings, we decided that if we recruited members from a branch, the secretary must be informed that one of his members was now with MK.

One warm December afternoon, while I sat in the kitchen at Liliesleaf Farm, I listened on the radio to the announcement that Chief Luthuli had been awarded the Nobel Peace Prize at a ceremony in Oslo. The government had issued him with a ten-day visa to leave the country and accept the award. I was – we all were – enormously pleased. It was, first of all, an acknowledgment of our struggle, and of the achievements of the chief as the leader of that struggle and as a man. It represented a recognition in the West that our struggle was a moral one, one too long ignored by the great powers. The award was an affront to the Nationalists, whose propaganda portrayed Luthuli as a dangerous agitator at the head of a communist conspiracy. Afrikaners were dumbfounded; to them the award was another example of the perversity of Western liberals and their bias against white South Africans. When the award was announced, the chief was in the third year of a five-year ban restricting him to the district of Stanger in Natal. He was also unwell; his heart was strained and his memory was poor. But the award cheered him and all of us as well.

The honour came at an awkward time for it was juxtaposed against an announcement that seemed to call the award itself into question. The day after Luthuli returned from Oslo, MK dramatically announced its emergence. On the orders of the MK High Command, in the early morning hours of 16 December – the day white South Africans used to celebrate as Dingane's

Day – homemade bombs were exploded at electric power stations and government offices in Johannesburg, Port Elizabeth and Durban. One of our men, Petrus Molife, was inadvertently killed, the first death of an MK soldier. Death in war is unfortunate, but unavoidable. Every man who joined MK knew that he might be called on to pay the ultimate sacrifice.

At the time of the explosions, thousands of leaflets with the new MK Manifesto were circulated all over the country announcing the birth of Umkhonto we Sizwe.

Units of Umkhonto we Sizwe today carried out planned attacks against government installations, particularly those connected with the policy of apartheid and race discrimination. Umkhonto we Sizwe is a new, independent body, formed by Africans. It includes in its ranks South Africans of all races . . . Umkhonto we Sizwe will carry on the struggle for freedom and democracy by new methods, which are necessary to complement the actions of the established national liberation movement . . .

The time comes in the life of any nation when there remain only two choices: submit or fight. That time has now come to South Africa. We shall not submit and we have no choice but to hit back by all means within our power in defence of our people, our future and our freedom . . .

We of Umkhonto have always sought – as the liberation movement has sought – to achieve liberation without bloodshed and civil clash. We hope, even at this late hour, that our first actions will awaken everyone to a realization of the disastrous situation to which the Nationalist policy is leading. We hope that we will bring the government and its supporters to their senses before it is too late, so that both the government and its policies can be changed before matters reach the desperate stage of civil war . . .

We chose 16 December, Dingane's Day, for a reason. That day, white South Africans celebrate the defeat of the great Zulu leader Dingane at the Battle of Blood River in 1838. Dingane, the half-brother of Shaka, then ruled the most powerful African state that ever existed south of the Limpopo River. That day, the bullets of the Boers were too much for the assegais of the Zulu *impis* and the water of the nearby river ran red with their blood. Afrikaners celebrated 16 December as the triumph of the Afrikaner over the African and the demonstration that God was on their side, while Africans mourned this day of the massacre of their people. We chose 16 December to show that the African had only begun to fight, and that we had righteousness – and dynamite – on our side.

The explosions took the government by surprise. They condemned the sabotage as heinous crimes while at the same time deriding it as the work of foolish amateurs. The explosions also shocked white South Africans into the realization that they were sitting on top of a volcano. Black South Africans realized that the ANC was no longer an organization of passive resistance, but a powerful spear that would take the struggle to the heart of white power. We planned and executed another set of explosions two weeks later on New Year's Eve. The combined sound of bells tolling and sirens wailing seemed not just a cacophonous way to ring in the new year, but a sound that symbolized a new era in our freedom struggle.

The announcement of Umkhonto spurred a vicious and unrelenting government counter-offensive on a scale that we had never before seen. The Special Branch of the police now made it their number one mission to capture members of MK, and they would spare no effort to do so. We had shown them we were not going to sit back any longer; they would show us that nothing would stop them from rooting out what they saw as the greatest threat to their own survival.

46

When Winnie visited, I had the illusion, however briefly, that the family was still intact. Her visits were becoming less frequent, as the police were becoming more vigilant. Winnie would bring Zindzi and Zenani to Rivonia, but the children were too young to know that I was in hiding. Makgatho, then eleven, was old enough to know, and he had been instructed never to reveal my real name in front of anyone. I could tell that he was determined, in his own small way, to keep my identity a secret.

But one day, towards the end of that year, he was at the farm playing with Nicholas Goldreich, Arthur's eleven-year-old son. Winnie had brought me a copy of the magazine *Drum*, and Makgatho and Nicholas stumbled upon it while they were playing. They began leafing through it when suddenly Makgatho stopped at a picture of me taken before I had gone underground. 'That's my father,' he exclaimed. Nicholas did not believe him, and his scepticism made Makgatho even keener to prove it was true. Makgatho then told his friend that my real name was Nelson Mandela. 'No, your father's name is David,' Nicholas replied. The boy then ran to his mother and asked her whether or not my name was David. She replied, 'Yes, it is David.' Nicholas then explained to his mother that Makgatho had told him that his father's real name was Nelson. This alarmed Hazel, and I soon learned of this lapse.

Once again I had the feeling that I had remained too long in one place. But I stayed put, for in a little over a week I was to leave on a mission that would take me to places that I had only ever dreamed of. Now, the struggle would for the first time take me outside the borders of my country.

In December the ANC received an invitation from the Pan-African Freedom Movement for East, Central and Southern Africa (PAFMECSA) to attend its conference in Addis Ababa in February 1962. PAFMECSA, which later became the Organization of African Unity, aimed to draw together the independent states of Africa and promote the liberation movements on the continent. The conference would furnish important connections for the ANC and be the first and best chance for us to enlist support, money, and training for MK.

The underground Executive asked me to lead the ANC delegation to the conference. Although I was eager to see the rest of Africa and meet freedom fighters from my own continent, I was greatly concerned that I would be violating the promise I had made not to leave the country but operate from underground. My colleagues, including Chief Luthuli, insisted that I go, but were adamant that I return immediately afterwards. I decided to make the trip.

My mission in Africa was broader than simply attending the conference; I was to arrange political and economic support for our new military force and, more important, military training for our men in as many places on the continent as possible. I was also determined to boost our reputation in the rest of Africa where we were still relatively unknown. The PAC had launched its own propaganda campaign and I was delegated to make our case wherever possible.

Before leaving, I secretly drove to Groutville to confer with the chief. Our meeting – at a safe house in town – was disconcerting. As I have related, the chief was present at the creation of MK, and was as informed as any member of the National Executive about its development. But the chief was not well and his memory was not what it had once been. He chastised me for not consulting him about the formation of MK. I attempted to remind him of the discussions that we had in Durban about taking up violence, but he did not recall them. This is in large part why the story has gained currency that Chief Luthuli was not informed about the creation of MK and was deeply opposed to the ANC taking up violence. Nothing could be further from the truth.

I had spent the night before my departure with Winnie at the house of white friends in the northern suburbs, and she brought me a new suitcase that she had packed. She was anxious about my leaving the country, but once again remained stoic. She behaved as much like a soldier as a wife.

The ANC had to arrange for me to travel to Dar es Salaam in Tanganyika, from where the flight to Addis Ababa would originate. The plan was for Walter, Kathrada, and Duma Nokwe to meet me at a secret rendezvous in Soweto and bring me my credentials for the trip. It would also be a moment for last-minute consultations before I left the country.

Ahmed Kathrada arrived at the appointed hour, but Walter and Duma were extremely late. I finally had to make alternative arrangements and Kathy managed to locate someone to drive me to Bechuanaland, where I would charter a plane. I later learned that Walter and Duma had been arrested on their way.

The drive to Bechuanaland was trying, as I was nervous both about the police and the fact that I had never crossed the boundaries of my country before. Our destination was Lobatse, near the South African border. We passed through the border without a problem and arrived in Lobatse in the late afternoon, where there was a telegram for me from Dar es Salaam postponing my trip for a fortnight. I stayed with my fellow Treason Trialist Fish Keitsing, who had since moved to Lobatse.

That afternoon I met Professor K.T. Motsete, the president of the Bechuanaland People's Party, which had been formed mainly by ex-ANC members. I now had unexpected spare time, which I used for reading, preparing my speech for the conference and hiking through the wild and beautiful hills above the town. Although I was not far outside my own country's borders, I felt as though I were in an exotic land. I was often accompanied by Max Mlonyeni, the son of a friend from the Transkei and a young member of the PAC. It was as though we were on safari, for we encountered all manner of animals, including a battalion of sprightly baboons, which I followed for some time, admiring their military-like organization and movements.

I was soon joined by Joe Matthews, who had come from Basutoland, and I insisted we should make haste for Dar es Salaam. An ANC colleague in Lobatse had recently been kidnapped by the South African police and I thought the sooner we could leave, the better. A plane was arranged, and our first destination was a town in northern Bechuanaland called Kasane, strategically situated near a point where the borders of four countries met – Bechuanaland, Northern and Southern Rhodesia, and South West Africa, as these colonies were then known. The landing strip at Kasane was waterlogged and we came in at a drier strip several miles away in the middle of the bush. The manager of a local hotel, armed with rifles, came to fetch us and reported that he had been delayed by a herd of rogue elephants. He was in an open van and Joe and I sat in the back, and I watched a lioness lazily emerge from the bush. I felt far from my home streets of Johannesburg; I was in the Africa of myth and legend for the first time.

Early the next morning we left for Mbeya, a Tanganyikan town near the Northern Rhodesian border. We flew near Victoria Falls and then headed north through a mountain range. While over the mountains, the pilot tried to contact Mbeya, but there was no answer. 'Mbeya, Mbeya!' he kept saying into the microphone. The weather had changed and the mountains were full of air pockets that made the plane bounce up and down like a cork on a rough sea. We were now flying through clouds and mists and in desperation the pilot descended and followed a twisting road through the mountains. By this time the mist had become so thick we could not see the road and when the pilot abruptly turned the plane I realized that we had narrowly missed a mountain that seemed to rear up out of nowhere. The emergency alarm went off, and I remember saying to myself, 'That's the end of us.' Even the ever-loquacious Joe was stone silent. But then just as we could see no further in the clouds and I imagined we were about to crash into a mountain, we emerged from the bad weather into a gloriously clear sky. I have never enjoyed flying much, and while this was the most frightening episode I have ever had on a plane, I am sometimes adept at appearing brave and I pretended that I was unconcerned.

We booked in a local hotel and found a crowd of blacks and whites sitting on the veranda making polite conversation. Never before had I been in a public place or hotel where there was no colour bar. We were waiting for Mr Mwakangale of the Tanganyika African National Union, a member of Parliament, and unbeknown to us he had already arrived and was looking for us. An African guest approached the white receptionist. 'Madam, did a Mr Mwakangale inquire after these two gentlemen?' he asked, pointing to us. 'I'm sorry, sir,' she replied. 'He did, but I forgot to tell them.'

'Please be careful, madam,' he said in a polite but firm tone. 'These men are our guests and we would like them to receive proper attention.' I then truly realized that I was in a country ruled by Africans. For the first time in my life, I was a free man. Though I was a fugitive and wanted in my own land, I felt the burden of oppression lifting from my shoulders. Everywhere I went in Tanganyika my skin colour was automatically accepted rather than instantly reviled. I was being judged for the first time not by the colour of my skin but by the measure of my mind and character. Although I was often homesick during my travels, I nevertheless felt as though I were truly home for the first time.

We arrived in Dar es Salaam the next day and I met Julius Nyerere, the newly independent country's first president. We talked at his house, which was not at all grand, and I recall that he drove himself in a simple car, a little Austin. This impressed me, for it suggested that he was a man of the people. Class, Nyerere always insisted, was alien to Africa; socialism indigenous.

I reviewed our situation for him, ending with an appeal for help. He was a shrewd, soft-spoken man who was well disposed to our mission, but his perception of the situation surprised and dismayed me. He suggested we postpone the armed struggle until Sobukwe came out of prison. This was the first of many occasions when I learned of the PAC's appeal in the rest of Africa. I described the weakness of the PAC, and argued that a postponement would be a setback for the struggle as a whole. He suggested I seek the favour of Emperor Haile Selassie and promised to arrange an introduction.

I was meant to meet Oliver Tambo in Dar, but because of my delay he was unable to wait and left a message for me to follow him to Lagos, where he was to attend the Lagos Conference of Independent States. On the flight to Accra I ran into Hymie Basner and his wife. Basner, who had once been my employer, had been offered a position in Accra. His radical politics and left-wing activities in South Africa had made him *persona non grata* there and he was seeking political asylum in Ghana.

The plane stopped in Khartoum and we lined up to go through customs. Joe Matthews was first, then myself, followed by Basner and his wife. Because I did not have a passport, I carried with me a rudimentary document from Tanganyika that merely said, 'This is Nelson Mandela, a citizen of the Republic of South Africa. He has permission to leave Tanganyika and return here.' I handed this paper to the old Sudanese man behind the immigration counter, and he looked up with a smile and said, 'My son, welcome to the Sudan.' He then shook my hand and stamped my document. Basner was behind me and handed the old man the same type of document. The old man looked at it for a moment, and then said in a rather agitated manner: 'What is this? What is this piece of paper? It is not official!'

Basner calmly explained that it was a document he had been given in Tanganyika because he did not have a passport. 'Not have a passport?' the immigration official said with disdain. 'How can you not have a passport – you are a white man!' Basner replied that he was persecuted in his own country because he fought for the rights of blacks. The Sudanese looked sceptical: 'But you are a white man!' Joe looked at me and knew what I was thinking: he whispered to me not to intervene, as we were guests in Sudan and did not want to offend our host's hospitality. But apart from being my employer, Basner was one of those whites who had truly taken risks on the behalf of black emancipation, and I could not desert him. Instead of leaving with Joe, I remained and stood close to the official and every time Basner said something, I simply bowed and nodded to the official as if to verify what he was saying. The old man realized what I was doing, softened his manner, and finally stamped his document and said quietly, 'Welcome to the Sudan.'

* * *

I had not seen Oliver for nearly two years, and when he met me at the airport in Accra I barely recognized him. Once clean-shaven and conservatively groomed, he now had a beard and longish hair and affected the military-style clothing characteristic of freedom fighters around the continent. (He probably had exactly the same reaction to me.) It was a happy reunion, and I complimented him on the tremendous work he had done abroad. He had already established ANC offices in Ghana, England, Egypt and Tanganyika, and had made valuable contacts for us in many other countries. Everywhere I subsequently travelled, I discovered the positive impression Oliver had made on diplomats and statesmen. He was the best possible ambassador for the organization.

The goal of the Lagos Conference of Independent States was to unite all African states, but it eventually disintegrated into bickering about which states to include or exclude. I kept a low profile and avoided the conference, for we did not want the South African government to know that I was abroad until I appeared at the PAFMECSA conference in Addis.

On the plane from Accra to Addis, we found Gaur Radebe, Peter Molotsi and other members of the PAC who were also on their way to PAFMECSA. They were all surprised to see me, and we immediately plunged into discussions concerning South Africa. The atmosphere was enjoyable and relaxed. Though I had been dismayed to learn of Gaur's leaving the ANC, that did not diminish my pleasure in seeing him. High above the ground and far from home, we had much more that united us than separated us.

We put down briefly in Khartoum, where we changed to an Ethiopian Airways flight to Addis. Here I experienced a rather strange sensation. As I was boarding the plane I saw that the pilot was black. I had never seen a black pilot before, and the instant I did I had to quell my panic. How could a black man fly a plane? But a moment later I caught myself: I had fallen into the apartheid mind-set, thinking Africans were inferior and that flying was a white man's job. I sat back in my seat, and chided myself for such thoughts. Once we were in the air, I lost my nervousness and studied the geography of Ethiopia, thinking how guerrilla forces had hidden in these very forests to fight the Italian imperialists.

47

Formerly known as Abyssinia, Ethiopia, according to tradition, was founded long before the birth of Christ, supposedly by the son of Solomon and the Queen of Sheba. Although it had been conquered dozens of times, Ethiopia was the birthplace of African nationalism. Unlike so many other African states, it had fought colonialism at every turn. Menelik had rebuffed the Italians in the last century, though Ethiopia failed to halt them in this one. In 1930 Haile Selassie became emperor and the shaping force of contemporary Ethiopian history. I was seventeen when Mussolini attacked Ethiopia, an invasion that spurred not only my hatred of that despot but of fascism in general. Although Selassie was forced to flee when the Italians conquered Ethiopia in 1936, he returned after the Allied forces drove the Italians out in 1941.

Ethiopia has always held a special place in my own imagination and the prospect of visiting Ethiopia attracted me more strongly than a trip to France, England and America combined. I felt I would be visiting my own genesis, unearthing the roots of what made me an African. Meeting the emperor himself would be like shaking hands with history.

Our first stop was Addis Ababa, the Imperial City, which did not live up to its title, for it was the opposite of grand, with only a few tarred streets, and more goats and sheep than cars. Apart from the Imperial Palace, the university and the Ras Hotel, where we stayed, there were few structures that could compare with even the least impressive buildings of Johannesburg. Contemporary Ethiopia was not a model when it came to democracy, either. There were no political parties, no popular organs of government, no separation of powers; only the emperor, who was supreme.

Before the opening of the conference, the delegates assembled at the tiny town of Debra Zaid. A grandstand had been erected in the central square and Oliver and I sat off to the side, away from the main podium. Suddenly we heard the distant music of a lone bugle and then the strains of a brass band accompanied by the steady beating of African drums. As the music came closer, I could hear – and feel – the rumbling of hundreds of marching feet. From behind a building at the edge of the square, an officer appeared brandishing a gleaming sword; at his heels marched five hundred black soldiers in ranks of four, each carrying a polished rifle against his uniformed shoulder. When the troops had marched directly in front of the grandstand, an order rang out in Amharic, and the five hundred soldiers halted as one man, spun round, and executed a precise salute to an elderly man in a dazzling uniform, His Highness the Emperor of Ethiopia, Haile Selassie, the Lion of Judah.

Here, for the first time in my life, I was witnessing black soldiers commanded by black generals applauded by black leaders who were all guests of a black head of state. It was a heady moment. I only hoped it was a vision of what lay in the future for my own country.

On the morning after the parade, Oliver and I

attended a meeting where each organization had to apply for accreditation. We were unpleasantly surprised to find that our application was blocked by a delegate from Uganda who complained that we were a tribal organization of Xhosas. My impulse was to dismiss this claim contemptuously, but Oliver's notion was that we should simply explain that our organization was formed to unite Africans and our membership was drawn from all sections of the people. This I did, adding that the president of our organization, Chief Luthuli, was a Zulu. Our application was accepted. I realized that many people on the continent knew about the ANC only from the PAC's description of us.

The conference was officially opened by our host, His Imperial Majesty, who was dressed in an elaborate brocaded army uniform. I was surprised by how small the emperor appeared, but his dignity and confidence made him seem like the African giant that he was. It was the first time I had witnessed a head of state go through the formalities of his office, and I was fascinated. He stood perfectly straight, and inclined his head only slightly to indicate that he was listening. Dignity was the hallmark of all his actions.

I was scheduled to speak after the emperor, the only other speaker that morning. For the first time in many months, I flung aside the identity of David Motsamayi and became Nelson Mandela. In my speech, I reviewed the history of the freedom struggle in South Africa and listed the brutal massacres that had been committed against our people, from Bulhoek in 1921, when the army and police killed 183 unarmed peasants, to Sharpeville forty years later. I thanked the assembled nations for exerting pressure on South Africa, citing in particular Ghana, Nigeria and Tanganyika, who spear-headed the successful drive to oust South Africa from the British Commonwealth. I retraced the birth of Umkhonto we Sizwe, explaining that all opportunities for peaceful struggle had been closed to us. 'A leader-ship commits a crime against its own people if it hesitates to sharpen its political weapons where they have become less effective . . . On the night of 16 December last year, the whole of South Africa vibrated under the heavy blows of Umkhonto we Sizwe.' I had no sooner said this than the chief minister of Uganda cried out: 'Give it to them again!'

I then related my own experience:

I have just come out of South Africa, having for the last ten months lived in my own country as an outlaw, away from family and friends. When I was compelled to lead this sort of life, I made a public statement in which I announced that I would not leave the country but would continue working underground. I meant it and I will honour that undertaking.

The announcement that I would return to South Africa was met with loud cheers. We had been encouraged to speak first so that PAFMECSA could evaluate our cause and decide how much support to give it. There was a natural reluctance among many African states to sup-port violent struggles elsewhere, but the speech per-suaded people that freedom fighters in South Africa had no alternative but to take up arms.

Oliver and I had a private discussion with Kenneth Kaunda, the leader of the United National Independence Party of Northern Rhodesia and the future president of Zambia. Like Julius Nyerere, Kaunda was worried about the lack of unity among South African freedom fighters and suggested that when Sobukwe emerged from jail, we might all join forces. Among Africans, the PAC had captured the spotlight at Sharpeville in a way that far exceeded their influence as an organization. Kaunda, who had once been a member of the ANC, told us he was concerned about our alliance with white communists and indicated that this reflected poorly on us in Africa. Communism was suspect not only in the West but in Africa. This came as something of a revelation to me, and it was a view that I was to hear over and over during my trip.

When I attempted to make the case that UNIP's support of the PAC was misguided, Kaunda put his hand on my shoulder and said, 'Nelson, speaking to me on this subject is like carrying coals to Newcastle. I am your supporter and a follower of Chief Luthuli. But I am not the sole voice of UNIP. You must speak to Simon Kapwepwe. If you persuade him, you will make my job easier.' Kapwepwe was the second in command of UNIP, and I made arrangements to see him the following day. I asked Oliver to join me but he said, 'Nel, you must see him on your own. Then you can be completely frank.'

I spent the entire day with Kapwepwe and heard from him the most astonishing tale. 'We were mightily impressed by your speech,' he said, 'and indeed by your entire ANC delegation. If we were to judge your organization by these two things, we would certainly be in your camp. But we have heard disturbing reports from the PAC to the effect that Umkhonto we Sizwe is the brainchild of the Communist Party and the Liberal Party, and that the idea of the organization is merely to use Africans as cannon fodder.'

I was nonplussed, and I blurted out that I was astounded that he could not see himself how damnably false this story was. 'First of all,' I said, 'it is well known that the Liberal Party and the Communist Party are arch-enemies and could not come together to play a game of cards. Second, I am here to tell you at the risk of immodesty that I myself was the prime mover behind MK's formation.' Finally, I said I was greatly disappointed in the PAC for spreading such lies.

By the end of the day I had converted Kapwepwe, and he said he would call a meeting and make our case himself – and he did so. But it was another example of both the lack of knowledge about South Africa in the rest of Africa and the extraordinary lengths the PAC would go to besmirch the ANC. Kapwepwe bade me good luck, for the conference was now over. It had been successful, but we had our work cut out for us.

As a student, I had fantasized about visiting Egypt, the cradle of African civilization, the treasure chest of so much beauty in art and design, about seeing the pyramids and the sphinx, and crossing the Nile, the greatest of African rivers. From Addis, Oliver, Robert Resha – who was to accompany me on the rest of my travels – and I flew to Cairo. I spent the whole morning of my first day in Cairo at the museum, looking at art, examining artifacts, making notes, learning about the type of men who founded the ancient civilization of the Nile Valley. This was not amateur archaeological interest; it is important for African nationalists to be armed with evidence to refute the fictitious claims of whites that Africans are without a civilized past that compares with that of the West. In a single morning, I discovered that Egyptians were creating great works of art and architecture when whites were still living in caves.

Egypt was an important model for us, for we could witness at firsthand the programme of socialist economic reforms being launched by President Nasser. He had reduced private ownership of land, nationalized certain sectors of the economy, pioneered rapid industrialization, democratized education and built a modern army. Many of these reforms were precisely the sorts of things that we in the ANC someday hoped to enact. At that time, however, it was more important to us that Egypt was the only African state with an army, navy and air force that could in any way compare with those of South Africa.

After a day, Oliver left for London, promising to join Robbie and me in Ghana. Before Robbie and I left on our tour, we discussed the presentation we would make in each country. My inclination was to explain the political situation as truthfully and objectively as possible and not omit the accomplishments of the PAC. In each new country, I would initially seal myself away in our hotel to familiarize myself with information about the country's policies, history and leadership. Robbie did the opposite. A natural extrovert, he would leave the hotel as soon as we arrived and hit the streets, learning by seeing and talking to people. We were an odd couple, for I affected the informal dress I had got used to underground and wore khakis and fatigues, while Robbie was always smartly turned out in a suit.

In Tunis, our first stop, we met the minister of defence, who bore a striking resemblance to Chief Luthuli. But I'm afraid that is where the similarity ended, for when I was explaining to him the situation in our country with PAC leaders such as Robert Sobukwe in jail, he interrupted me and said, 'When that chap returns, he will finish you!' Robbie raised his eyebrows at this (later he said, 'Man, you were putting the case for the PAC better than they could!'), but I insisted on giving the minister the full picture. When the following day we met President Habib Bourguiba, his response was utterly positive and immediate: he offered training for our soldiers and £5,000 for weapons.

Rabat in Morocco, our next stop, with its ancient and mysterious walls, its fashionable shops and medieval mosques, seemed a charming mixture of Africa, Europe and the Middle East. Apparently freedom fighters thought so as well, for Rabat was the crossroads of virtually every liberation movement on the continent. While there, we met freedom fighters from Mozambique, Angola, Algeria and Cape Verde. It was also the headquarters of the Algerian revolutionary army, and we spent several days with Dr Mustafa, head of the Algerian mission in Morocco, who briefed us on the history of the Algerian resistance to the French.

The situation in Algeria was the closest model to our own in that the rebels faced a large white settler community that ruled the indigenous majority. He related how the FLN had begun their struggle with a handful of guerrilla attacks in 1954, having been heartened by the defeat of the French at Dien Bien Phu in Vietnam. At first, the FLN believed they could defeat the French militarily, Dr Mustafa said, then realized that a purely military victory was impossible.

Instead, they resorted to guerrilla warfare. Guerrilla warfare, he explained, was not designed to win a military victory so much as to unleash political and economic forces that would bring down the enemy. Dr Mustafa advised us not to neglect the political side of war while planning the military effort. International public opinion, he said, is sometimes worth more than a fleet of jet fighters.

At the end of three days, he sent us to Oujda, a dusty little town just across the border from Algeria and the headquarters of the Algerian army in Morocco. We visited an army unit at the front, and at one point I took a pair of field glasses and could actually see French troops across the border. I confess I imagined that I was looking at the uniforms of the South African Defence Force.

A day or two later I was a guest at a military parade in honour of Ahmed Ben Bella, who was to become the first prime minister of independent Algeria and who had recently emerged from a French prison. A far cry from the military parade I had witnessed in Addis Ababa, this parade was not the crisp, well-drilled, handsomely uniformed force of Ethiopia but a kind of walking history of the guerrilla movement in Algeria.

At its head sauntered proud, battle-hardened veterans in turbans, long tunics and sandals, who had started the struggle many years before. They carried the weapons they had used: sabres, old flintlock rifles, battle-axes and assegais. They were followed in turn by younger soldiers, all carrying modern arms and equally proud. Some held heavy anti-tank and anti-aircraft guns. But even these soldiers did not march with the smartness and precision of the Ethiopians. This was a guerrilla force, and they were soldiers who had won their stripes in the fire of battle, who cared more about fighting and tactics than dress uniforms and parades. Inspired as I was by the troops in Addis, I knew that our own force would be more like these troops here in Oujda, and I could only hope they would fight as valiantly.

At the rear was a rather rag-tag military band that was led by a man called Sudani. Tall, well built and confident, he was as black as the night. He was swinging a ceremonial mace, and when we saw him, our whole party stood up and started clapping and cheering. I looked around and noticed others staring at us, and I realized that we were only cheering because this fellow was a black man and black faces were quite rare in Morocco. Once again I was struck by the great power of nationalism and ethnicity. We reacted instantly, for we felt as though we were seeing a brother African. Later, our hosts informed us that Sudani had been a legendary soldier, and had even reputedly captured an entire French unit single-handedly. But we were cheering him because of his colour not his exploits.

From Morocco, I flew across the Sahara to Bamako, the capital of Mali, and then on to Guinea. The flight from Mali to Guinea was more like a local bus than a plane. Chickens wandered the aisles, women walked back and forth carrying packages on their heads and selling bags of peanuts and dried vegetables. It was flying democratic-style, and I admired it very much.

My next stop was Sierre Leone and, when I arrived, I discovered that Parliament was in session and decided to attend the proceedings. I entered as any tourist would and was given a seat not far from the Speaker. The clerk of the House approached me and asked me to identify myself. I whispered to him, 'I am the representative of Chief Luthuli of South Africa.' He shook my hand warmly and proceeded to report to the Speaker. The clerk then explained that I had inadvertently been given a seat not normally allowed to visitors, but in this case it was an honour for them to make an exception.

Within an hour there was an adjournment, and as I stood among the members and dignitaries drinking tea, a queue formed in front of me and I saw to my amazement that the entire Parliament had lined up to shake hands with me. I was very gratified, until the third or fourth person in line mumbled something to the effect of, 'It is a great honour to shake the hand of the revered Chief Luthuli, winner of the Nobel Peace Prize.' I was an impostor! The clerk had misunderstood. The prime minister, Sir Milton Margai, was then brought over to meet me, and the clerk introduced me as the chief. I immediately attempted to inform the clerk that I was not Chief Luthuli, but he would have none of it, and I decided that in the interests of hospitality I would continue the charade. I later met the president, explained the case of mistaken identity, and he offered generous material assistance.

In Liberia, I met President Tubman, who not only gave me $5,000 for weapons and training, but said in a quiet voice, 'Have you any pocket money?' I confessed that I was a bit low, and instantly an aide came back with an envelope containing $400 in cash. From Liberia, I went to Ghana, where I was met by Oliver and entertained by Guinea's resident minister, Abdoulaye Diallo. When I told him that I had not seen Sekou Touré when I was in Guinea, he arranged for us to return immediately to that arid land. Oliver and I were impressed with Touré. He lived in a modest bungalow, and wore an old faded suit that could have done with a visit to the dry cleaner's. We made our case to him, explained the history of the ANC and MK, and asked for $5,000 for the support of MK. He listened very carefully, and replied in a rather formal way. 'The government and the people of Guinea,' he said, as though giving a speech, 'fully support the struggle of our brothers in South Africa, and we have made statements at the UN to that effect.' He went to the bookcase, where he removed two books of his, which he autographed to Oliver and me. He then said thank you, and we were dismissed.

Oliver and I were annoyed: we had been called back from another country, and all he gave us were signed copies of his book? We had wasted our time. A short while later, we were in our hotel room when an official from the Foreign Affairs Department knocked on our door and presented us with a suitcase. We opened it and it was filled with banknotes; Oliver and I looked at each other in glee. But then Oliver's expression changed. 'Nelson, this is Guinean currency,' he said. 'It is worthless outside here; it is just paper.' But Oliver had an idea: we took the money to the Czech embassy, where he had a friend who exchanged it for a convertible currency.

The gracefulness of the slender fishing boats that glided into the harbour in Dakar was equalled only by the elegance of the Senegalese women who sailed through the city in flowing robes and turbanned heads. I wandered through the nearby market place, intoxicated by the exotic spices and perfumes. The Senegalese are a handsome people and I enjoyed the brief time that Oliver and I spent in their country. Their society showed how disparate elements – French, Islamic and African – can mingle to create a unique and distinctive culture.

On our way to a meeting with President Léopold Senghor, Oliver suffered a severe attack of asthma. He refused to return to the hotel, and I carried him on my back up the stairs to the president's office. Senghor was greatly concerned by Oliver's condition and insisted that he be attended to by his personal physician.

I had been told to be wary of Senghor, for there were reports that Senegalese soldiers were serving with the French in Algeria, and that he was a bit too taken with the customs and charms of the *ancien régime*. There will always be, in emerging nations, an enduring attraction to the ways of the colonizer – I myself was not immune to it. President Senghor was a scholar and poet, and he told us he was collecting research material on Shaka, flattering us by asking numerous questions about that great South African warrior. We summarized the situation in South Africa and made our request for military training and money. Senghor replied that his hands were tied until Parliament met.

In the meantime, he wanted us to talk with the minister of justice, a M. Daboussier, about military training, and the president introduced me to a beautiful white French girl who, he explained, would interpret for me in my meeting with him. I said nothing, but was disturbed. I did not feel comfortable discussing the very sensitive issues of military training in front of a young woman I did not know and was not sure I could trust. Senghor sensed my uneasiness, for he said, 'Mandela, do not worry, the French here identify themselves completely with our African aspirations.'

When we reached the minister's office, we found some African secretaries in the reception area. One of the black secretaries asked the Frenchwoman what she was doing there. She said she had been sent by the president to interpret. An argument ensued and in the middle of it, one of the African secretaries turned to me and said, 'Sir, can you speak English?' I said I could, and she replied, 'The minister speaks English and you can talk with him directly. You don't need an interpreter.' The French girl, now quite miffed, stood aside as I went in to speak to the minister, who promised to fulfil our requests. In the end, although Senghor did not then provide us with what we asked for, he furnished me with a diplomatic passport and paid for our plane fares from Dakar to our next destination: London.

48

I confess to being something of an Anglophile. When I thought of Western democracy and freedom, I thought of the British parliamentary system. In so many ways, the very model of the gentleman for me was an Englishman. Despite Britain being the home of parliamentary democracy, it was that democracy that had helped to inflict a pernicious system of iniquity on my people. While I abhorred the notion of British imperialism, I never rejected the trappings of British style and manners.

I had several reasons for wanting to go to England, apart from my desire to see the country I had so long read and heard about. I was concerned about Oliver's health and wanted to persuade him to receive treatment. I very much wanted to see Adelaide, his wife, and their children, as well as Yusuf Dadoo, who was now living there and representing the Congress movement. I also knew that in London I would be able to obtain literature on guerrilla warfare that I had been unable to acquire elsewhere.

In London, I resumed my old underground ways, not wanting word to leak back to South Africa that I was there. The tentacles of South African security forces reached all the way to London. But I was not a recluse; my ten days there were divided among ANC business, seeing old friends and occasional jaunts as a conventional tourist. With Mary Benson, a Pretoria-born friend who had written about our struggle, Oliver and I saw the sights of the city that had once commanded nearly two-thirds of the globe: Westminster Abbey, Big Ben, the Houses of Parliament. While I gloried in the beauty of these buildings, I was ambivalent about what they represented. When we saw the statue of General Smuts near Westminster Abbey, Oliver and I joked that perhaps some day there would be a statue of us in its stead.

I had been informed by numerous people that the *Observer* newspaper, run by David Astor, had been tilting towards the PAC in its coverage, its editorials implying that the ANC was the party of the past. Oliver arranged for me to meet Astor at his house, and we talked at length about the ANC. I do not know if I had an effect on him, but the coverage certainly changed. He also recommended that I talk to a number of prominent politicians, and in the company of the Labour MP Denis Healey, I met Hugh Gaitskell, leader of the Labour Party, and Jo Grimond, leader of the Liberal Party.

It was only towards the end of my stay that I saw Yusuf, but it was not a happy reunion. Oliver and I had encountered a recurring difficulty in our travels: one African leader after another had questioned us about our relations with white and Indian communists, sometimes suggesting that they controlled the ANC. Our non-racialism would have been less of a problem had it not been for the formation of the explicitly nationalistic and anti-white PAC. In the rest of Africa, most African leaders could understand the views of the PAC better than those of the ANC. Oliver had discussed these things with Yusuf, who was unhappy about Oliver's conclusions. Oliver had resolved that the ANC had to appear more independent, taking certain actions unilaterally without the involvement of the other members of the Alliance, and I agreed.

I spent my last night in London discussing these issues with Yusuf. I explained that now that we were embarking on an armed struggle we would be relying on other African nations for money, training and support, and therefore had to take their views into account more than we did in the past. Yusuf believed that Oliver and I were changing ANC policy, that we were preparing to depart from the non-racialism that was the core of the Freedom Charter. I told him he was mistaken; we were not rejecting non-racialism; we were simply saying the ANC must stand more on its own and make statements that were not part of the Congress Alliance. Often the ANC, the South African Indian Congress and the Coloured People's Congress would make a collective statement on an issue affecting only Africans. That would have to change. Yusuf was unhappy about this. 'What about policy?' he kept asking. I told him I was not talking about policy, I was talking about image. We would still work together, only the ANC had to appear to be the first among equals.

Although I was sad to leave my friends in London, I was now embarking on what was to be the most unfamiliar part of my trip: military training. I had arranged to receive six months of training in Addis Ababa. I was met there by Foreign Minister Yefu, who warmly greeted me and took me to a suburb called Kolfe, the headquarters of the Ethiopian Riot Battalion, where I was to learn the art and science of soldiering.

While I was a fair amateur boxer, I had very little knowledge of even the rudiments of combat. My trainer was a Lieutenant Wondoni Befikadu, an experienced soldier, who had fought with the underground against the Italians. Our programme was strenuous: we trained from 8 a.m. until 1 p.m., broke for a shower and lunch, and then again from 2 to 4 p.m. From 4 p.m. into the evening I was lectured on military science by Colonel Tadesse, who was also assistant commissioner of police and had been instrumental in foiling a recent coup attempt against the emperor.

I learned how to use an automatic rifle and a pistol and took target practice both in Kolfe with the Emperor's Guard and at a shooting range about fifty miles away with the entire battalion. I was taught about demolition and mortar-firing and I learned how to make small bombs and mines – and how to avoid them. I felt myself being moulded into a soldier and began to think as a soldier thinks – a far cry from the way a politician thinks.

What I enjoyed most were the 'fatigue marches' in which you are equipped with only a gun, bullets and some water, and must reach a distant point within a certain time. During these marches I got a sense of the landscape, which was very beautiful, with dense forests and spare highlands. The country was extremely backward: people used wooden ploughs and lived on a very simple diet supplemented by home-brewed beer. Their existence was similar to the life in rural South Africa; poor people everywhere are more alike than they are different.

In my study sessions, Colonel Tadesse discussed matters such as how to create a guerrilla force, how to command an army and how to enforce discipline. One evening, during supper, he said to me, 'Now, Mandela, you are creating a liberation army not a conventional capitalist army. A liberation army is an egalitarian army. You must treat your men entirely differently from how you would in a capitalist army. When you are on duty, you must exercise your authority with assurance and control. That is no different from a capitalist command. But when you are off duty, you must conduct yourself on the basis of perfect equality, even with the lowliest soldier. You must eat what they eat; you must not take your food in your office, but eat with them, drink with them, not isolate yourself.'

All this seemed admirable and sensible, but while he was talking to me, a sergeant came into the hall and asked the colonel where he could find a certain lieutenant. The colonel regarded him with ill-concealed contempt and said, 'Can't you see that I am talking to an important individual here? Don't you know not to interrupt me when I am eating? Now, get out of my sight!' Then he continued with his discussion in the same didactic tone as before.

The training course was meant to be six months long, but after eight weeks I received a telegram from the ANC urgently requesting that I return home. The internal armed struggle was escalating and they wanted the commander of MK on the scene.

Colonel Tadesse rapidly arranged for me to take an Ethiopian flight to Khartoum. Before I left, he presented me with a gift: an automatic pistol and two hundred rounds of ammunition. I was grateful, both for the gun and his instruction. Despite my fatigue marches, I found it wearying to carry around all that ammunition. A single bullet is surprisingly heavy: hauling around two hundred is like carrying a small child on one's back.

In Khartoum I was met by a British Airways official who told me that my connecting flight to Dar es Salaam would not leave until the following day and they had taken the liberty of booking me into a posh hotel in town. I was dismayed, for I would have preferred to stay in a less conspicuous third-class hotel.

When I was dropped off, I had to walk across the hotel's long and elegant veranda, where several dozen whites were sitting and drinking. This was long before metal detectors and security checks, and I was carrying my pistol in a holster inside my jacket and the two hundred rounds wrapped around my waist inside my trousers. I also had several thousand pounds in cash. I had the feeling that all these well-dressed whites had X-ray vision and that I was going to be arrested at any moment. But I was escorted safely to my room, where I ordered room service; even the footsteps of the waiters put me on edge.

From Khartoum I went direct to Dar es Salaam, where I greeted the first group of twenty-one Umkhonto recruits who were headed for Ethiopia to train as soldiers. It was a proud moment, for these men had volunteered for duty in an army I was then attempting to create. They were risking their lives in a battle that was only just beginning, a battle that would be most dangerous for those who were its first soldiers. They were young men, mainly from the cities, and they were proud and eager. We had a dinner in Addis; the men slaughtered a goat in my honour, and I addressed them about my trip and told them of the necessity of good behaviour and discipline abroad, because they were representatives of the South African freedom struggle. Military training, I said, must go hand in hand with political training, for a revolution is not just a question of pulling a trigger; its purpose is to create a fair and just society. It was the first time that I was ever saluted by my own soldiers.

President Nyerere gave me a private plane to Mbeya, and I then flew directly to Lobatse. The pilot informed me that we would be landing in Kanye. This concerned me: why was the plan altered? In Kanye, I was met by the local magistrate and a security man, both of whom were white. The magistrate approached me and asked me my name. David Motsamayi, I replied. No, he said, please tell me your real name. Again, I said David Motsamayi. The magistrate said, 'Please tell me your real name because I was given instructions to meet Mr Mandela here and provide him with help and transportation. If you are not Mr Nelson Mandela, I am afraid I will have to arrest you for you have no permit to enter the country. Are you Nelson Mandela?'

This was a quandary; I might be arrested either way. 'If you insist that I am Nelson Mandela and not David Motsamayi,' I said, 'I will not challenge you.' He smiled and said simply, 'We expected you yesterday.' He then offered me a lift to where my comrades would be waiting for me. We drove to Lobatse, where I met Joe Modise and an ANC supporter named Jonas Matlou, who was then living there. The magistrate told me that the South African police were aware that I was returning, and he suggested that I leave the next day. I thanked him for his help and advice, but when I arrived at Matlou's house, I said that I would leave that night. I was to drive back to South Africa with Cecil Williams, a white theatre director and member of MK. Posing as his chauffeur, I got behind the wheel and we left that night for Johannesburg.

49

After crossing the border, I breathed in deeply. The air of one's home always smells sweet after one has been away. It was a clear winter night and somehow even the stars looked more welcoming here than from elsewhere on the continent. Though I was leaving a world where I experienced freedom for the first time and returning to one where I was a fugitive, I was profoundly relieved to be back in the land of my birth and destiny.

Between Bechuanaland and the northwestern Transvaal, dozens of unmarked roads transverse the border, and Cecil knew just which ones to take. During the drive, he filled me in on many of the events I had missed. We drove all night, slipping across the border just after midnight and reaching Liliesleaf Farm at dawn. I was still wearing my beat-up khaki training uniform.

Once at the farm, I did not have time for rest and reflection because the following night we held a secret meeting for me to brief the Working Committee on my trip. Walter, Moses Kotane, Govan Mbeki, Dan Tloome, J.B. Marks and Duma Nokwe all arrived at the farm, a rare reunion. I first gave a general overview of my travels, itemizing the money we had received and the offers of training. At the same time, I reported in detail the reservations I had encountered about the ANC's co-operation with whites, Indians and particularly communists. Still ringing in my ears was my final meeting with the Zambian leaders, who told me that while they knew the ANC was stronger and more popular than the PAC, they understood the PAC's pure African nationalism but were bewildered by the ANC's non-racialism and communist ties. I informed them that Oliver and I believed the ANC had to appear more independent to reassure our new allies on the continent, for they were the ones who would be financing and training Umkhonto we Sizwe. I proposed reshaping the Congress Alliance so that the ANC would clearly be seen as the leader, especially on issues directly affecting Africans.

This was a serious proposition, and the entire leadership had to be consulted. The Working Committee urged me to go down to Durban and brief Chief Luthuli. All agreed except Govan Mbeki, who was not then living at Liliesleaf Farm but was present as part of the High Command of MK. He urged me to send someone else. It was simply too risky, he said, and the organization should not jeopardize my safety, especially as I was newly returned and ready to push ahead with MK. This wise advice was overruled by everyone, including myself.

I left the next night from Rivonia in the company of Cecil, again posing as his chauffeur. I had planned a series of secret meetings in Durban, the first of which was with Monty Naicker and Ismail Meer to brief them about my trip and to discuss the new proposal. Monty and Ismail were extremely close to the chief, and the chief trusted their views. I wanted to be able to tell Luthuli I had spoken to his friends and convey their reaction. Ismail and Monty, however, were disturbed by my belief that the ANC needed to take the lead among the Congress Alliance and make statements on its own concerning affairs that affected Africans. They were against anything that unravelled the Alliance.

I was taken to Groutville, where the chief lived, and we met in the house of an Indian lady in town. I explained the situation to the chief at some length, and he listened without speaking. When I was done, he said he did not like the idea of foreign politicians dictating policy to the ANC. He said we had evolved the policy of non-racialism for good reasons and he did not think that we should alter our policy because it did not suit a few foreign leaders.

I told the chief that these foreign politicians were not dictating our policy, but merely saying that they did not understand it. My plan, I told him, was simply to effect essentially cosmetic changes in order to make the ANC more intelligible – and more palatable – to our allies. I saw this as a defensive manoeuvre, for if African states decided to support the PAC, a small and weak organization could suddenly become a large and potent one.

The chief did not make decisions on the spur of the moment. I could see he wanted to think about what I had said and talk to some of his friends about it. I said farewell, and he advised me to be careful. I still had a number of clandestine meetings in the city and townships that evening. My last meeting that evening was with the MK Regional Command in Durban.

The Durban Command was led by a sabotage expert named Bruno Mtolo, whom I had never met before, but would come across again under dramatically different circumstances. I briefed them on my trip around Africa, about the support we had received and the offers of training. I explained that for the moment MK was limited to sabotage, but that if sabotage did not have the desired effect we would probably move on to guerrilla warfare.

Later that same evening, at the home of the photo-journalist G. R. Naidoo, where I was staying, I was joined by Ismail and Fatima Meer, Monty Naicker, and J. N. Singh for what was a combination welcome-home and going-away party, for I was leaving the next day for Johannesburg. It was a pleasant evening and my first night of relaxation in a long while. I slept well and I met Cecil on Sunday afternoon – 5 August – for the long drive back to Johannesburg in his trusty Austin.

I wore my chauffeur's white dust-coat and sat next to Cecil as he drove. We often took turns behind the wheel. It was a clear, cool day and I revelled in the beauty of the Natal countryside; even in winter, Natal remains green. Now that I was returning to Johannesburg I would have some time to see Winnie and the children. I had often wished that Winnie could share with me the wonders of Africa, but the best I could do was to tell her what I had seen and done.

Once we left the industrial precincts of Durban, we moved through hills that offered majestic views of the surrounding valleys and the blue-black waters of the Indian Ocean. Durban is the principal port for the country's main industrial area, and the highway that leads to Johannesburg runs parallel to the railway line for a great distance. I went from contemplating the natural beauty to ruminating on the fact that the

railway line, being so close to the highway, offered a
convenient place for sabotage. I made a note of this in
the small notebook I always carried with me.

Cecil and I were engrossed in discussions of sabotage
plans as we passed through Howick, twenty miles north-
west of Pietermaritzburg. At Cedara, a small town just
past Howick, I noticed a Ford V-8 filled with white men
shoot past us on the right. I instinctively turned round
to look behind and I saw two more cars filled with white
men. Suddenly, in front of us, the Ford was signalling to
us to stop. I knew in that instant that my life on the run
was over; my seventeen months of 'freedom' were
about to end.

As Cecil slowed down, he turned to me and said,
'Who are these men?' I did not answer because we both
knew very well who they were. They had chosen their
hiding-spot well; to the left of us was a steep wooded
bank they could have forced us into had we tried to
elude them. I was in the left-hand passenger seat, and
for a moment I thought about jumping out and making
an escape into the woods, but I would have been shot in
a matter of seconds.

When our car stopped, a tall slender man with a
stern expression came directly over to the window on
the passenger side. He was unshaven and it appeared
that he had not slept in quite a while. I immediately
assumed he had been waiting for us for several days. In
a calm voice, he introduced himself as Sergeant Vorster
of the Pietermaritzburg police and produced an arrest
warrant. He asked me to identify myself. I told him my
name was David Motsamayi. He nodded, and then, in a
very proper way, he asked me a few questions about
where I had been and where I was going. I parried

these without giving him much information. He seemed a bit irritated and then he said, 'Ag, you're Nelson Mandela, and this is Cecil Williams, and you are under arrest!'

He informed us that a police major from the other car would accompany us back to Pietermaritzburg. The police were not yet so vigilant in those days, and Sergeant Vorster did not bother searching me. I had my loaded revolver, and again I thought of escape, but I would have been greatly outnumbered. I secretly put the revolver – and my notebook – in the upholstery between my seat and Cecil's. For some reason, the police never found the gun or the small notebook, which was fortunate, for many more people would have been arrested if they had.

At the police station I was led into Sergeant Vorster's office, where I saw a number of officers, one of whom was Warrant Officer Truter, who had testified in the Treason Trial. Truter had made a favourable impression on the accused because he had accurately explained the policy of the ANC, and had not exaggerated or lied. We greeted each other in a friendly way.

I had still not admitted to anything other than the name David Motsamayi, and Truter said to me, 'Nelson, why do you keep up this farce? You know I know who you are. We all know who you are.' I told him simply that I had given a name, and that was the name I was standing by. I asked for a lawyer and was curtly refused. I then declined to make a statement.

Cecil and I were locked in separate cells. I now had time to ruminate on my situation. I had always known that arrest was a possibility, but even freedom fighters practise denial, and in my cell that night I realized I was not prepared for the reality of capture and confinement. I was upset and agitated. Someone had tipped the police off about my whereabouts; they had known I was in Durban and that I would be returning to Johannesburg. For weeks before my return, the police believed that I was already back in the country. In June, newspaper headlines blared 'RETURN OF THE BLACK PIMPERNEL' while I was still in Addis Ababa. Perhaps that had been a bluff?

The authorities had been harassing Winnie in the belief that she would know whether I was back. I knew that they had followed her and searched the house on a number of occasions. I guessed they had figured I would visit Chief Luthuli directly upon my return, and they were correct. But I also suspected they had information that I was in Durban at that time. The movement had been infiltrated with informers, and even well-intentioned people were generally not as tight-lipped as they should have been. I had also been lax. Too many people had known I was in Durban. I had even had a party the night before I left, and I chastised myself for letting down my guard. My mind ricocheted among the possibilities. Was it an informer in Durban? Someone from Johannesburg? Someone from the movement? Or even a friend or member of the family? But such speculation about unknowns is futile, and with the combination of mental and physical exhaustion, I soon fell deeply asleep. At least on this night – 5 August 1962 – I did not have to worry about whether the police would find me. They already had.

In the morning I felt restored and braced myself for the new ordeal that lay ahead of me. I would not, under any circumstances, seem despairing or even disappointed to my captors. At 8.30 I appeared before the local magistrate and was formally remanded to Johannesburg. It was low-key, and the magistrate seemed no more concerned than if he were handling a traffic summons. The police had not taken elaborate precautions for the trip back to Johannesburg or for my security, and I merely sat in the back seat of a sedan, un-handcuffed, with two officers riding in front. My arrest had been discovered by my friends; Fatima Meer brought some food to the jail and I shared it with the two officers in the car. We even stopped at Volksrust, a town along the way, and they allowed me to take a brief walk to stretch my legs. I did not contemplate escape when people were kind to me; I did not want to take advantage of the trust they placed in me.

But as we approached Johannesburg, the atmosphere changed. I heard an announcement over the police radio of my capture and the order to fold up the road-blocks to and from Natal. At sunset, on the outskirts of Johannesburg, we were met by a sizable police escort. I was abruptly handcuffed, taken from the car, and placed in a sealed police van with small opaque windows reinforced with wire netting. The motorcade then took a circuitous and unfamiliar route to Marshall Square as if they were concerned we might be ambushed.

I was locked in a cell by myself. In the quiet, I was planning my strategy for the next day, when I heard a cough from a nearby cell. I did not realize a prisoner was close by, but more than that, there was something about this cough, something that struck me as curiously familiar. I sat up in sudden recognition and called out, 'Walter?'

'Nelson, is that you?' he said, and we laughed with an indescribable mixture of relief, surprise, disappointment and happiness. Walter, I learned, had been arrested shortly after my own arrest. We did not think that the arrests were unrelated. While this was not the most auspicious place for a meeting of the National Working Committee, it was certainly convenient, and the night sped by as I gave him a full account of my arrest, as well as my meetings in Durban.

The next day I appeared in court before a senior magistrate for formal remand. Harold Wolpe and Joe Slovo had come to court after hearing of my arrest, and we conferred in the basement. I had appeared before this magistrate on numerous occasions in my professional capacity and we had grown to respect one another. A number of attorneys were also present, some of whom I knew quite well. It is curious how one can be easily flattered in certain situations by otherwise insignificant incidents. I am by no means immune to flattery in normal circumstances, but there I was, a fugitive, No. 1 on the state's Most Wanted list, a handcuffed outlaw who had been underground for more than a year, and yet the judge, the other attorneys and the spectators all greeted me with deference and professional courtesy. They knew me as Nelson Mandela, attorney-at-law, not Nelson Mandela, outlaw. It lifted my spirits immensely.

During the proceedings, the magistrate was diffident and uneasy, and would not look at me directly. The other attorneys also seemed embarrassed, and at that moment I had something of a revelation. These men were not only uncomfortable because I was a colleague brought low, but because I was an ordinary man being punished for his beliefs. In a way I had never quite comprehended before, I realized the role I could play in court and the possibilities before me as a defendant. I was the symbol of justice in the court of the oppressor, the representative of the great ideals of freedom, fairness and democracy in a society that dishonoured those virtues. I realized then and there that I could carry on the fight even within the fortress of the enemy.

When I was asked the name of my counsel, I announced that I would represent myself, with Joe Slovo as legal adviser. By representing myself I would enhance the symbolism of my role. I would use my trial as a showcase for the ANC's moral opposition to racism. I would not attempt to defend myself so much as put the state itself on trial. That day, I answered only the questions as to my name and choice of counsel. I listened silently to the charges: inciting African workers to strike and leaving the country without valid travel documents. In apartheid South Africa, the penalties for these 'crimes' could be as much as ten years in prison. Yet the charges were something of a relief: the state clearly did not have enough evidence to link me with Umkhonto we Sizwe or I would have been charged with the far more serious crimes of treason or sabotage.

Only as I was leaving the courtroom did I see Winnie in the spectators' gallery. She looked distressed and gloomy; she was undoubtedly considering the difficult months and years ahead, of life on her own, raising two small children, in an often hard and forbidding city. It is one thing to be told of possible hardships ahead, it is entirely another to have to confront them in reality. All I could do, as I descended the steps to the basement, was to give her a wide smile, as if to show her that I was not worried and that she should not be either. I cannot imagine that it helped very much.

From the court, I was taken to the Johannesburg Fort. When I emerged from the courthouse to enter the sealed van, there was a crowd of hundreds of people cheering and shouting '*Amandla!*' followed by '*Ngawethu!*' a popular ANC call-and-response meaning 'Power!' and 'The power is ours!' People yelled and sang and pounded their fists on the sides of the van as the vehicle crawled out of the courthouse exit. My capture and case had made headlines in every paper: 'POLICE SWOOP ENDS TWO YEARS ON THE RUN' was one; 'NELSON MANDELA UNDER ARREST' was another. The so-called Black Pimpernel was no longer at large.

A few days later Winnie was granted permission to visit me. She had dressed up and now, at least on the face of it, appeared less glum than before. She brought me a new pair of expensive pyjamas and a lovely silk dressing gown more appropriate to a salon than a prison. I did not have the heart to tell her it was wholly inappropriate for me to wear such things in jail. I knew, however, that the parcel was a way of expressing her love and a pledge of solidarity. I thanked her, and although we did not have much time we quickly discussed family matters, especially how she would support herself and the children. I mentioned the names of friends who would help her and also clients of mine who still owed me money. I told her to tell the children the truth of my capture, and how I would be away for a long time. I said we were not the first family in this situation, and that those who underwent such hardships came out the stronger. I assured her of the strength of our cause, the loyalty of our friends, and how it would be her love and devotion that would see me through whatever transpired. The officer supervising the visit turned a blind eye, and we embraced and clung to each other with all the strength and pent-up emotion inside each of us, as if this were to be the final parting. In a way it was, for we were to be separated for much longer than either of us could then have imagined. The warrant officer allowed me to accompany Winnie part of the way to the main gate where I was able to watch her, alone and proud, disappear round the corner.

50

At the Fort I was being supervised by Colonel Minnaar, a courtly Afrikaner considered something of a liberal by his more *verkrampte* (hard-line) colleagues. He explained that he was placing me in the prison hospital because it was the most comfortable area and I would be able to have a chair and table on which I could prepare my case. While the hospital was indeed comfortable – I was able to sleep in a proper bed, something I had never done before in prison – the real reason for his generosity was that the hospital was the safest place to keep me. To reach it one had to pass through two impregnable walls, each with armed guards; and, once inside, four massive gates had to be unlocked before one even reached the area where I was kept. There was speculation in the press that the movement was going to attempt to rescue me, and the authorities were doing their utmost to prevent it.

There had also been wild speculations, in the press and within the ANC, that I had been betrayed by someone in the movement. I knew that some people blamed G. R. Naidoo, my Durban host, a suggestion I believe was unfounded. The press trumpeted the notion that I had been betrayed by white and Indian communists who were unsettled by my suggestions that the ANC must become more Africanist-oriented. But I believed these stories were planted by the government to divide the Congress movement, and I regarded it as malicious mischief. I later discussed the matter not only with Walter, Duma, Joe Slovo and Ahmed Kathrada, but Winnie, and I was gratified to see that they shared my feelings. Winnie had been invited to open the annual conference of the Transvaal Indian Youth Congress, and at my instigation she repudiated these rumours in no uncertain terms. The newspapers were filled with stories of her beauty and eloquence. 'We shall not waste time looking for evidence as to who betrayed Mandela,' she told the audience. 'Such propaganda is calculated to keep us fighting one another instead of uniting to combat Nationalist oppression.'

The most oft-cited story was that an American consular official with connections to the CIA had tipped off the authorities. This story has never been confirmed and I have never seen any reliable evidence as to the truth of it. Although the CIA has been responsible for many contemptible activities in its support of American imperialism, I cannot lay my capture at its door. In truth, I had been imprudent about maintaining the secrecy of my movements. In retrospect, I realized that the authorities could have had a myriad of ways of locating me on my trip to Durban. It was a wonder in fact that I wasn't captured sooner.

I spent only a few days in the Fort's hospital before being transferred to Pretoria. There had been no restrictions on visits in Johannesburg, and I had had a continuous stream of people coming to see me. Visitors keep one's spirits up in prison, and the absence of them can be disheartening. In transferring me to Pretoria, the authorities wanted to get me away from my home turf to a place where I would have fewer friends dropping in.

I was handcuffed and taken to Pretoria in an old van in the company of another prisoner. The inside of the van was filthy and we sat on a greasy spare tyre, which slid from side to side as the van rumbled on its way. The choice of companion was curious: his name was Nka-dimeng and he was a member of one of Soweto's fiercest gangs. Normally, officials would not permit a political prisoner to share the same vehicle with a common-law criminal, but I suspect they were hoping I would be intimidated by Nkadimeng, who I assumed was a police informer. I was dirty and annoyed by the time I reached prison, and my irritation was aggravated by the fact that I was put in a single cell with this fellow. I demanded and eventually received separate space so that I could prepare my case.

I was now permitted visitors only twice a week. Despite the distance, Winnie came regularly and always brought clean clothes and delicious food. This was another way of showing her support, and every time I put on a fresh shirt I felt her love and devotion. I was aware of how difficult it must have been to get to Pretoria in the middle of the day in the middle of the week with two small children at home. I was visited by many others who brought food, including the ever-faithful Mrs Pillay who supplied me with a spicy lunch every day.

Because of the generosity of my visitors I had an embarrassment of riches and wanted to share my food with the other prisoners on my floor. This was strictly forbidden. In order to circumvent the restrictions, I offered food to the warders, who might then relent. With this in mind I presented a shiny red apple to an African warder who looked at it and stonily rebuffed

me with the phrase '*Angiyifuni*' ('I don't want it').
African warders tend to be either much more sympathetic than white warders, or even more severe, as
though to outdo their masters. But, a short while later,
the black warder saw a white warder take the apple he
had rejected, and changed his mind. Soon I was
supplying all my fellow prisoners with food.

Through the prison grapevine, I learned that Walter
had been brought to Pretoria as well, and although we
were isolated from each other we did manage to communicate. Walter had applied for bail – a decision I fully
supported. Bail had long been a sensitive issue within
the ANC. There are those who believed we should
always reject bail, as it could be interpreted that we
were fainthearted rebels who accepted the racist stric-
tures of the legal system. I did not think this view should
be universally applied and believed we should examine
the issue on a case-by-case basis. Ever since Walter had
become secretary-general of the ANC, I had felt that
every effort should be made to bail him out of prison. He
was simply too vital to the organization to be allowed to
languish in jail. In his case, bail was a practical not a
theoretical issue. It was different with me. I had been
underground; Walter had not. I had become a public
symbol of rebellion and struggle; Walter operated behind the scenes. He agreed that no application for bail
should be made for me. For one thing, it would not have
been granted and I did not want to do anything that
might suggest that I was not prepared for the consequences of the underground life I had chosen.

Not long after Walter and I reached this decision I
was again transferred back to the hospital at the Fort. A
hearing had been set for October. Little can be said in

favour of prison, but enforced isolation is conducive to study. I had begun correspondence studies for my LL B degree, which allows one to practise as an advocate. One of the first things I had done after arriving at Pretoria Local was to send a letter to the authorities notifying them of my intention to study and requesting permission to purchase a copy of *The Law of Torts*, part of my syllabus.

A few days later, Colonel Aucamp, commanding officer of Pretoria Local and one of the more notorious of prison officials, marched into my cell and in a gloating manner said, 'Mandela, we have got you now!' Then he said, 'Why do you want a book about torches, man, unless you plan to use it for your damn sabotage?' I had no idea what he was talking about, until he produced my letter requesting a book about what he called 'the Law of Torches'. I smiled at this and he became angry that I was not taking him seriously. The Afrikaans word for 'torch' is *toorts*, very similar to tort, and I explained to him that in English *tort* was a branch of law, not a burning stick of wood that could be used to set off a bomb. He went away in a huff.

One day I was in the prison courtyard at the Fort doing my daily exercises, which consisted of jogging, running on the spot, push-ups and sit-ups, when I was approached by a tall, handsome Indian fellow named Moosa Dinath whom I had known slightly as a prosperous, even flamboyant, businessman. He was serving a two-year sentence for fraud. On the outside we would have remained acquaintances, but prison is an incubator of friendship. Dinath would often accompany me on my jogs around the courtyard. One day he asked whether I would have any objection if he obtained permission from the commanding officer to be near me in the prison hospital. I told him that I would welcome it, but I thought to myself that the authorities would never permit it. I was wrong.

It was exceedingly odd that a convicted prisoner like Dinath was permitted to stay together with a political prisoner awaiting trial. But I said nothing as I was glad to have company. Dinath was wealthy and had a private payroll for the prison authorities. In return for his money, he received many privileges: he wore clothes meant for white prisoners, ate their diet and did no jail work at all.

One night, to my astonishment, I observed Colonel Minnaar, who was the head of prison and a well-known Afrikaner advocate, come to fetch him. Dinath then left prison for the night and did not come back again until the morning. If I had not seen it with my own eyes I would not have believed it.

Dinath regaled me with tales of financial shenanigans and corruption among cabinet ministers, which I found fascinating. It confirmed to me how apartheid was a poison that bred moral decay in all areas. I scrupulously avoided discussing with him any matters of a political or sensitive nature on the grounds that he might also have been an informer. He once asked me to tell him about my African trip and I simply glossed over it. In the end, Dinath pulled enough strings to speed up his release and left after serving only four months of his two-year sentence.

Escape serves a double purpose: it liberates a freedom fighter from jail so that he can continue to fight, but offers a tremendous psychological boost to the struggle and a great publicity blow against the enemy. As a prisoner, I always contemplated escape, and during my various trips to and from the commanding officer's office, I carefully surveyed the walls, the movements of the guards, the types of keys and locks used in the doors. I made a detailed sketch of the prison grounds with particular emphasis on the exact location of the prison hospital and the gates leading out of it. This map was smuggled out to the movement with instructions to destroy it immediately after it was perused.

There were two plans, one hatched by Moosa Dinath, which I ignored; the second was conceived by the ANC and communicated to me by Joe Slovo. It involved bribes, copies of keys and even a false beard that was to be sewn into the shoulder pad of one of my jackets brought to me in prison. The idea was that I would don the beard after I had made my escape. I carefully considered the plan and concluded that it was premature, and the likelihood of its failure unacceptably high. Such a failure would be fatal to the organization. During a meeting with Joe, I passed him a note communicating my views. I wrote that MK was not ready for such an operation; even an elite and trained force would probably not be able to accomplish such a mission. I suggested that such a gambit be postponed until I was a convicted prisoner and the authorities were less cautious. At the end, I wrote, 'Please destroy this after you have finished reading it.' Joe and the others took my advice about not attempting the escape, but he decided the note should be saved as a historical document, and it later turned up at a very unfortunate time.

51

The initial hearing was set for Monday 15 October 1962. The organization had set up a Free Mandela Committee and launched a lively campaign with the slogan 'Free Mandela'. Protests were held throughout the country and the slogan began to appear scrawled on the sides of buildings. The government retaliated by banning all gatherings relating to my imprisonment, but this restriction was ignored by the liberation movement.

In preparation for Monday's hearing, the Free Mandela Committee had organized a mass demonstration at the courthouse. The plan was for people to line both sides of the road along the route my van would take. From press reports, conversations with visitors and even the remarks of prison guards, I learned that a large and vociferous turnout was expected.

On Saturday, while I was preparing myself for the Monday hearing, I was ordered to pack my things immediately: the hearing had been shifted to Pretoria. The authorities had made no announcement, and had I not managed to get word out through a sympathetic jailer, no one would have known that I had left Johannesburg.

But the movement reacted quickly, and by the time my case began on Monday morning, the Old Synagogue was packed with supporters. The synagogue was like a second home to me after four years of the

Treason Trial. My legal adviser, Joe Slovo, could not be present as he was confined to Johannesburg by bans and I was ably assisted instead by Bob Hepple.

I entered the court that Monday morning wearing a traditional Xhosa leopard-skin *kaross* instead of a suit and tie. The crowd of supporters rose as one and with raised clenched fists shouted '*Amandla!*' and '*Ngawethu!*' The *kaross* electrified the spectators, many of whom were friends and family, some of whom had come all the way from the Transkei. Winnie also wore a traditional beaded headdress and an ankle-length Xhosa skirt.

I had chosen traditional dress to emphasize the symbolism that I was a black African walking into a white man's court. I was literally carrying on my back the history, culture and heritage of my people. That day, I felt myself to be the embodiment of African nationalism, the inheritor of Africa's difficult but noble past and her uncertain future. The *kaross* was also a sign of contempt for the niceties of white justice. I well knew the authorities would feel threatened by my *kaross* as so many whites feel threatened by the true culture of Africa.

When the crowd had quietened down and the case was called, I formally greeted the prosecutor, Mr Bosch, whom I had known from my attorney days, and the magistrate, Mr von Heerden, who was also familiar to me. I then immediately applied for a two-week remand on the grounds that I had been transferred to Pretoria without being given the opportunity of notifying my attorneys. I was granted a week's postponement.

When I was on my way back to my cell, a very nervous

white warder said that the commanding officer, Colonel Jacobs, had ordered me to hand over the *kaross*. I said, 'You can tell him that he is not going to have it.' This warder was a weak fellow, and he started trembling. He practically begged me for it and said he would be fired if he did not bring it back. I felt sorry for him and said, 'Look, here, just tell your commanding officer that it is Mandela speaking, not you.' A short while later Colonel Jacobs himself appeared and ordered me to turn over what he referred to as my 'blanket'. I told him that he had no jurisdiction over the attire I chose to wear in court and if he tried to confiscate my *kaross* I would take the matter all the way to the Supreme Court. The colonel never again tried to take my 'blanket', but the authorities would permit me to wear it only in court, not on my way to or from court for fear it would 'incite' other prisoners.

When the case resumed a week later I was given permission to address the court before I was asked to plead. 'I hope to be able to indicate,' I explained, 'that this case is a trial of the aspirations of the African people, and because of that I thought it proper to conduct my own defence.' I wanted to make it clear to the bench, the gallery, and the press that I intended to put the state on trial. I then made application for the recusal of the magistrate on the grounds that I did not consider myself morally bound to obey laws made by a Parliament in which I had no representation. Nor was it possible to receive a fair trial from a white judge:

Why is it that in this courtroom I am facing a white magistrate, confronted by a white prosecutor, escorted by white orderlies? Can anybody honestly and seriously suggest that in this type of atmosphere the scales of justice are evenly balanced? Why is it that no African in the history of this country has ever had the honour of being tried by his own kith and kin, by his own flesh and blood? I will tell Your Worship why: the real purpose of this rigid colour bar is to ensure that the justice dispensed by the courts should conform to the policy of the country, however much that policy might be in conflict with the norms of justice accepted in judiciaries throughout the civilized world. . . . Your Worship, I hate racial discrimination most intensely and in all its manifestations. I have fought it all my life. I fight it now, and I will do so until the end of my days. I detest most intensely the set-up that surrounds me here. It makes me feel that I am a black man in a white man's court. This should not be.

During the trial the prosecutor called more than a hundred witnesses from all over the country, including the Transkei and South West Africa. They were policemen, journalists, township superintendents, printers. Most of them gave technical evidence to show that I had left the country illegally and that I had incited African workers to strike during the three-day stay-at-home in May 1961. It was indisputable – and in fact I did not dispute – that I was technically guilty of both charges.

The prosecutor had called Mr Barnard, the private secretary to the prime minister, to testify to the letter I had sent the prime minister demanding that he call a national convention and informing him that if he did not, we would organize a three-day strike. In my cross-examination of Mr Barnard I first read the court the letter I sent requesting that the prime minister call a national convention for all South Africans to write a new non-racial constitution.

NM: Did you place this letter before your prime minister?

WITNESS: Yes.

NM: Now was any reply given to this letter by the prime minister?

WITNESS: He did not reply to the writer.

NM: He did not reply to the letter. Now, will you agree that this letter raises matters of vital concern to the vast majority of the citizens of this country?

WITNESS: I do not agree.

NM: You don't agree? You don't agree that the question of human rights, of civil liberties, is a matter of vital importance to the African people?

WITNESS: Yes, that is so, indeed.

NM: Are these things mentioned here?

WITNESS: Yes, I think so.

NM: . . . You have already agreed that this letter raises questions like the rights of freedom, civil liberties, and so on?

WITNESS: Yes, the letter raises it.

NM: Now, you know of course that Africans don't enjoy the rights demanded in this letter? They are denied these rights of government.

WITNESS: Some rights.

NM: No African is a member of Parliament?

WITNESS: That is right.

NM: No African can be a member of the provincial council, of the municipal councils?

WITNESS: Yes.

NM: Africans have no vote in this country?

WITNESS: They have got no vote as far as Parliament is concerned.

NM: Yes, that is what I am talking about, I am talking about Parliament and other government bodies of the country, the provincial councils, the municipal councils. They have no vote?

WITNESS: That is right.

NM: Would you agree with me that in any civilized country in the world it would be scandalous for a prime minister to fail to reply to a letter raising vital issues affecting the majority of the citizens of that country. Would you agree with that?

WITNESS: I don't agree with that.

NM: You don't agree that it would be irregular for a prime minister to ignore a letter raising vital issues affecting the vast majority of the citizens of that country?

WITNESS: This letter has not been ignored by the prime minister.

NM: Just answer the question. Do you regard it as proper for a prime minister not to respond to pleas made in regard to vital issues by the vast majority of the citizens of the country? You say that is wrong?

WITNESS: The prime minister did respond to the letter.

NM: Mr Barnard, I don't want to be rude to you. Will you confine yourself to answering my questions. The question I am putting to you is, do you agree that it is most improper on the part of a prime minister not to reply to a communication raising vital issues affecting the vast majority of the country?

Mr Barnard and I never did agree. In the end, he simply said that the tone of the letter was aggressive and discourteous and for that reason the prime minister did not answer it.

Throughout the proceedings the prosecutor and the magistrate repeatedly inquired about the number of witnesses I intended to call. I would always reply, 'I plan to call as many witnesses as the state, if not more.' When the state finally concluded its case, there was a stillness in the courtroom in anticipation of the beginning of my defence. I rose, and instead of calling my first witness I declared quite matter-of-factly that I was not calling any witnesses at all, at which point I abruptly closed my case. There was a murmur in the courtroom and the prosecutor could not help exclaiming, 'Lord!'

I had misled the court from the beginning because I knew the charge was accurate and the state's case was solid, and I saw no point in attempting to call witnesses and defend myself. Through my cross-examination and attempts to force the judge to recuse himself, I had made the statements I wanted about the unfairness of the court. I saw no advantage in calling witnesses to try to disprove something that was incontrovertible.

The magistrate was taken by surprise by my action and asked me with some incredulity, 'Have you anything more to say?'

'Your Worship, I submit that I am guilty of no crime.'

'Is that all you have to say?'

'Your Worship, with respect, if I had something more to say I would have said it.'

The prosecutor then shuffled through his papers attempting to get ready for an address he did not expect to have to make. He briefly addressed the court and asked the magistrate to find me guilty on both counts. The court was then adjourned until the following day, when I would have a chance to address it in what is known as the plea in mitigation before the magistrate gave his sentence.

The following morning, before court was called into session, I was in an office off the courtroom talking with Bob Hepple, who had been advising me on the case, and we were praising the fact that the day before, the General Assembly of the UN had voted in favour of sanctions against South Africa for the first time. Bob also told me that acts of sabotage in Port Elizabeth and Durban had occurred, both celebrating the UN vote and in protest at my trial. We were in the midst of this discussion when the prosecutor, Mr Bosch, entered the room and then asked Bob to excuse himself.

'Mandela,' he said, after Bob had left, 'I did not want to come to court today. For the first time in my career, I despise what I am doing. It hurts me that I should be asking the court to send you to prison.' He then reached out and shook my hand, and expressed the hope that everything would turn out well for me. I thanked him for his sentiments, and assured him that I would never forget what he had said.

The authorities were on alert that day. The crowd inside the courtroom seemed even larger than on the first day of the case. All 150 'Non-European' seats were filled. Winnie was present, in Xhosa dress, as well as a number of my relatives from the Transkei. Hundreds of demonstrators stood a block from the courthouse, and there seemed to be as many policemen as spectators.

When I walked into the courtroom, I raised my right fist and called out 'Amandla!' which was met by a mighty 'Ngawethu!' The magistrate pounded his gavel and cried for order. When the court was quiet, he summed up the charges, after which I had my opportunity to speak.

My plea in mitigation lasted over an hour. It was not a judicial appeal at all but a political testament. I wanted to explain to the court how and why I had become the man I was, why I had done what I had done, and why, if given the chance, I would do it again.

Many years ago, when I was a boy brought up in my village in the Transkei, I listened to the elders of the tribe telling stories about the good old days before the arrival of the white man. Then our people lived peacefully, under the democratic rule of their kings and their *amapakati* [literally 'insiders', but meaning those closest in rank to the king], and moved freely and confidently up and down the country without let or hindrance. The country was our own, in name and right. We occupied the land, the forests, the rivers; we extracted the mineral wealth beneath the soil and all the riches of this beautiful country. We set up and operated our own government, we controlled our own arms and we organized our trade and commerce. The elders would tell tales of the wars fought by our ancestors in defence of the Fatherland, as well as the acts of valour by generals and soldiers during these epic days. . . .

The structure and organization of early African societies in this country fascinated me very much and greatly influenced the evolution of my political outlook. The land, then the main means of production, belonged to the whole tribe and there was no individual ownership whatsoever. There were no classes, no rich or poor and no exploitation of man by man. All men were free and equal and this was the foundation of government. Recognition of this general principle found expression in the constitution of the council, variously called 'Imbizo' or 'Pitso' or 'Kgotla', which governs the affairs of the tribe. The council was so completely democratic that all members of the tribe could participate in its deliberations. Chief and subject, warrior and medicine man, all took part and endeavoured to influence its decisions. It was so weighty and influential a body that no step of any importance could ever be taken by the tribe without reference to it.

There was much in such a society that was primitive and insecure and it certainly could never measure up to the demands of the present epoch. But in such a society are contained the seeds of revolutionary democracy in which none will be held in slavery or servitude, and in which poverty, want and insecurity shall be no more. This is the history which, even today, inspires me and my colleagues in our political struggle.

I told the court how I had joined the African National Congress and how its policy of democracy and non-racialism reflected my own deepest convictions. I explained how as a lawyer I was often forced to choose between compliance with the law or accommodating my conscience.

I would say that the whole life of any thinking African in this country drives him continuously to a conflict between his conscience on the one hand and the law on the other. This is not a conflict peculiar to this country. The conflict arises for men of conscience, for men who think and who feel deeply in every country. Recently in Britain, a peer of the realm, Earl [Bertrand] Russell, probably the most respected philosopher of the Western world, was sentenced and convicted for precisely the type of activities for which I stand before you today – for following his conscience in defiance of the law, as a protest against the nuclear weapons policy being pursued by his own government. He could do no other than to oppose the law and to suffer the consequences for it. Nor can I. Nor can many Africans in this country. The law as it is applied, the law as it has been developed over a long period of history, and especially the law as it is written and designed by the Nationalist government is a law which, in our views, is immoral, unjust and intolerable. Our consciences dictate that we must protest against it, that we must oppose it and that we must attempt to alter it. . . . Men, I think, are not capable of doing nothing, of saying nothing, of not reacting to injustice, of not protesting against oppression, of not striving for the good society and the good life in the ways they see it.

I recounted in detail the numerous times the government had used the law to hamper my life, career and political work, through bannings, restrictions and trials.

I was made, by the law, a criminal, not because of what I had done, but because of what I stood for, because of what I thought, because of my conscience. Can it be any wonder to anybody that such conditions make a man an outlaw of society? Can it be wondered that such a man, having been outlawed by the government, should be prepared to lead the life of an outlaw, as I have led for some months, according to the evidence before this court?

It has not been easy for me during the past period to separate myself from my wife and children, to say good-bye to the good old days when, at the end of a strenuous day at an office, I could look forward to joining my family at the dinner-table, and instead to take up the life of a man hunted continuously by the police, living separated from those who are closest to me, in my own country, facing continually the hazards of detection and of arrest. This has been a life infinitely more difficult than serving a prison sentence. No man in his right senses would voluntarily choose such a life in preference to the one of normal, family, social life which exists in every civilized community.

But there comes a time, as it came in my life, when a man is denied the right to live a normal life, when he can only live the life of an outlaw because the government has so decreed to use the law to impose a state of outlawry upon him. I was driven to this situation, and I do not regret having taken the decisions that I did take. Other people will be driven in the same way in this country, by this very same force of police persecution and of administrative action by the government, to follow my course, of that I am certain.

I enumerated the many times that we had brought our grievances before the government and the equal number of times that we were ignored or shunted aside. I described our stay-away of 1961 as a last resort after the government showed no signs of taking any steps to either talk with us or meet our demands. It was the government that provoked violence by employing violence to meet our non-violent demands. I explained that because of the government's actions we had taken a more militant stance. I said that I had been privileged throughout my political life to fight alongside colleagues whose abilities and contributions were far greater than my own. Many others had paid the price of their beliefs before me, and many more would do so after me.

Before sentencing, I informed the court that whatever sentence the state imposed, it would do nothing to change my devotion to the struggle.

I do not believe, Your Worship, that this court, in inflicting penalties on me for the crimes for which

I am convicted should be moved by the belief that penalties will deter men from the course that they believe is right. History shows that penalties do not deter men when their conscience is aroused, nor will they deter my people or the colleagues with whom I have worked before.

I am prepared to pay the penalty even though I know how bitter and desperate is the situation of an African in the prisons of this country. I have been in these prisons and I know how gross is the discrimination, even behind the prison wall, against Africans. . . . Nevertheless these considerations do not sway me from the path that I have taken nor will they sway others like me. For to men, freedom in their own land is the pinnacle of their ambitions, from which nothing can turn men of conviction aside. More powerful than my fear of the dreadful conditions to which I might be subjected in prison is my hatred for the dreadful conditions to which my people are subjected outside prison throughout this country. . . .

Whatever sentence Your Worship sees fit to impose upon me for the crime for which I have been convicted before this court, may it rest assured that when my sentence has been completed I will still be moved, as men are always moved, by their conscience; I will still be moved by my dislike of the race discrimination against my people when I come out from serving my sentence, to take up again, as best I can, the struggle for the removal of those injustices until they are finally abolished once and for all. . . .

I have done my duty to my people and to South

Africa. I have no doubt that posterity will pronounce that I was innocent and that the criminals that should have been brought before this court are the members of the government.

When I had finished, the magistrate ordered a ten-minute recess to consider the sentence. I turned and looked out at the crowd before leaving the courtroom. I had no illusions about the sentence I would receive. Exactly ten minutes later, in a courtroom heavy with tension, the magistrate pronounced sentence: three years for inciting people to strike and two years for leaving the country without a passport; five years in all, with no possibility of parole. It was a stern sentence, and there was wailing among the spectators. As the court rose, I turned to the gallery and again made a clenched fist, shouting '*Amandla!*' three times. Then, on its own, the crowd began to sing our beautiful anthem, '*Nkosi Sikelel' iAfrika*'. People sang and danced and the women ululated as I was led away. The uproar among the gallery made me forget for a moment that I would be going to prison to serve what was then the stiffest sentence yet imposed in South Africa for a political offence.

Downstairs, I was permitted a brief good-bye to Winnie, and on this occasion she was not at all grim: she was in high spirits and shed no tears. She seemed confident, as much a comrade as a wife. She was determined to brace me. As I was driven away in the police van I could still hear the people outside singing '*Nkosi Sikelel' iAfrika*'.

INDEX